So Many Miles to Paradise

ABOUT THE AUTHOR

Christine Breen was born in America. In 1985, she moved from New York with her husband, novelist Niall Williams, to the cottage in the west of Ireland where her grandfather was born. They have two children, Deirdre and Joseph. She is a registered member of The Irish Society of Homeopaths and is currently working on a novel.

So Many Miles to Paradise

to Paradise

From Clare to There

CHRISTINE BREEN

TOWN
HOUSE
DUBLIN

First published in 2005 by

TownHouse, Dublin
THCH Ltd
Trinity House
Charleston Road
Ranelagh
Dublin 6
Ireland

www.townhouse.ie

1 2 3 4 5 6 7 8 9 10

ISBN: 1-86059-236-8

Cover design by Vivid

Typeset by Typeform
Printed by Nørhaven Paperback A/S, Denmark

CONTENTS

ITINERARY

September
Port Washington, NY, USA
Amagansett, NY
West Glacier, MT
Bozeman, MT
West Yellowstone, MT

October
Sun Valley, ID
Seattle, WA
Canon Beach, OR
Florence, OR
Brookings, OR
Eureka, CA
Mendocino, CA

November
San Francisco, CA
Los Angeles, CA
Coronado Beach, San Diego, CA
San José, Costa Rica
Manuel Antonio, Costa Rica
Lima, Peru
Cusco, Peru
Machu Picchu, Peru

December
Puno, Peru
Lake Titicaca, Peru
Floating Islands, Peru
Isla del Sol, Bolivia
Copacobana, Bolivia
La Paz, Bolivia
Santiago, Chile
Torres del Paine, Chile
Punto Arenas, Chile
Parque Pumalin, Chile
Puerto Varas, Chile
Fundo Chacaipulli, Los Lagos, Chile

January

Las Condes, Santiago, Chile
Auckland, New Zealand
Waiheke Island, New Zealand
Rotorua, New Zealand
Nelson, New Zealand
Punakaiki, New Zealand
Queenstown, New Zealand

February

Waiheke Island, New Zealand
The Rocks, Sydney, Australia

March

Hamilton Island, Queensland, Australia
Uluru, Ayers Rock, Central Australia
Melbourne, Victoria, Australia

April

Sayan, Ubud, Bali
Singapore
Frankfurt, Germany
Heidelburg, Germany
Augsburg, Germany
Salzburg, Austria
Prague, The Czech Republic
Paris, France
Giverny, France

May

Valbonne, France
Cap d'Antibes, France

June

Kiltumper, Ireland

DEDICATION

In memory of my mother and to mothers everywhere

ACKNOWLEDGEMENTS

To all those who travelled with us in spirit. To my friend Marie for the Christmas box and the phone calls along the way. To Concorde Travel for their help in arranging our tickets. To Martin for minding Huckleberry. To Diarmuid for taking care of my cats. To Lucy and Larry for being there. To Hawthorn Nursery for their work in the garden. To Ian and Maggie Staples for the Christmas cheer. To Stephen and Jane Burn for the bach and the great coffee and the chat. And mostly I acknowledge my wonderful family, Joseph, Deirdre and Niall, because no journey would be worth it without them.

Prologue

Many years ago, before my children Deirdre and Joseph were born, a calendar of one hundred days lay on an office desk. It was 1985. The desk was in an office building in midtown Manhattan where I worked as a copy editor for a well-known medical journal. Five days a week, my husband and I travelled to Manhattan. Niall was a copywriter for a large paperback publishing house. We commuted home on the Harlem River Line, the 5.26 from Grand Central. We were living in Mt Kisco, an hour's commute from New York City, renting an apartment in an old turn-of-the-century house on top of a hill. The statue of Kisco, the Indian Chief of the Mohicans, saluted us every morning as we passed him on our way to the station.

We were in our twenties, had no children, and were on the yuppie ladder of the 1980s. Mid-level jobs in publishing promised careers that led to offices with windows. Niall was heading towards 'senior copywriter' and eventually I would move from 'assistant editor' to 'editor'. It was only a matter of time. Yet, we couldn't quite see ourselves fulfilling that destiny. Niall, especially, wanted to write. From his earliest days as a student in Dublin it was always his wish for himself. He had a couple of short stories published already by the time I met him in university in Dublin, where I was studying in a master's programme in Irish literature, and he was working on a novel. After we married, I had persuaded Niall to live in New York, my home state, and eventually we were both of us working in New York City. During many lunches together we grumbled about the commute, the lack of personal time, and we fantasised about living another life. A life somewhere else. After a year, a moment came to us – you could call it an epiphany – and we took advantage of an opportunity that was to change our lives.

Discreetly, then, we ticked off the disappearing days on that calendar back in late winter of 1985, keeping at bay the enquiring eyes of our comrades at work. Days mounted up like building blocks to a new life. As the marked-off days passed, we gradually let people know that we were leaving our jobs, leaving our lives as we knew them. For not only were we quitting our jobs, we were moving. Not to some rural retreat on the coast of the Northeast – we were moving to the other side of the Atlantic. One hundred crossed-off days later, we moved – lock, stock and barrel, with no jobs to go to – to the west coast of Ireland, arriving in our new home just in time for spring. The 5.26 had blown its last whistle for us. The song of the cuckoo was singing instead. Our lives were changed forever.

~

Nearly twenty years have passed since we moved from New York to Kiltumper, to this 200-year-old farmhouse in County Clare we call home. Many wonderful and exciting things have happened for us. We've written four non-fiction books about our life in Ireland and Niall has had four novels published to worldwide acclaim. Before writing fiction, three stage plays written by Niall were seen on the Irish stage. I helped found a craft co-operative shop in Ennis, where my own paintings were sold. I've undergone training as a professional homeopath in Ireland and homeopathy has become a steady companion for us. But most importantly, two delightful children have joined us and now lay claim to the small bedrooms that have been built for them in the roof of the cottage.

We moved to Ireland during the mid-1980s when so many Irish

were emigrating to North America and Australia. (Now, they're all returning, to a new, prosperous Ireland, having made it in a way that was not possible for them ten years ago.) But the life we have made in Kiltumper was quite different from the upwardly mobile one of the new Dubliners. Ours is country living, built from the soil up, so to speak. First attempting self-sufficiency, then suckler cows, a few horses and farmyard animals until, finally, we progressed along the path we had initially envisioned for ourselves. We had started our lives in Ireland as 'small farmers' and tried to eke out an existence in boggy ground where, if rushes were a cash crop, we'd have been millionaires. (Mind you, we have yet to discard the wellies, which fall just inside the back kitchen door ready to be slipped on for a wander around the farm, or a walk down to our neighbours, or a stint in the garden.) But we have given up the farming. Much has changed, yet much remains the same since that day in April in '85 when we arrived to a bare stone cottage in the west of Ireland with ten suitcases and less than a fistful of money.

As we wrote in our first book, we wanted to make a house of words, and paintings, and music and flowers. And we have done so. Now, Niall's books line the shelves in several languages, music drifts through the house, Joseph's fiddle sings traditional tunes while the deep notes of Deirdre's cello hum in the red music room. A garden surrounds the house on all sides. It is a little piece of heaven, albeit a wet one.

The joys and pains of country living are the boundaries by which we have come to know our lives, experiencing a rural life on an intimate level. From pulling new born calves from the backside of a cow to spraying blighted potatoes. From saving hay to saving turf. From bringing bags of turf home from the bog by hand instead of by tractor – because of a wet summer – to making silage in the rain or hay in the sunshine. We have witnessed the magic of a foal being born in the field at the back of the house under a starry night and christened him Magic Star. As our children have grown, we have sent them on bicycles down the whitethorn-edged road to a two-roomed schoolhouse. We have listened, enraptured, to our daughter playing cello in a string quartet at a music school in Ennis. Our son, Joseph, has taken part in the Willie Clancy Summer School in Miltown Malbay among 400 other fiddlers. For nearly twenty years, we have lived a very rural country life from within this old cottage sitting remotely in the green and wet landscape on the west coast of Ireland. It has given voice to a wellspring of creativity.

The house in Kiltumper has been home to several generations of my father's family, the long, tall Breens as they were known. My grandfather was born and raised here, eventually leaving in his teenage years for New York City, never to return except once. They remember he came by bicycle from the village in his fine suit. His father, too, was born in the cottage. And before that, a great-great-grandfather who is remembered locally as 'Jack of the Grove'. The long, tall Breens walked barefoot to school, saved turf on the bog, dug new potatoes in summer. The memory of that way of life is also a part of our lives. When I look out across the meadows, it is through a veil of a hundred years because it is the same view my grandfather gazed on from a kitchen table. The south-sloping garden patch in front of the cottage has gone from potatoes and cabbages in his day to delphiniums, daisies and poppies in mine; the gardeners themselves have gone from self-sufficiency to designing herbaceous borders. But the earth has a memory, same as the stone. A long memory and one of which we are now a part.

Deirdre and Joseph's primary school years were spent in a 100-year-old schoolhouse. It has had a bit of a facelift, but birds still nest above the ceiling causing Martin, the principal, to stand on a chair with the broom handle in his hand, tapping the space above him, calling out to the birds, 'Stop that now. Do ye hear?' The eighteen children giggle. The school's stone walls have welcomed children from the local townlands for over ten decades. I find security in that. The ground beneath yields a message of its own that can't be bought for any price. A message that speaks of continuity and a sense of place. Our children will have experienced that amidst a world that is changing almost too rapidly to keep track of. And, although they don't know it yet, it has been an anchor in their growing lives.

The cottage itself, although having seen modern changes, is very much the same. The ten-foot wide, open hearth still bellows in and out with a turf fire glowing from the grate on the floor at its centre almost daily. An old crane still swings, soot covered and black. That

4

old fireplace is a testament to a way of life – and one of the last surviving open hearths in the county – and another anchor in our lives. (It was only fifteen years ago that the village phone system went direct dial.) Now we have a computer, two laptops, and satellite television. The rural primary school may close as the population of the countryside continues to dwindle. But one day I'll be sitting on a sofa in a place far from Ireland and telling a man in black suede loafers sitting beside me that there were only four other children in Joseph's class. He will marvel at me and shake his head eyeing us enviously. One day Deirdre and Joseph will cherish the memory of playing at break-time with only the bog fields in sight, hearing the wind whistle a somewhat melancholic song through the weather-pruned hedgerows, the cows calling for their calves and the buzz of tractors murmuring in the distance. We will all always cherish those memories as parts of ourselves. And, it has been plenty and enough for all of us.

Until now.

While the circumference of our physical life here has been small, with much of it lived within a village community, there is no denying that it has been rewarding and fulfilling. But I, for one, am getting restless. After nearly twenty years, the meadow at the back of the house is in danger of becoming just another field to me. The May blossoms of the whitethorn and the yellow, coconut-scented gorse are blooming as they do every summer, rain or shine, but where once they sparkled in rain-mist now the mind's eye records them like the second hand of the clock, simply marking the season's change from spring to summer. We have watched the wind shape trees and hedgerows until we have groaned with that relentless wind. We have driven down too many rain-spilled roads. Even the freshness seems damp. Red and purple blossoms of fuchsia line the boreens like thrown confetti and, although the twilight of a July evening can still infuse them with a glow that is electrifying, I am eager for new visions of flowered hedgerows in a place beyond this house. Somewhere else. Kiltumper is in danger of becoming commonplace, ordinary in a way that signals to me that I am ready for and need a new perspective. After working hard for nearly two decades here in Ireland, starting from scratch, tending the small farm, learning to paint, writing, practising homeopathy, I am ready for a change. In fact, I *need* a change in order to continue living my life as a mother, as a wife, as an American woman in the west of Ireland, and I need to reconnect with the person inside me that is more than all these things. I am like an old wet dishrag that needs a good airing in the sun and air.

Moving to Ireland was a measure of the depth of our commitment to each other and to a life consciously lived, and during those years our lives have gone in the direction we had always intended for ourselves. Grateful for this rural way of life, we have built from our experiences a richness for ourselves and our children. A richness that has been the fountain of inspiration for Niall's novels and for my mixed creativities. It is not that the wellspring is dry but the fountain needs an overhaul of sorts. It is sputtering and spurting. Its parts are rusty. It needs more than a paint job.

We've always had a yardstick to measure this life against the life we had in Manhattan and in Westchester, but our children haven't. And, while their lives are still in our hands, we want to create a new yardstick, with new experiences for all of us to share. I am keenly aware that Deirdre is quickly nearing the end of her teenage years and will likely be heading off to university soon. Our life together will never be the same. I want to spend time with her in ways that will bring us closer together. I want her all to myself. This time will never come again. So, we have had an idea, another epiphany. We are on the move and, not unlike the last time, we have decided on an adventure.

Epiphany

Like the last time, I make another calendar. It begins in mid-May. The cuckoo has arrived and sings in the back garden. It is 2002. The calendar holds centre stage on the blue refrigerator in the kitchen. We can each tick off the days as we count down to another departure date: this time, 1 September 2002. We are stepping out of our lives as of this date. All four of us together. We are taking a year off. We are going to leave behind the scaffolding and the structures that we erect around our days, the timetables, the routines of work, of school and homework, of music lessons, of travelling the same route to and from the same shops, of eating the same foods, watching the same television programmes, experiencing the same weather and responding in the same way. As of 1 September, we are going to leave it all. We are going to take our family and put it elsewhere. We are going to learn about different places in the world and learn more about ourselves in the process. In so doing, we may find new perspectives, and find ourselves anew.

As so many of my emails of enquiry read these days, I write the words, 'We are an Irish family of four about to embark on a nine-month journey around the world…' It is a journey that will take us across five continents and into at least ten different countries. We are making over thirty stops by air. Visiting places with names that tickle the imagination. Kalispell, Eureka, Fundo Chacaipulli, Waiheke Island, Uluru. Whispered images – glimpsed at from dozens of travel catalogues spread on the floor in corners of the cottage – beckon the adventurer in me. Faraway landscapes thrill and excite and tempt fear from the unknowable. Some people think we are crazy to leave the comfort of our lives. But comfortable living can become like a life with small windows. We think it is time to open the windows and fly out, extend our horizons, *carpe diem*… The excitement alone of planning the trip has already given me a new perspective. Like they say in America, *You go girl*. I feel alive and the possibility of freedom is intoxicating.

At first we told no one about our plans – our escape, our holiday from the business of our lives. It was just an idea, undulating like a wave, rising and falling. Curling and subsiding. Sometimes wild with the hurricane winds, other days flat and ripple-less. Over the course of a year we began to talk more and more seriously about it.

Once before, some years ago, I had had the same idea of a year out of our lives, but Niall was hesitant then. To be fair, my plan was to go to the Yellow River in China and live along the banks with a Chinese family. He had smiled in a kind of frown at me. Very often the dreams we all dream seem so far from reality when you speak of them, especially if you are alone in that dream. You lose your enthusiasm for them, and they disappear. But this time the idea is somewhat different. This time it's a winner. And this time I had a conspirator. How did it come about? I cannot quite say any one thing triggered it. It was a combination of many things, including the stuck-ness I found myself in. But for Niall, who can say? Perhaps it was born one day the previous summer when he collapsed in Ennis and had to go by ambulance to the Casualty Department after the lights in the opticians seemed to cause a fit; perhaps it was the Hydrogen remedy his homeopath gave him; or the exhaustion he felt from completing his third novel. Perhaps it was watching Deirdre exhaust herself studying long, hard hours in the evenings preparing for her Junior Certificate exams. For myself, I was only waiting for the word.

One evening after the children were in bed, Niall, sitting across the turf fire from me, lowered the book he was reading and said:

'Why don't we do it?'

'What?'

'Take the year. Just go.'

'Really?' I looked up from the laptop where I was researching remedies for a new client.

'Yes.'

'Could we?'

'We could. We just go.'

'Really, really?' My voice was like a rising crescendo. Huckleberry's ears twitched listening to me.

'Yes.'

'When?'

'When summer's over. Go in September before school starts up again.'

And like that, in the middle of the evening, I saw the window opening.

'Well,' I hesitated, remembering the Yellow River, 'here's actually what *I have* been thinking.'

'Yes?' He raised his eyebrows at me. Was this my plan after all? Hadn't I slipped it like sugar into his tea without his noticing?

'What about going to, say, ten places around the world?' I said, closing the laptop.

'Ten?'

'Or more.' I laughed. 'Not trying to see everything exactly. Just going somewhere else…to be, to try…. Well, just to live in some other places.' The words stumbled from my lips excitedly.

'I think we could do it,' Niall said. I could see he was serious this time. It was a huge step for him. I remembered the first time we travelled together, before we were married, while we were living in Normandy for six months. We had a week off his teaching schedule

9

and we spread the map of Europe open before us and I said, 'where should we go?' And he said 'Belgium' proudly. And I laughed and said 'Belgium? It's only over there. No, let's go to Vienna!' It was as far as we could go east on the map of Europe. So we spent a week in February in freezing Vienna without proper winter coats, eating large white sausages because we couldn't read the menus. It was Valentine's Day and we went to the Staatsopera to hear *Tristan und Isolde*. So, this time, in the beginning, I didn't tell him just where I had in mind. But I began buying maps.

~

In the beginning we didn't tell the children. We wanted to let the plan develop sufficiently before declaring a proposal to them of such enormous dimensions. Could they even comprehend it? Then we told them. I said some place names: Machu Picchu, Patagonia, Waiheke, and showed them the maps. Our son, Joseph, already an armchair explorer, held the globe in his hands.

'Do you know that there are eleven time zones in Russia?' he said. 'Are we going there?'

'No, I don't think so.'

'The city of Auckland was built on seventy inactive volcanoes. Did you know that?'

Hmmm. We could already see that we didn't need to bring an atlas with us! Our daughter, Deirdre, always the observer, was stunned. She had so many thoughts running through her head. What about school? What about my friends? Can we bring anyone with us? What clothes will I pack?

The first step in deciding to make this commitment to ourselves, was for Niall to request a sabbatical from his teaching position. Once his request was accepted a few months later, we knew we had made our first big step. I was also taking a sabbatical from my homeopathic practice, most likely putting on hold an international postgraduate course I had taken up in Bologna, Italy.

For many months, this idea of travelling to places around the world was held in our mouths like a secret too precious to utter to anyone outside the family. Eventually we told my sister in New York. She was stunned but not surprised. She said she could never leave home for that long but she was thrilled and excited nonetheless. 'All I want to know is when are you coming to New York?'

Here and there, then, we started to drop hints. People thought we'd naturally be going to America for a year, I being an American, and we let them think that. But quietly in the cottage we were unrolling the world map we had bought, putting a book in each corner to pin it, and planning. Meanwhile, I was writing and emailing for brochures offered by tour companies from Patagonia to Alaska, from Tasmania to Beijing. From the tailor-made and ultra de luxe to the barest economy. Journeys with titles like *Beyond the Clouds – A Twelve-day Excursion through the Yunnan Region of Southern China*, 'taking to the road to explore landscapes and cultures scarcely touched by the modern world' excited our imaginations but proved unaffordable. Names like Black Dragoon Pool and Tiger Leaping Gorge made Ang Lee's film, *Crouching Tiger, Hidden Dragon* leap off the page. At Stg£4,250 for two weeks, such a de luxe journey promised luxury amidst snow-capped mountains, traditional hill tribes and the remains of ancient Chinese empires, but at a price beyond our reach. Another tour brochure came through the post called 'GAP Adventures – The Great Adventure People' and was more in keeping with our budgetary parameters and offered 'glimpses of the real world though travel experience. Trips designed to transport you from the familiar surroundings of home to a world completely different from your own. 'We don't try to take out the surprises when you travel with GAP Adventures – it's the surprises that make your experience unique and different from that of every other traveller.' I wondered what surprises would be in store for us. Sounded great on paper. We were all for sustainable travel and low-impact eco-tourism. They were aimed mostly at the independent twenty-five to thirty-five-year-old traveller, children had to be over thirteen and those over sixty needed a medical. There was even a 'comfort class' for people requiring a little bit more from their accommodation than a hostel-like arrangement. The prices were very reasonable and departure dates were frequent. Only one thing really stopped us – the age requirement. Joseph would be eleven at the time of travelling.

Brochures arrived steadily in the post box. PJ our postman must have been the first in the village to get an inkling of what was ahead for us. He was probably secretly delighted at the prospect of not having to drive the extra quarter of a mile back the road to our house to deliver our mail. Research for the trip took many forms: from the travel brochures to visits to bookstores to endless hours on the Internet. We've got one guide each from various travel book publishers: *Footprints, Rough Guide, Lonely Planet, Fodor's, National Geographic,* and *Dorling Kindersley.* Clippings from magazines like *Wanderlust* and Conde Nast's *Traveller* fill a notebook.

~~~

Once we had decided that we were going, the next big question was where. Where would *you* go if you gave yourself a year off? It's an interesting question and we began to ask people. Italy and India were resounding answers, but I was thinking more along the lines of Bolivia and New Zealand.

The more we looked at our own priorities the answers materialised. We decided that we would do most of our long-haul travelling by air and that began to focus our possibilities too. We investigated Round the World tickets. There is any number of companies offering such tickets, especially on the web, and we settled with Oneworld Alliance, a partnership of airlines that offered flights to destinations around the world. Initially we had thought of starting our trip in Alaska, in a place called Homer on the Kenai Peninsula. We hoped to time it to arrive as the black bear were feeding on the salmon runs. But, as it turned out, Alaska was not on our Oneworld Alliance destination map and we decided to save it for a trip all its own. I've heard it said, 'Save Alaska for last'. So we looked at the airline partners in the Oneworld Alliance and charted our trip around them. Originally we planned to go to Brazil, Niall being a soccer aficionado and the World Cup of 2002 being in our midst day and night on the television. (After Ireland, we were cheering for Brazil.) We learned that Lan Chile was the carrier for South America, but with the recent unrest in Argentina and with Brazil not being extensively catered for, we explored Chile, the long thin country, as a major destination. A big bonus was that we also found we could fly Lan Chile from Santiago to Auckland, New Zealand. American Airlines would get us across North America from New York City to Seattle after British Airways flew us to New York. Between Chile and Seattle, we would visit Montana, Wyoming and Idaho, in a 1,500-mile loop. Then drive the Pacific Coast, Highway 101 from Oregon to San Francisco where we hoped to spend a month renting an apartment. Out came the calendar again. Two months in North America, two weeks in Central America, six weeks in South America…that would mean spending Christmas where exactly? We put that down under 'yet to be determined'. It was too exciting at times and kept me awake.

With the arrival of each new brochure on the kitchen table we told perhaps one more person that we were thinking of travelling. Remarks ranged from surprise to disbelief. Sometimes we found ourselves telling people who, because of their own place in time, weren't able to join in the excitement we were feeling. And still others, perhaps envious, prevented themselves from celebrating the idea itself. Imagine, a family of four, travelling for nine months away from home, leaving jobs, skipping school. A young friend of ours from the village, Tommy Kilkenny, who was visiting from Germany where he had moved after falling in love with a *Fräulein*, stopped by to see us a few weeks before our departure. He had travelled around North America by Greyhound and was keen to do a bit more travelling himself. He had trained as a carpenter and was happily working in Germany. Places change us. Tommy was changed since his young days in the village, his hair was spiked and blond and you could sense the move away from Ireland had been good for him. He was confident and happy in himself. He wasn't ready to come back.

'So where are you off to?' he asked, sitting on the sofa in the conservatory surveying the garden that he had helped dig just a few years before.

'At the moment, we're thinking of New York, Washington, Montana, Wyoming, Idaho and California before heading to Costa Rica. Then maybe Peru and Bolivia. Chile is also a possibility. Don't know yet about Argentina. We want to go to New Zealand and Australia and China and Southeast Asia too.'

Cool as a cucumber, blasé as anything, he nodded his head and turned to us and said, 'So, you're taking a year of holidays?'

'Yeah,' I said looking to Niall, 'I guess we are. I guess you could say that.'

'How does it sound to you, Martin? I asked our good friend and confidant, who during his working hours had been Joseph and Deirdre's primary school teacher.

'Exhausting. I'm tired just listening to you!' he said with a smile, 'But you never know, I may meet up with you somewhere.'

I was surprised at the reaction we got from some people. There were those who seemed to have no interest at all, and those who seemed stunned. Perhaps they thought we hadn't thought it through, but I couldn't help feeling that there was a touch of envy there also. I repeated to myself the words I kept hearing, *all that travelling…* But what I was thinking instead was: we are going to spend a year somewhere else. Call it a year of holidays, call it a year off, call it looking for paradise, call it anything you want. I am going on an adventure and bringing my family with me.

~

So, sketchily, we began planning the first four months. The next logical question for me that needed to be answered, considering that we were leaving Ireland in the beginning of September, was where to observe the first anniversary of 9/11. The answer came when Niall suggested that rather than blowing our budget on round-trip tickets to Alaska and back to a Oneworld Partner Hub, we spend three weeks on Long Island instead and rent a house near the ocean. We had always wanted to holiday out near the end of Long Island but, 'the Hamptons' being what they are, could never afford it during the 'season'. Admittedly, we went from one extreme to the other, from the wilderness to the *haute couture* of beachcombing, equal in cost undoubtedly. But our first adventure together saw us leaving New York to move to Ireland and so, in a way, it was fitting that we return to New York to begin another. Being a New Yorker myself and familiar with downtown Manhattan, having spent a summer during high school working on Wall Street with my father, it felt right to want to be in New York on 11 September 2002. Just

14

to be in the vicinity of the Greater New York area would allow us to observe with reverence and appreciation and highlight its importance to our children as well as to ourselves.

~

I had been on the way home from Clonakilty in the southwest of Ireland that morning. I had passed a garden nursery on the way and stopped to buy a bag of 100 daffodils, not knowing then that havoc was being wreaked upon New York. By the time I walked in the door of my home, the phone was already ringing with a voice telling me to turn on CNN, the daffodils in a yellow, netted bag at my feet. Joseph was coming in the door from school. We stood shocked like the rest of the world. Days later, Niall, Deirdre, Joseph and I found a spot alongside the Calf's Cabin, as we call it, bordering the road, and planted the daffodils in a place where everyone would see them the following spring. First throwing handfuls of them up in the air and watching them fall at random, we planted each one in its own hole of sand and fertiliser, carefully covering up each bulb. When the planting was finished, we held hands and said a prayer for the dead.

~

When thinking of a place to live somewhere else, the sea is among the first of my considerations. That we could begin this year on Long Island seemed a dream come true. As young children, before my parents divorced, we spent a few summer holidays out in Montauk, the most westerly point of Long Island. I learned to body surf at Ditch Plains. I had my first taste of beer and my first taste of cherrystone clams at Gossman's Dock long before it became the landmark hot spot it now is. My father and I sat on stools at the outdoor counter in the summer afternoon breeze. He taught me how to eat clams and introduced me to my first cold beer. I remember the sensation on my skin, sun-tired and glowing with heat. Sand-slippered feet swinging from the stool. Hair, salty soft. I was sixteen. It was a hallmark memory for me as is Montauk itself. In those summers we stayed out in little cabins overlooking the beach out at Shagwong Cove and watched the fishing boats going out past the point. There were eight of us. We played running races on the sand and ate tuna-fish sandwiches – sand being the operative word.

From those days to this, beaches hold for me the greatest promise of possibilities. From a beach's shores I can sail away, in my mind if not my body, or stay anchored in the sanctity of the sand. When the light is cool and violet in the twilight I am comforted and peaceful of mind. Some people like mountains and lakes. I prefer the ocean. Niall is an ocean lover too which, his having come from the island of Ireland, is no surprise. Really it was too good to be true. I had to pinch myself. Deirdre, my sister, would help us arrange a house rental and was particularly delighted as it meant that she would get to see us, and with my brother Joe living in Manhattan, we'd see him too.

~

Second stop, Glacier National Park, Montana. We hoped to arrive before the snow made travel along the Going-to-the-Sun Road impassable. It mightn't be Alaska but hey, by all accounts it is meant to be spectacular. Deirdre and Joseph will get to say they were in Canada. Next, Seattle, after a drive though Montana, Wyoming and Idaho with a stop in Sun Valley.... I am getting ahead of myself. As I write it is the beginning of summer.... There is a mountain of work ahead.

~

Eighty-four days and counting. Niall has just celebrated birthday number forty-four. Deirdre is in the throes of her Junior Certificate exams, twelve exams over two and half weeks, some of them double papers, and Joseph has two weeks left of primary school. I have taken a sabbatical from my practice as a homeopath. The clouds refuse to part to let the sun shine. Farmers are wearing winter coats and it's the middle of June! We look across the meadow at fields uncut and wonder how the farmers will get the silage made and the turf cut, albeit by machine. Our neighbour Michael said, buttoning up his coat, 'It'll all have to be done at once. No second cuts of silage this year.'

Niall asks me to consider something as I bemoan the sugar-snap peas that have sat still rather than climb the pea fence:

'What do you think it will be like,' he says, 'to spend a year without winter?'

'Paradise,' I smiled.

Things were happening fast and furious; our leave-taking was quickly approaching. The calendar on the blue refrigerator was showing only nine days left. Friends were calling to say good luck and goodbye. Dinners were shared among neighbours. And last-minute details were being checked off the list that greeted us every morning as we opened the refrigerator door:

Call Electricity Supply Board

Call Eircom

Downgrade the satellite television subscription

Order nine months of cat food for Freckles and Neidín

Get a fill of oil

Talk to Gregory and Lillian, the postmasters

Schedule Hawthorn Nurseries for garden maintenance

Get a year's worth of homework assignments for Joseph and Deirdre

And, saddest of all,

Say goodbye to Huckleberry, our golden retriever

I read a story where a family like ours took a similar journey but sold their house and cars first! We wanted to come back to the cottage next summer. (Two miserable summers couldn't follow back to back, could they? In 2001, Europe had experienced the worst summer in decades. Luckily for Ireland, well used to the rain, there weren't the floods that plagued Dresden and Prague.)

Just two weeks before our departure, we heard about a young teacher who had accepted a year's posting in the secondary school in the village. He happened to be looking for a cottage to rent from 1 September to 1 June. The dates fitted like a glove. We imagined that our house might be too much for him, but glad of the possibility of someone living in our home while we were gone, we thought the idea was well worth exploring. His name was Diarmuid. He came to the house on one of the rare nice days at the end of August. The garden was sparkling white and green with daisies and agapanthus nodding in the breeze. The conservatory had just been painted. It looked a little piece of heaven. He was just as curious about us as we were about him.

'And you'd leave your house to a perfect stranger?' He asked when Niall telephoned him to arrange a day for his visit.

'Well, you won't be a stranger by then, will you?' replied Niall.

I could see straight away that our place appealed to him. Most houses that are for rent are not very homey and welcoming. Here was a cosy, funky kind of space full of books and music. He was finishing a master's degree himself and I could see him in a month's time sitting before the fire, with the cat on his lap, sipping a cup of tea and ruminating over early Celtic religion in Ireland. But first things first. I enquired rather coyly, 'How do you feel about cats?' That was more important than anything and would determine how happy I would feel with him as our tenant.

He hesitated at first, probably thrown by the unanticipated question, rather expecting me to ask for references or something. He looked about him. No, no sign of cats in abundance.

'I'm a dog person myself.' Hoping, I think, for me to say, 'oh yes, the dog comes with the house.' Huckleberry was galloping around the garden, playing with Joseph.

'But I'll look after your cats if that's what you're asking.'

We were delighted and went about tidying for him, removing photos of ourselves and touches that spoke too strongly of us, so he could put his own stamp on the house. It was a comfort to know that our cats and cottage would be minded during our long absence, and at the same time a little terrifying that now we really had to go. Up into the garret room at the top of the stairs I carried a box of photographs of us, pictures of nearly twenty years of our life here. I came out and closed the door.

~

'Did you have to get a whole load of shots?' This was one of the two most frequently asked questions. The other was, 'How do you pack for nine months? What will you bring?'

The first question is an ongoing debate with the simple answer, *No, no shots, not for the moment.* As for the second question, Niall and I had flown over to London in July of that year to celebrate twenty-one years of married life and bought some travel bags from the Nomad shop in Covent Garden. (Talk about romantic, hey?) The salesman emptied the stuffing out of every single bag and we deliberated over how we were going to fit our lives for nine months into suitcases that would travel with us. And, more importantly, could we fit ourselves and our belongings *together* into a rental car *and* Joseph's viola too? Niall and I decided we would share a suitcase and bought an enormous one. A kind of duffel-cum-pulley black yoke that was so big, Deirdre could fit inside. For Joseph we bought a smaller blue duffel-pulley bag with zillions of pockets and zips, and for Deirdre, the sophisticate among us, we bought an aubergine-coloured pulley case from the British Airways travel shop, with wheels that spun in all directions. Very cool and classy. We each of us had one carry-on bag. There wasn't a chance it was going to work! Where were the two laptops, cables, CDs, plugs and phone jacks going to fit? And the cameras? It was going to be a tight squeeze. Martin came over and we did a trial run. We fitted all the bags into the boot of our four-door Toyota, imagining it would be like a rental car. With the three large bags fitting, we thought we had scored 100 per cent. Again, only time would tell if our strategy worked. When it came to the real showdown, Niall packed his half of the bag first and I was already complaining that he had taken up more than his fair share. After all, besides my clothes, I had to pack my hot-water bottle, my travel pillow, an outfit for Christmas, my remedy kit, the first-aid kit, the mosquito net and all the supplements for keeping us healthy. (I could already see there might be bag trouble ahead.)

Deirdre announced, 'I don't know *how* you can share a bag with Dad! I mean just look at the size of his shoes!'

Perhaps she was right. This trip was going to see the four us spending a lot of quality time together *in quantity*! Maybe we should reserve some private space for ourselves wherever we could get it.

We left it until three days before leaving to say goodbye to

Huckleberry. It felt a bit like Dorothy in *The Wizard of Oz* when she turns to say goodbye to Scarecrow, 'And you, Scarecrow, I think I'm going to miss you most of all!' Martin arrived and, after coffee and some of Joseph's homemade ice-cream, we all walked out to the car. This wasn't the first time Martin had agreed to mind Huck for us. Mind you, nine months is testing the friendship just a wee bit. Whenever Martin stopped by, Huck was delighted to see him. We felt comfortable knowing that he was in good hands. And Martin, too, who would miss us and our Sunday evening soirées, would be in good hands with Huck to love him. We walked out to the car together, Deirdre and Joseph, Martin, Niall and I, and Huck with his 'baby', which he held securely in his mouth. Baby this time was a little stuffed Mr Bump from the Mr Man Series. Out too, came the huge blanket that Huckleberry sleeps on in the house, scents of Kiltumper Cottage kitchen attached. We ever so slowly walked out in the still evening. As we neared the back of Martin's station wagon, Huck knowingly paused, waiting for Martin to lift the boot. Up and in he jumped to everyone's surprise and to no one's surprise, dogs possessing an awareness that we forget to credit them with. As we put in his mat and he lay down, Baby Mr Bump held gingerly in his mouth, I wondered did he know he wouldn't see us for nine months. Deirdre and I cried, but the boys were manly. We listened into the night sky as the car disappeared down the road. Bye bye, Huckleberry. See you in June.

On the morning of our departure, we stood in our cottage for a final time. Talk about emotional. The house was beautiful and for a moment I wondered what the hell we were doing. Too late to go back now. A couple of friends had agreed to meet us at the airport for a send-off, a version of the Irish wake, waving the emigrants off to better fortunes. Our ticket had been booked through British Airways. To get to Kennedy on 1 September, we had to travel through Heathrow. It would be a long day with two stops and a four-hour layover. Good practice, we told ourselves. We piled into Martin's station wagon (already we had had to move to a bigger car!) and drove off down our Kiltumper road hooting the neighbours as we passed.

There was no fanfare at the airport. I wasn't expecting a television crew, although I thought we were worthy of one, but the great sense of departure we were feeling was unmatched at the check-in desk at the airport. Who could feel what we were feeling? To expect anything else was only a measure of how full of emotion we were. We would share it in time, I reminded myself. Once check-in was over and our bags ticketed through to Kennedy, we sat for breakfast with the small band of well-wishers who had come to see us off. Martin had said goodbye to us outside.

'Good luck. Hopefully you won't need it!'

During the hour or so we waited together, I could see that Deirdre was in trouble. She had cried most of the night saying goodbye to some of her friends who had called over for last-minute hugs. Suddenly, the child who had been so excited since the get-go didn't want to go. I mean, *seriously* didn't want to go. My heart broke for her. *What the hell are we doing?* How could I assure her that what was before us was going to be magical? That magic would strike its spell in many ways, sometimes obvious and sometimes not. That she would never be the same again but that the year held promises that would yield mostly treasures. I watched her gather herself as she walked with tear-filled eyes to the departure lounge and said goodbye to her friend, Kate, her favourite flute-playing pal, whom she would miss terribly. I said goodbye to Marie, and Jane and Jack, and Carmel and their children, holding each one separately. Marie, my great friend in the last year, who herself had spent two years travelling the world before settling down in west Clare to raise a family and practise as an osteopath, pushed us off like we were birds ready to fly. Soaring into the unknown in a way. We waved one last goodbye and disappeared into the departure lounge. It was really happening. No time to turn back. I held Deirdre tightly and navigated her towards the gate, thinking, *O my God, here we go.*

First Stop: New York

I t had been a long journey because of the four-hour stopover in London and we were all tired. We arrived at Kennedy Airport at a different entry point from usual because we generally pass immigration control in Shannon. Having arrived via Heathrow, however, Niall and the children had to follow a long line of non-Americans in another direction while I went along with the American passport holders. We always have to separate at immigration checkpoints in EU countries and in America. My children are not entitled to American passports because they are adopted and not related by blood to me, even though Deirdre and Joseph are legally mine and carry my name as their mother. Every time we fly, we travel as a family of one American and three Irish. Nothing to be done. The US Embassy in Dublin denied my application. But that's a whole other story.

I realised as I neared the head of my queue at immigration that Niall had the customs card, the one-to-a-family customs form they ask you to fill out. I sidestepped my line to find Niall and within seconds a security policeman enquired what I was doing. After I had explained, he motioned for Niall and the children to join me.

They glided past the long weary line of 'aliens' who eyed them suspiciously. It was a gesture that I wasn't expecting. Equally obliging, at first glance, was the passport control officer with overtly good cheer for us. Perhaps it was a trained approach because her friendliness soon revealed a skill of interrogation that was coy and cunning. She asked us a couple of times when were we last in America and how long we had stayed in a way that seemed designed to trip us up if we didn't have our stories straight. Perhaps Niall, who is bearded, Irish, and a writer, could be mistaken (at a stretch) as an Irish terrorist. Who knows what she was thinking. Maybe she was practising her skills on small fry.

'Last time we were here was when?' I sleepily asked Niall.

'April, Mum,' Deirdre replied with a teenage like-how-could-you-forget look. We had visited my father in Amelia Island and swum with the dolphins.

'How long did you stay?' she asked.

'Two weeks,' I replied, trying to get my jet-lagged head around her questions.

'Ten days,' Joseph replied. 'We stayed for *ten* days.'

The officer looked at me and then to Niall and asked him, 'Well, which was it, how long did you stay?' She was very friendly during the exchange but curious. We were just an Irish family. Nothing threatening here. Was it that their Irish passports were like a red rag to a bull? Hardly. It was the heightened security since 9/11 that we were face to face with. And Deirdre, Joseph and Niall were non-green-card-bearing aliens. I shook my fuzzy head and tried to concentrate. When exactly *did* we last visit and how long *did* we stay, anyway? After we got our previous itinerary straightened out, she chatted easily with Joseph.

'Are you going anywhere special?' she asked, while stamping our passports.

'I'm going to my cousins' house in Port Washington,' he said proudly.

'Oh, I thought you were staying in the city.'

'Enough with the trick questions,' I wanted to shout. 'Just let us get to our beds!'

'No, but we are going *into* the city,' he said, 'to see *Aida* on Broadway and then to Montana and Yellowstone National Park and Idaho and…'

'Hmm…' She smiled sweetly, waving us forward. 'Have a nice holiday.'

~

Port Washington, thirty miles from Manhattan, like so many towns in the Tri State area, was one of those many places affected by the tragedy of September 2001. My nephew's girlfriend's father was on the plane that crashed into Rockaway Beach just days after 9/11. So close to Manhattan, the air was potent with memories of somebody who knew somebody. My own cousin's husband was mid-way down Building Two when he made a decision that changed his life. A voice on a megaphone told workers it was all right, the fire was contained, they could go back to their offices. More than half of his co-workers climbed the stairs and returned to their desks. They never came down. My cousin's husband continued his rapid flee and was saved. We were aware that things would be different in New York.

We left in rain and arrived in rain. It rained solidly for the following two days. Labor Day picnics and barbecues were called off. The Anaheim Angels were playing the New York Yankees in Yankee Stadium in the final games leading up to the World Series. The weather was not up to standard for New Yorkers. The Irish were well used to it although Deirdre complained that she had brought all the wrong outfits.

'Where's the sun? I thought I'd be wearing shorts! I don't have clothes for this weather. I left them behind in Ireland, Mum.'

It was a dismal start. Some places you go to for the weather and Labor Day Weekend in New York was one of them. The roadside gullies were flooding with rain. Labor Day was spent in Roosevelt Field, the giant shopping mall in Southern Long Island, strolling the shiny, waxed corridors with hundreds of others. We had expecta-tions of sunshine and shorts, sunglasses and string tops, hotdogs and lemonade, sweet corn and tomatoes – all the ingredients for the beginning of a year of holidays – but instead of the barbecue we had the mall. We had the hotdogs and lemonade indoors. Expectations deflated, it seemed to telegraph a pattern that if left unchecked could have tremendous power to disappoint during the coming year. I knew that I, for one, needed to learn to live more in the moment, to reduce my expectations by staying focused on the here and now. Having done so much planning I was especially in danger of anticipating places, people and things to be other than they might in reality. Half the motivation to travel revolves around the excitement of imagining each new destination. As my sister is fond of imparting to me, 'there is no right way or wrong way, only a different way.' We had traded in the barbecue on the summer lawn for the mall and a different slice of Americana. Miraculously, we kept the lid capped on our piggybanks and bought nothing, marvelling instead at the enormity of the American consumers' marketplace.

After two days, the clouds parted and the sun shone. Deirdre and her cousin Julia sported their shorts and belly tops and rejoiced in the heat from the rainless, beautiful blue sky. They walked to town and went shopping along Port Washington's main street. Strutting their stuff, as we used to say, and feeling the freedom that comes from being young adults trusted by their parents. Julia's brother, Daniel, meanwhile instructed Joseph about baseball in the backyard.

'Hey Joe,' he said, 'catch this!' and he threw the softball up and swung with his bat hitting a perfect slammer right at Joseph who ducked in time and fell to the ground laughing. My nephew is enormously athletic and energetic when it comes to sports while Joseph is more interested in books and discussions. They're a perfect pair for the first couple of days they get together. My sister Deirdre showed me her garden and the delphiniums she was coaxing along. We sat under an old dogwood tree and waited for Larry, her husband, who walked home from the station – his jacket free and his tie loosened. The American dream was being played out right in front of me. Pastoral and tree-laden streets greeted homeward-bound commuters in a welcoming September evening.

Later, Julia and Daniel got ready for the first day of school while Deirdre and Joseph counted their lucky stars because their fellow classmates in Ireland were already busy back at their desks. My sister needed to shift gear now that summer was officially over and early wake-ups, last-minute homework, and making lunch would once again busy the first part of her morning. For Larry, it was same ol', same ol'. His routine was least affected with a demanding position as manager/owner in a business in the garment district, the constant lifeblood of their family. We, on the other hand, were in effect playing hooky, 'mitchin'' as they say in Ireland, cutting classes, taking a time-out, going on a gap year, and we felt good if a little guilty. Free from the constraints of work and school and the ties that bound us to our life, we stepped into a new sense of freedom like crossing the road in a shower of rain when the sun suddenly appears. We had begun the holiday of a lifetime.

'How are you feeling now that you are here?' my sister asked me over tea one morning. It was 7.30 a.m., Larry had already left for Manhattan and our kids were still asleep. Niall hadn't come down yet. We were sitting in her kitchen by the cupboard that holds her collection of the Irish potter, Nicholas Mosse, some pen-and-ink sketches from our Irish books and a watercolour of my garden. Deirdre calls it her Kiltumper corner.

'Well, Dee, I can't exactly say. It feels kind of numb to be honest. Sometimes I think a lot about it and sometimes I surprise myself by not thinking about it at all. Does that make sense?'

She handed me a tea mug, one with yellow pears, and said, 'Yes, of course it makes sense. You're trying to live in the moment!' We both laughed because as she knew well it was a new way of being for me. We had both been avid initiates to Eckhart Tolle's *The Power of Now*. It was an approach that came more easily to her. Between the two of us, I was gifted with the organisation skills, while Deirdre had people skills oozing from her pores. It felt right to be with her for the beginning of our adventure. Deirdre had always been particularly supportive from the start.

'As Niall will tell you,' I continued, 'it is thrilling and terrifying. That's how he describes it.'

'I can understand that,' she said. We were neatly snug on her window seat, still in our nightgowns. The sun hit a hanging crystal slantwise. 'It's thrilling and terrifying for me and I'm just sticking pins on a map and threading your journey across the globe with string!'

'Oh, what fun. I hope you keep it for us when we're finished.' She looked at me then and said seriously, 'You know, Chrissie, I really admire what you and Niall are doing.' She paused considering what she was going to say next. 'I don't know if Larry and I could spend that much time with Julia and Daniel.'

'Hmmm,' I responded. 'I know what you mean and thank you for being so honest, but it's actually one of the things I'm most looking forward to. Can you just imagine it? 24/7 together for nine months!'

'Yeah,' she said, 'that's just it. I can imagine it.' And we both laughed.

~

Something on the landscape of New York was definitely different, and it heralded the change in American patriotism the world had been witnessing since 9/11. Flying from building tops, shop fronts and green spaces was the American flag. Hundreds of them. And more appeared daily as the first anniversary of the tragedy approached. Pocket-size flags; plastic grocery bags bearing the emblem of the flag above the printed words 'United We Stand' with 'This bag was made in New York City' emblazoned as a footnote at the bottom. Beach umbrellas fashioned with stars and stripes. Red, white and blue fairy lights sparkling in the shape of the flag, lit up by night, stood outside the Farmer's Market on Montauk Highway. It took a few days of flag-flying afternoons for me to understand that the point being made was for all Americans to be reminded of the words of their national anthem, 'O say can you see...our flag is still there'. And yes, it was. It was everywhere.

We had left no time to visit New York City. It was a decision based mostly on the fact that we visited New York State at least once a year anyway.

'But Mum,' Joseph complained, 'you never take us in to *see* the city. I want to see the Statue of Liberty. The Empire State Building. Someone's apartment. Central Park. What's Brooklyn like? And Queens? I want to go there! And where's Harlem?'

'Yeah,' Deirdre was joining in now. 'I want to go to Wall Street and see the Stock Exchange. And where are the cool shops?' They were right. It occurred to me that while I knew New York, having lived there for thirty years and having worked in Manhattan, I hadn't shown it to my children, preferring instead to visit with my sister over cups of tea out in the leafy 'burbs of Long Island.

'Okay, I promise, next time we come to New York, I'll show you around. Is that all right?' I pleaded.

'Yeah, whatever,' Deirdre answered with a shoulder shrug.

'Besides, we are going to be in San Francisco for three weeks. It'll be great.'

To make it up to them my sister orchestrated a full day's activities in the city for the last day of our visit before we headed out to the Hamptons. She chose the Gauguin Exhibit at the Metropolitan, a Broadway show, and dinner with my brother Joe and his daughter Caitlin. We were happy to follow her lead and hailed two taxis outside Penn Station to take us up to Central Park.

'Madison Square Garden's over there, Joseph.' I pointed from the taxi cab, energised to be in Manhattan and to be sharing it with my son.

'Well, it's not square and it's not a garden, Mum. So why is it called that?' He looked knowingly at me. 'I bet you don't know!'

He was right. I didn't know. I reflected that from now on I had better have the correct knowledge to back up my points of interest if I intended on travelling with Joseph for the next nine months. We arrived at the Met in the blazing sunshine, and climbed the white steps into the cool, sunless foyer. My kids had never been to a museum as big as the Metropolitan. We decided to be selective and headed to the Gauguin exhibition, stopping first to see the Impressionists on the second floor. It seems we were all fans of Van Gogh. As for the Gauguin, I was personally expecting a bit more until I realised it was an individual's collection on exhibit and never intended as a retrospective. Julia and Deirdre, happy to be together, went along arm in arm in whispered giggles, admiring the naked pink breasts of Gauguin's Tahitians while Daniel and Joseph weaved in and out of museum-goers like characters in a video game. My sister and I caught up with them and smiled, envying them the chance to be in an art museum at all at their age. Any impression it would make would be a good one. The only museum Deirdre and I ever saw the inside of as young teenagers was the Museum of Natural History which my father used to like to take us to.

'Hey Mum, look what it says here!' My daughter pulled me over to the exhibition notes and read: 'Gauguin crisscrossed the globe in search of inspiration, and ultimately ensured his legacy – to quote an early critic for the New York Sun – as a "bold initiator, one who shipwrecked himself in his efforts to fully express his art."'

'Aren't we crisscrossing the globe ourselves. Isn't that good?' It struck a chord like a tuning fork. How could it not? *In search of inspiration.* 'Hopefully we won't have to shipwreck ourselves in order to achieve *our* goals.' I said to her. 'Better mind ourselves in boats just in case, hey?'

~

The entire summer of 2002 was sunless in Ireland, making the long hours of sunshine in Long Island seem like a gift to us. After Labor Day Weekend we drove to the Hamptons to the house in Amagansett that we had booked for three weeks. When I was planning this part of the trip, I had imagined large glass windows, bleached wooden floors and checked blue cushions on a white sofa, but what we got instead was a three-bedroom colonial family house that you could have found anywhere in mid-Long Island. Inside, the floors were white tiled and the furniture was glass and chrome. There were prints of cats on the walls. If anything life-changing was to happen for me during this trip, I hoped it would be something along the lines of learning to prune my expectations and be accepting of *what was*. I was disappointed but what had I been thinking? That I had the income of Jerry Seinfield who had just bought Billy Joel's house on the water for $32 million? Get with the programme girlfriend, I chided myself. At $6,500, this is what you get for three weeks in the Hamptons if you want to be *south* of the highway – in other words, by the water – even in September. After our initial impressions settled, we found ourselves pleased with the house that was to become our first home away from home. Out came our bits and bobs to make our surroundings a bit familiar, and away to the cupboards went the kitsch that spoke too strongly of the owner's taste. Deirdre and Joseph each had their own bedrooms and, after a little readjusting of an abundance of white wicker furniture, Deirdre made a room for herself and decorated it with hanging beach sarongs. The long porch at the back of the house and the twenty-foot pool were not to be sneered at and, although the water was cold, the children made straight for it once we had unpacked. There were a few lounge chairs and we sat warming in the afternoon sun while Joseph cannon-balled into the pool.

The great beauty of the rental was its location. The house was on one of those streets that links Moutauk Highway with the beach road and was within easy walking distance of the town. A three-minute walk saw us at the Farmers' Market or at the café. The beach itself – the reason we had come – was only a mile away. The two entrances to the Greater East Hampton Beach, recently named one of the top ten beaches in America by *National Geographic Traveller,* were equidistant from our front door.

Starting with our first morning, we walked nearly every day into the town of Amagansett to Mary's Marvellous! for our morning café latte and freshly made blueberry muffin. Mary, the owner, was often behind the counter. Friendliness out in the Hamptons is not generally in abundance, we found, but Mary and her staff showed us otherwise. Sipping tall lattes, we flipped-flopped with our towels down Indian Wells Road to the beach. Once weekenders went back to work, the beaches cleared and the sand along the shore carried simply the footprints of seagulls and sandpipers. Half past ten in the morning, we stood on the crest of the sand looking into the horizon in either direction across an empty beach It was sheer heaven. The weather was God's own. We had entered a golden world I had longed for. I felt safe as I gazed on the enormity of the Atlantic. The sheer vastness of the sky and sea and sand enveloped us in softness and warmth. The surf was gentle but the waves rideable, encouraging Deirdre to body surf to her heart's content. We spent days like this, heading to the beach where the sun wasn't so strong that we needed to take cover, bringing picnics with us. Reading. Swimming in the sea and beachcombing. One day Deirdre and I collected about thirty starfish that had washed up the night before. Deirdre decided she would walk everyday to the beach, especially on those days when we drove with the towels and boogie boards and food hamper. It was a complete novelty for her – old enough to walk to the beach alone, she enjoyed a new sense of personal freedom. In Ireland we don't often get the kind of shorts-and T-shirt-wearing weather that we were getting in Amagansett and it added to her independence. Free as the air she freewheeled her way to the ocean. It was the perfect holiday atmosphere for all of us and, to paraphrase Dorothy in *The Wizard of Oz*, there were telltale signs everywhere that were weren't in Ireland anymore.

My brother Joe came out from Manhattan to spend a week with us. I was delighted for my children as they don't often get to be with my rather crazy family. There was a downstairs to the house that we didn't use which had a fourth bedroom and bath and Joe slept there happily. It was the kind of holiday I always envisioned we might have – beaches and families going together like summer and barbecues. We went to the Farmers' Market and bought large-petalled zinnias in pinks and oranges and reds for the table, big, ripe tomatoes and mozzarella for salads, and fresh sweet corn for dinner. The summer lingering on in the season of sweet corn and tomatoes. Already the trip was satisfying one of my greatest wishes and we had hardly begun.

September might be the best time to be out at the Hamptons. The crowds are gone, the people who *have* to be seen are back in the city, although you can still occasionally bump into the skinny, rich and famous at Citarella's in East Hampton. But best of all is the weather. Gone is the harsh heat of July and August. The sea has warmed up and is perfect for swimming. And you have the beach to yourself.

'I want to live here,' I announced to Joe and Niall.

'Ha-aagh! Ha-aagh! Ha-aagh!' laughed my brother whose trained operatic voice bellowed and echoed down the street.

'You do, do you? And just how do you think you could afford it?' We were picnicking outside Citarella's. People paused when my brother laughed, in the way they do when they don't want to be noticed noticing (he had been an actor in New York for many years). But he was right to query the depth of my purse. The price of houses wasn't keeping pace with the current downturn in the economy.

'The good old-fashioned American way,' I said. 'I'll borrow money from the bank and rent out the house in July and August.'

'Oh,' he laughed, 'and use what for collateral? Your good looks?'

'No, I'll borrow yours,' I said. 'But seriously, you never know when one of Niall's novels might…' I turned to Niall as he rolled his eyes, shook his head and smiled. But I knew that, in the back of his mind, he was juggling a dozen combinations of money, school, weather, ocean, and family.

'I know it's got the high-power brokers from Manhattan and the nouveau riche and the glitterati, but look at the beach and the wealth of fresh vegetables and the flowers in summer and my sister and…okay,' I realised I was rambling and thought I'd better stop torturing Niall with what ifs, 'I guess it doesn't have to be *exactly* here, but somewhere where the sun is shining, and the sand and sea are near. 'In the meantime,' I said pointedly to Joe for a bit of deflection, 'you keep your eyes peeled for any of those movie directors you recognise from your days in the business.'

'Yeah,' he said, 'I'll grab them in a neck-hold and wrestle them to the ground and we'll feed 'em Niall's script page by page. Will that make you happy?'

'It's a start,' I said.

'Aaaghh!' Niall roared. 'You see, Joe, if only I had the good sense to marry a nice Irish country girl, one without any of what my mother would have called your sister's "notions".'

'I know,' Joe agreed, 'you poor man. She's going to be like this everywhere you go. You realise that? "Niall, I want to live here," and "Niall, I love it here."'

'Well,' Niall said, 'could we just finish our lunch so I can get back to the house and get a bit of writing done, just so I can first afford to *pay* for this lunch, never mind a whole house?'

~

My sister Deirdre and her family came out for a long weekend to Larry's father's house in East Amagansett, a proper beach house within a stone's throw of the ocean. It had the big white sofa and bleached wooden feeling and full-length glass windows and high ceilings. Larry's nephew Jacob was celebrating his Bar Mitzvah and we were invited to the reception back at the house. It was early evening when Laura and Bruce, Jacob's parents, welcomed their friends. It was an interesting mix of people and there were plenty of young people for Joseph and Deirdre to meet. We gave Jacob a book of Irish poetry and a tin whistle to celebrate his coming-of-age party and later we saw him fully engrossed as Deirdre taught him a tune. Joseph was in heaven with a crew of boys his own age. I stood with my back to Niall and listened as one of Bruce's friends talked about what was on everyone's mind at the time: War in Iraq.

'I think we should go in there and blast Saddam and his regime to pieces. I don't want to hear any of that liberal shit. And don't tell me they aren't plotting our destruction every moment of every day.'

'So you think Bush *would* go to war?' Niall asked. 'And the American people, would they support that?'

'Not only do I think Bush *would* go to war, I think we *will* go to war. And I think we *should* go to war.'

Niall nodded and I stayed fixed to my eavesdropping spot.

'You see, you don't understand. Only a New Yorker could understand. It is *my* city they tried to destroy.'

'What does Iraq have to do with September 11?' Niall asked quietly but pointedly.

The guy paused, looking at Niall, and was probably measuring up in his mind that Niall was one of those liberals who walks around with blinkers on because to do otherwise would offend his artistic sensibilities. He finally said, 'Does it really matter? America has to show the world that it won't be messed with.'

I was reminded of the movie where Jack Nicholson tells Tom Cruise, 'You want the truth? You can't handle the truth!' At what price does the free world pay for its freedom?

Later, Niall asked Larry what he thought about the possibility of war.

'It won't happen. They're bluffing.'

33

Leonard, who was showing Niall how to cook the perfect sweet corn, agreed.

'It's a show of strength. A bullying tactic. I understand from Larry that you were caught in the crossfire of one of Bruce's friends?'

'Yes, he felt very strongly in support of a war.'

'I see. That's very interesting. Would you be in support of war?'

'No. Definitely not. I think it would be mistake,' said Niall.

'I agree with you,' replied Leonard. 'It would be a mistake.'

'What would be a mistake?' asked Joseph who had entered the kitchen.

'War in Iraq,' Niall said.

'What do you think, Joseph?' asked Leonard, who was quick to spot the conversationalist in Joseph and thoughtfully gave him his full attention.

'I think it's a bad idea. War doesn't solve anything. Kids would be able to work out something like this. It's wrong.'

'Speaking of wrong-doing, Joseph,' Leonard said, 'Daniel tells me that you are going to join us in our fast on Yom Kippur.'

'Ah huh,' replied Joseph. 'I think it's a good idea. It's a completely different religion to mine and I might as well learn something about it while I'm here at Jacob's Bar Mitzvah.'

'That's very admirable of you, Joseph. And I'm grateful of your support,' said Leonard with a smile. 'We begin our fast at sunset.'

~

Hurricane Gustav flew through Long Island over the days of the September 11 commemoration. Suitably, the ocean rolled with tumultuous waves, creating a surf of crashing breakwater. The sea roared and churned as wave upon wave collided with the outgoing tide. The grey clouds swirled in giant mists just above the water. We drove out early that morning to Ditch Plains, one of the great surfing beaches in America, to see the surf before attending a commemorative service in Montauk. There were already a dozen people at the beach, presumably doing the same as ourselves. When

34

we were young, my parents took us for a couple of summers to Ditch Plains and it held fond memories for us. We braved a good few waves in our day, but this sea was too rough. No swimmer braved the waves without a board. None that is except my brother. Some might call him crazy. All I know is that not a single other swimmer dared. It's the kind of thing he does. We joked as he entered the water that maybe we wouldn't see him again, alive.

'Do you want to be buried or cremated?' I said with an older sister's mix of concern and fear, carrying, I hoped, a warning tone that might dissuade him.

'Cremated,' he shouted, his great big hearty laugh echoing across the waves.

'Yeah, okay,' Joseph was quick to add and he shouted out to him, 'but that's if we can *find* your body!'

While I was nervous as I watched him duck and dive, I admired his spirit. Memories are made from these moments, good and bad, but a boy's got to do what a boy's got to do. One grey-haired gentleman on the beach came running over to us. He was about sixty and tanned.

'I don't want to tell you your business, but your friend's too far out.' It was true and everyone watching from the shoreline probably felt the same way, but for my brother it was exhilarating and also for him, I imagined, life-affirming. And if there was ever a day for a New Yorker to celebrate life, it was this one. So I let him off and didn't give out to him when he finally emerged from the grey sea, red-chested and sand encrusted. He towelled off, warmed up and we drove back into Montauk town to St Thérèse of Lisieux Church to commemorate the tragedy of a year ago. There were almost 400 people gathered in the basement-cum-church of the local Catholic school. We noticed that, as more and more people arrived, the colours of the flag were being well represented by over half the congregation. Red sweaters, blue jeans, white shirts and every combination of navy Bermudas, red polo shirts and white sneakers were like beacons of a hundred lighthouses flashing. The celebrant paused for a minute's silence at 8.43 a.m. to observe the first crash into the towers. A blue New York Fireman's cap lay on a small table near the altar with a single candle. It was eerie and deathly quiet.

Tears fell freely amid small, soft murmurs of muffled crying. Again at 9.03 a.m., the congregation paused to observe the second crash. Another minute's silence. It was as if we all held our breath, willing the day undone, hoping against hope that the horror was only a nightmare. With the schoolchildren of the United States in school, Deirdre and Joseph stood out amongst the retired couples of Montauk, but the gravity of the day of remembrance was just as potent for them. A year ago, Joseph and I had watched on television as the second tower fell while we sat in the safety of Kiltumper Cottage. It is a moment that I will never get my head around – watching it *live*. Joseph still shakes his head and says he is not able to comprehend it. He chooses not to think about what he cannot understand. Niall and Deirdre were still at school. It was afternoon in Ireland. One of those moments that you remember. Where were you when JFK was shot? Do you remember where you were when John Lennon was shot? What were you doing when Bobby Kennedy was shot? Where were you on September 11?

'...If you walk amid the burning flames, you shall not be harmed. If you stand before the power of hell and death is at your side, know that I am with you through it all. Be not afraid. I go before you always. Come follow me and I will give you rest.'

The words of 'Be Not Afraid' wafted like a rich vapour through the air of Montauk. My brother's voice was like a ship's horn guiding other singers in the direction of the remembrance of the power of the human spirit. Here was ample evidence that we were right in feeling that we wanted to be in New York for 11 September 2002. And with flags flying everywhere, it was a fitting choice of hymn to end the commemorative service, although a surprising one, when the priest announced that we would close with the 'Star-Spangled Banner'. I looked down to Joseph, whom I knew would be chuffed. He had learned the words just a few weeks earlier and had played it at our piano in Kiltumper. In perfect unison, the red white and blue congregation rose. There was nothing that could be said, but it made the hairs rise on the back of my neck as the small church filled with the National Anthem, beginning with the words:

'God Bless America...'

Montana, Idaho and Yellowstone

After three weeks in New York it was time to leave. But in many ways, none of us wanted to. Although Deirdre and Joseph have been to New York often, it still held for them a fascination that will likely be lifelong. The shops with everything in the world in them, the black, paved, pothole-less roads of the tree-lined suburbs, perfect for cycling or skateboarding, the sense of seasons changing, neighbours to play with. Not to mention Starbucks and The Gap. The old joke that Ireland has four seasons: wet, rainy, showery, and damp, isn't funny after you live there for a while. Here there was everything for them, including sunshine. Asking them to appreciate the quietness of Kiltumper, the safety, the education system, and an altogether less hectic lifestyle was putting too much on their young shoulders.

'I hear you Joseph,' I said. 'But do you know that Larry doesn't get home from work until half past six in the evening and he's away before Daniel gets up for school?'

'I know that. I know Americans work ten hours a day and seven days a week! But, but I still want to live here.' I could see that he was thinking about it. 'And in a way it's a good thing,' he added, 'because you can't take your parents for granted then. Daniel and Uncle Larry spend quality time together.'

Oh, oh, where was this going? There was no getting around it. I found it hard to disagree with Joseph. There were many times in the last few years, especially when my mother was suffering with cancer before she died, that I wanted to return to New York. I needed to talk to someone who would tell me the downside.

'We could have a house in Milford, Connecticut, for $300,000,' Joseph continued. 'Four bedrooms.' He was reading this in a copy of *New York* from an article, 'Ten Suburbs You Can Afford'. 'You could have a house in Katonah, Mum, where you grew up, for $700,000. Wouldn't you like that?' His blue eyes looked directly at me as he tried to work out why his Dad and I weren't phoning an Irish real estate agent to put our house on the market.

'Well, all I can say now Joseph is that the world is a big, beautiful place and there are lots of nice places in it to live. Let's wait until the end of trip, okay? We have many places to see first.'

But in my mind I was like Joseph. Those were my words he was speaking. There were many reasons why we lived in Ireland, some of them past their sell-by date, but I was hopeful that at the end of the trip I would discover new reasons that reaffirmed our choice to continue living on the most western edge of Europe, if not forever, at least until Deirdre and Joseph finished secondary school.

Abundant tears fell the morning we left Deirdre and Larry's house for Kennedy Airport, as they always do when I have to leave my sister. Maybe we would see them again next summer; Joseph wanted to go to an American summer camp in Vermont. Instead, we headed to JFK. It was a year and a week and a few days since September 11 and it began to dawn on us as we approached the first security gate. We had arrived at the airport at half past six in the morning for a nine o'clock flight to Seattle, leaving plenty of time, or so we thought. Security was on high alert, so every single bit of stuff in our carry-ons was searched. We all had to take off our shoes. Joseph even had to take off his glasses and his watch! This is my eleven-year-old we're talking about. His viola case was opened, viola out on the table, pitch pipe, chin rest too. We were all in different sections. A tall, threatening-looking guard opened my homeopathic remedy kit and took out the tiny bottles of pillules to investigate. Now here was something he obviously hadn't seen before: a remedy for high-altitude sickness that comes from the coca leaf, an illegal substance in its crude form. (My kit was from Helios in London where the laws aren't as strict for homeopathic medicines.) Trying to explain homeopathy to him while another guard took out my laptop and all its bits and bobs was infuriating. There were passengers and guards everywhere. A senior security lady finally said it was all right to let the remedy kit go through. 'But these could be drugs,' he whispered. (The bottle was tiny enough to fit in my pocket; it wouldn't set off any alarms. I made a mental note to do that from then on, while in the US anyway.) Shoeless – with my laptop left on one table, my remedies on another, Niall and Deirdre together, and poor Joseph on his own getting his gear back – I felt like Scarecrow in the haunted forest with Lion, Tin Man, and Dorothy when he says, 'And then they threw a bit of me over here and another bit of me over there!'

'Whoa! Can you believe that?' I said, exasperated, when I finally caught up with Niall and Deirdre who were tying the laces on their boots.

'Are you okay, Joseph?' Deirdre asked. He clearly was not.

'For f***'s sake, how *stupid* can you bloody be to think an eleven-year-old can have a bomb strapped to his glasses?' He was shouting, not caring how much noise he made. Passers-by smiled. We had made a little camp at the first available seating area. Our stuff was half in, half out of our bags. Still wound up, Joseph spoke agitatedly.

'Did you guys see that A-hole that was with Mum?' Joseph said. He mimicked the security man.

'"Ma'am, this is co*caine*". He said it to her as if her IQ was that of a cornflake,' Joseph continued. 'And then Mum said, somewhat heatedly, back to him, "This is *not* a drug, it is a *homeopathic remedy*."'

Deirdre turned to me then and said, 'Like he was really going to know what *that* was, Mum!'

'Yeah, well, it is New York!' I replied regaining my composure, just glad to have it over with.

Deirdre was laughing. 'Then what happened next, Joseph?'

'"Well, then," the guy said, "Can I see your medical licence please?" Then Mum started to get really bad, like you know, angry and she said, "You don't need a medical licence to practise homeopathy in Ireland."'

Niall said quietly but with some alarm, 'You were lucky. Can't you put the kit somewhere else?'

'No I can't.' I shouted over-loudly. 'The X-rays are really harmful to the remedies. It's just ridiculous. But I will hide the coca next time. Don't you worry,' I added.

When we had all finished venting and felt better, we headed to the departure gate, ready for the flight across the US to Seattle, where we would change planes for Kalispell, Montana. We were just in time and joined the queue only to find that the four of us were chosen by the computer for a random search. *Random, my eye!* Off came the jackets and the shoes. Out came the viola and the laptops. Deirdre's flute was fully investigated this time. Joseph went ballistic, noticing, he said, that most of us on the queue looked, how shall I say it, non-American? Even Joseph's school books from his knapsack were turned upside down and flicked through. I can't imagine what they thought might slip out that could initiate a terrorist act, but it was obviously time to take a step back, not to get too worked up about it. These people were only doing a job. A terrible thing had happened in the previous year and an ounce of prevention goes a long way. The jury was still out, however, on how effective these airport security screenings were.

'We'll have some queuing to do in North America,' Niall, the most relaxed among us, said. 'Better to get used to it, than to complain.'

'Surely we won't be *randomly* searched each time!' I said.

'We'll see, but I think we've been flagged in the computer.'

'Well that's just wonderful!' And off we marched down the runway to the plane where every last seat but ours was already taken.

~

By four o'clock 'mountain time', we were a world away. Kalispell, a small city airport, was like a breath of fresh air compared with what we had experienced that morning in JFK International. We hired an Isuzu Rodeo which just about fit all our gear, and headed out for West Glacier to the Glacier River Raft Company where we had booked a log cabin in the woods for three days.

The air was crisp with autumn and the tourist season was in its last days. Snow was not far away. We hardly passed a car the whole journey through to the mountains. What a complete change.

Yielding to the feeling too, Joseph, ever the witty fellow, said, 'Guys? Is it Cast-a-spell or Kalispell?'

We were booked on an overnight camping excursion with river-rafting in Chile, so didn't avail of the river-rafting trips offered at West Glacier, but it was a smart-looking operation all the same. Very professional. The cabins were tidy, spotless and warm. I had been emailing Deb Knapp, one of the owners, for months before our departure to arrange our dates and she had been most obliging. Now that we were meeting her, I was happy when she turned out to be as friendly as her emails. A young-spirited active woman in her forties, she showed us to our cabin and set us up with basic provisions.

'It's quiet this time of year,' Deb said. 'All the summer tourists have gone home. You'll have a nice time. The weather is looking good too.' She was wearing a yellow polo shirt with the Glacier River Raft company logo and khaki shorts. 'If you need anything, we're down at the centre.'

Deb matched her email voice. She was organised and mannerly and not falsely friendly. Considering that nearly every aspect of the trip was organised through the Internet, I was particularly curious as to how people in cyberspace were in real time. Cyberspace enables some people to be quite different from how they are ordinarily, and it was something I was particularly interested in. If less than 10 per cent of communication is verbal, or so they say, how would people match up to their email voice? I had a theory that you can tell a lot about a person by the way they email and twice as much when you meet them in relation to their Internet voice. I was also sure there were surprises in store for us because of my planning on the Internet, but whether or not I was prepared for them was an altogether different thing. We had heard over the radio before leaving Ireland of an English couple who had booked a holiday in Sydney, Australia and ended up in Sydney, Canada. Another couple had booked a trip to Goa over the Internet, ending up at the right destination, but with hotel vouchers for Genoa. Our round-trip tickets from Seattle to Kalispell had been organised by us over the Internet with Alaskan Air from the back bedroom of our cottage in the west of Ireland. All we had was an electronic confirmation number. But it had worked like a charm. So far so good. We settled into our cabin for the night.

I had researched Glacier National Park as a destination after Alaska had been bumped from the itinerary, and discovered that it is called the Land of Shining Mountains, by the Blackfeet Indians, and that, in their quest for the Pacific, Lewis and Clark had failed to find the route through these mighty glacier peaks. The view from our cabin in the woods was of the mountains in front of an ever-changing sky. We planned to experience the park's dramatic scenery from the roadways that followed along ancient routes used for centuries by native hunters. On the western slope was cedar forest, parried grasslands on the eastern side, and in between lay the glacier-carved peaks and lush alpine meadows of the Rocky Mountains.

The Going-to-the-Sun Road, a spectacular world-famous route, is listed as one of the best scenic drives in the US and traverses the heart of Glacier National Park. Fifty-five miles of scenic parkway winds its way up and over the Continental Divide from Lake McDonald to St Mary. Known for its glaciers, the park also encompasses several large lakes. Hiking is said to be superb and the high alpine terrain is accessible to almost everyone from the Going-to-the-Sun Road, which is open only in summer and early fall. We were there in the last week before most facilities close at the beginning of October, and headed out first thing in the morning to make the most of our first wilderness experience. But first we asked Deb about bear. Had she seen any or heard of anyone who had?

'Yeah, there are bear, but there haven't been any sightings in a few weeks,' she said.

'Uh, huh,' said Joseph not sure now if he wanted to go on a trek with us.

'Just stay on the trail, stick together and make noise as you go along. Oh, and don't leave any food anywhere. You'll be fine,' she said smiling.

Deirdre had spotted bear jingles, a leather wrist band with jingle bells, in the rafting shop, and, armed with these, we headed out to find Avalanche Lake *without* a picnic.

We were on the trail of the Great Bear that stretched all the way to Canada through these mountains and, from behind every tree, we expected a bear to jump out. What was that dark shape? Was it a bear or a tree? As the shapes we passed didn't move, we continued along the Avalanche trail, deep into the forest. Pine needles cushioned the path, tree trunks like thick, barked standing pencils stretched before us, behind us and beside us. We were enveloped in a green sky of branches. Occasionally, other hikers winding their way up to Avalanche Lake passed us and we felt comforted that we were not alone, although most of the time it felt like that. The trek took about two hours with Joseph feeling like he was being dragged every step of the way. Deirdre jingled her bear bells, teasing Joseph, singing, 'If you go down to the woods today, you're sure of a big surprise.'

'Shut up, Deirdre!' Joseph shouted. 'Leave me alone.' Just what we needed, sibling squabbles in the bear woods below the glaciers.

'Do you think that's a new one for the bear?' Niall asked jokingly, trying to deflect. This wasn't the place for a 'tweenager' temper tantrum. 'Keep singing, I'm sure they'll join in, if they're about. They probably even know the words!'

We were all relieved when we reached the lake and rested in the sunshine of an autumn afternoon. Chipmunks skipped along the rocky shoreline. The lake was low and impoverished-looking in the hollow with giant trees and stone-faced mountains rising above it.

Dead, bleached tree trunks crisscrossed the lake in a latticework design of skeletal remains. It would have been a bit eerie if the sun hadn't been above us. We imagined bear watching us, waiting for us to descend so they could carry on.

Curley Bear Wagner, an American Indian, wrote that according to the Blackfeet native people, the Great Bear serves as the overarching symbol of the most powerful image of indigenous human experience in relation to nature. 'Going back 5,000 years ago now,' he said 'you've got to understand that the American Indian and the Bear walked the same path. We fished the same streams. We dug the same Camus root. We picked the same berries in the same berry patch. And we as a people observed the Bear to learn how to survive.' Imbued with an ancient spiritual connection to the trees, the sacred mountains around us, the deep wilderness below the glaciers, we made our descent, at ease, listening to the peace of nature. Even Joseph was feeling relaxed and joined Niall in conversation about a book he was reading on Lewis and Clarke. Deirdre and I jingled the bear bells and lead the way down, deep, deep in a truly remarkable landscape, not another soul to be seen, not another sound to be heard.

~

People in this northernmost part of Montana must survive on frozen food, beef jerky and beer, because that's all we saw in the few shops we passed, along with an enormous array of knives. Hungry, not having had the foresight to bring supplies with us from Kalispell and not wanting to drive back, we fortuitously stumbled upon the Belton Chalet. A 1910 Railroad Hotel, Belton Chalet Hotel was the first chalet built by James and Louis Hill of the Great Northern Railway. An upscale hotel, it is an oasis for the hungry and tired and features old-style accommodation and a gourmet menu. In front of a roaring fire, we feasted on homemade pizzas and toasted brie and fruit salad, playing hearts with a young waiter from Idaho who said, with some surprise, 'Why are you going to Idaho? There's nothing there. I'm going to Switzerland myself this summer.'

The Going-to-the-Sun Road lived up to its expectations. Deirdre and I kept hopping out of the car to take photographs. Mountains pointed at the sky. There was Indian Chief Mountain, mightiest of the great glaciers. Clouds followed the contours of the peaks, gliding down like liquidy meringue. As we approached Logan's Pass, the highest summit, frozen fog descended and suddenly we were driving in white, cold mist. The vista completely disappeared. One minute there had been sunshine and blueness, and the next there was blankness. I was disappointed. We had finally arrived at the top and couldn't see anything. All those fabulous – okay, polarised and re-touched – photos of Glacier National Park I had seen with its jewelled mountain lakes and reflected blue skies were veiled in a frozen gauze. Winter was approaching before our very eyes. It came much like the rain of Ireland, making itself an element of the landscape that demanded attention and was not to be messed with.

After a family vote, we decided to continue and moved slowly down through the freezing white fog heading for St Mary's Lake on the other side. We had come prepared for a hike and a picnic, so we parked and climbed through the woods to the edge of the lake with its view of Goose Island. We sat on logs at the black water's edge and made out bear shapes across the lake until our eyes were satisfied they were shadowed rocks. We ate our peanut-butter sandwiches held with frozen fingertips and pictured the lake as it was on a nice day, surrounded by glacial peaks piercing the sky. It was for this kind of moment that we had packed the gloves, hats, jackets and our Timberland boots. My girl-scout training from the second grade had come in handy: be prepared.

'Hey guys, just two days ago we were lying on the beach in Amagansett!' Joseph mused. 'And we were still in the same country!'

At the visitor's centre at St Mary's, we saw from the maps that Canada was not far away.

'Can we go?' asked Deirdre excitedly.

'I don't know,' said Niall. Tired of driving and not one for experiencing the landscape by car, he was looking at a two-hour return journey *without* a side trip to Canada.

'We have to. It's right there!' she persisted.

Democracy is a tricky business in families, and on a trip like ours even trickier. Better get used to it, I was thinking, secretly delighted at Deirdre's speaking up. Fortunately we had brought along our passports, so, acquiescing to the Princess we crossed the border into Canada, driving to Waterton Lake. Just about everything was closed. The tourist season had officially ended the week before. The famous Prince of Wales Hotel had shut its doors just a few days earlier. It was a strange feeling with everyone getting ready for snow and winter like bears going into hibernation. Just part of the season of life here. We had lunch in Waterton and experienced some Canadian friendly service, Joseph listening intently to the accent, and then the children sent a few postcards to their classmates so they could prove they had been to Canada.

Crooked yellow aspens and pine trees stretched endlessly as we drove back through the grey rain, passing acres of nothing but trees. A 10" by 12" billboard saying 'Last shop in America' beside the most dilapidated-looking structure seemed an apt symbol of the isolation of this part of the world. Much of the landscape was barren and vast. Ted Turner hadn't bought any land out this way. Here were homesteads where ordinary people lived without luxury and seemingly without many neighbours. Where were the schools? We passed a Baptist church in need of repair, standing on its own in a yellowed field of dead grass. Republican placards for Mike Taylor abounded. Montana has a population of less than half a million with very few of them living in this northern part of the state, which made Glacier National Park an oddly serene wilderness, a kind of private park for those who ventured this far. A gift bestowed for the journey, I thought.

~

Education has undoubtedly changed in North American schools since I was a primary school student. I don't remember learning that much about the terrible treatment of the American Indian, and the John Wayne movies my brothers watched didn't do much to set the record straight. People of my age didn't learn about the disappearance of the Native Americans, which is sadly ironic when you think of the place names I grew up with: Katonah, Chappaqua, Mahopac, Kisco – all Indian names. I do remember searching for

Indian arrowheads in the maple woods beside our house when I was in grammar school. We drove through Browning, Montana over the great Indian plains, trying to envision the roaming herds of bison as they might really have been a hundred years ago. The heart-wrenching part was realising that, amongst this great vastness of land, the American Indians were segregated to the areas of poor land to the point of extinction. The map is designated with pink shapes denoting areas of Indian reservations. According to the map we were in the Blackfoot Indian Reservation protected land. I can't imagine what they were protecting. There was only tumbleweed and sage.

As a kind of homage I insisted that we get out and stop at a museum of the Blackfoot Indians called the Browning Museum of the Plains Indian. Founded in 1941, the Museum is now adminis-tered by the Indian Arts and Crafts Board, a separate agency of the US Department of the Interior that promotes the development of contemporary American Indian and Alaska Native Arts. Too little, too late it looked like to me. It was a redbrick rectangular two-storey building, standing on its own beside a cracked Tarmacadam parking area. No garden or shrubbery adorned it. Inside, historic clothing, horse gear, weapons, housekeeping implements, baby carriers and toys highlighted the exhibits. The intricate, artful beadwork was exceptional. Traditional crafts like beaded bags and moccasin shoes, still made by the Blackfoot Indian community, were for sale in a shop beside the museum staffed by Native American women. We went down into the basement shop to see it and to see them – the Indians. Silently we circled inside the shop. The moccasins and decorative beaded things were priced in the hundreds, so we could only admire the work and nod how good they were. We bought some sage and a beaded hair clip and returned to the car without a word amongst us. I felt remorse at the state of the museum and town that revealed a level of poverty that made me recognise the disproportionate distribution of wealth in remote places of this country. Niall turned on the engine and we drove away into the wilderness once more, each of us in a kind of hush.

~

Dear S,

We took your advice and headed to Helena, but what a place. We couldn't find its downtown! The headline movie in the cinema was Gone with the Wind. *Anyway, after a stop in an endearing little old-fashioned ice-cream parlour we drove out and headed further south. Incredible drive down through Montana. Stayed in Bozeman for two nights at the Best Western you recommended. Good facilities for us. Business centre, laundry room, pool. Joseph met a chap in the hot tub who has suggested a drive to Lamar Valley in Yellowstone. We're off tomorrow in search of Grizzlies. See you in Sun Valley.*

Love, C

~

We had agreed from the start that Niall would do most of the driving because for most of our married life I had been the driver every time we left Ireland. Niall hadn't learned to drive as a teenager, and driving on the *right* side of the road was too foreign. Not that I'm a daredevil on the road, but Niall's continued cautiousness was making me irritable in the car. It was the first test of how we held together as a family – in a car for a journey that extended through the whole day. It was not always pleasant. The kids felt squashed together in the back and baulked at the long hours, the countryside sometimes just a bothersome blur getting us to our next destination. They soon tired of me saying, 'Hey, look at that over there, isn't it wonderful? Pretty as a picture.' And asked me in so many words to shut-up already. Niall felt the burden of accustoming himself to the right-side driving and needed to ask at every junction 'Is this the right way?' as if I, being American, had been gifted with a kind of interior navigational programme. He rightfully, I might add, resented my reproaches. After all, he was doing the driving and I was free to look out the window at the moving pictures all around me. I found myself trying to block out the interruptions from the kids and biting my lips when I really wanted to shout: 'Will you just keep quiet and look at this beautiful place that we are driving through?' I probably had a bit to learn about allowing for different appreciations of the landscape we were *all* experiencing. Nonetheless I was beginning to realise that the natural environment affects me in a way that leaves others tired out. I don't know if it is inspiration I feel or just sheer wonderment.

The Old Faithful Lodge was booked months in advance so we booked a family room in a hotel in the town of West Yellowstone, a few miles from the western entrance to Yellowstone National Park. It may sound like a cliché, but Yellowstone is everything you imagine Montana to be. They don't call it Big Sky country for nothing. Stretches of golden grass separated by winding, silver threaded rivers extending into a horizon of hills and sky, horses and rolled hay bales. Suddenly there were designer log cabins and massive ranches obscured by trees and tucked into the hills. Lone fisherman stood thigh deep in waterways fly-casting amidst the tranquillity. A little piece of heaven dropped from the sky and landed beside the river. Why doesn't everyone live here? I thought. Here is where the movie *A River Runs Through It* was filmed. The area above Yellowstone on the northern entrance is aptly known as Paradise Valley. Yet again I wondered why I was living in Ireland when I could be living somewhere else.

Inside Yellowstone National Park, one gets the feeling, again, of the enormity of the American landscape. There isn't the Disneyesque interference that one often encounters in the US – sometimes called industrial tourism by the preservationists. A sense of protection emanates. Purists disagree, however, saying that the park is not protected enough, arguing that there is too much passive tourism inside the park. Recreational vehicles, they say, complete with satellite televisions, belong elsewhere – it being the latter they object to, saying the natural setting itself is enough entertainment. Let birdsong, far away from traffic jams, be your amusement. (Achieving a balance between the nature tourist and the nature purist is hotly debated by conservationists and 'industrial tourist operators' alike these days.) Personally, I think Yellowstone is big enough for everybody to enjoy. When North Americans do things right, they go all out. From the visitors' centres to the ranger stations everything radiates a respect for the wilderness and preservation of it. Yellowstone, the world's first National Park, was established in 1872 and became a model for other nations to refer to in establishing their own parks. Yellowstone, whose sole aim is to encourage preservation, education, and enjoyment of the natural landscape and wilderness, continues to fascinate visitors from all corners of the globe.

We, too, came in search of the wilderness and the geothermal features that make Yellowstone so unique. From the steaming thermal springs and boiling blue waters to bubbling mud pots and paint pots, boiling mud coloured by minerals. From meadows stippled with brown, hairy bison to lakes converged with elk. We sat for an hour in the rain with Japanese tourists waiting for Old Faithful to erupt. We drove to Mt Washburn, over 10,000 feet high, and experienced our first sense of the dizziness and light-headedness of high altitude. Or was it simply the awesome beauty that made us swoon? We drove from west to east and north to south inside the park following the two loop roads that make up the park's main transportation routes. We drove through the golden Lamar Valley and picnicked beside the river. We climbed Mammoth Springs, which, I noted with special interest, was covered in the calcified form of *Calcarea Carbonicum*, a commonly used homeopathic remedy.

The park is populated with so many elk, deer, and bison that wolves have been reintroduced to balance the wildlife. Bear and moose are scarcely seen from the inside of a car but, if you're lucky, you'll spot a slew of parked cars on the roadside which will lead you to a bear viewing. On our third day in Yellowstone, we finally spotted a black bear on the boundaries of the Lamar Valley. It was so far in the distance that it was indistinguishable from the rocks lying beside it. But for the gracious offer of a friendly couple with power zoom telescopes, we would never have seen it. We eventually drove off happy to at least have seen a bear, presuming that to be the end of our great bear hunt.

Joseph was keen to see the Petrified Tree, a redwood that was buried in volcanic ash some forty-five to fifty million years ago. *The Official Guide to Touring America's First National Park* says, 'For a tree to become petrified, it must be buried quickly, minimising decay. In addition, surrounding groundwater must have a high concentration of silica. Over time silica saturated water soaks into the tree, fills the spaces between the cells and hardens.' This is the kind of information that Joseph loves. We walked up to the tree, which was enclosed by a steel gate a few feet from the road. It was more of a ten-foot iron stump in the ground than the remnants of a once mighty tree, but Joseph said, 'Cool!'

Nothing else. Just 'Cool!' We stood and looked and took a photo. Joseph was happy. Deirdre looked sideways at me thinking, I'm sure, 'What else do you have up your sleeve, Mum?' 'Just you wait and see.' I smiled broadly back and waved goodbye to the tree. Niall and I were eager to hike a bit. The day was fine and we agreed to venture down into the valley to a signposted, easy hike. When we approached the start of the trail Deirdre noticed a small, brown wooden box like a bird box sitting on a pole. When she opened it she found a visitors' book inside and signed us in.

12.20 p.m. 4 visitors, The Breen Williams from Ireland.

'Hey, Mum,' she whispered in case Joseph heard, 'the visitors before us said they heard a bear in the woods. And another saw a wolf!'

'Yeah, we are in wolf territory. That's right.' I replied quietly, not sure what else to say, but secretly more cautious of grizzlies than wolves.

The air was crispy blue and autumn was dazzling me with its scents and colours. Thickets of pine trees and aspens guarded the tall amber grass of the valley. Cool air wafted with the green and wooden scents of timber, leaf and forest. There was a quiet, eerie calmness, the kind of stillness that can be easily shattered, however, like throwing a stone onto the tranquil surface of a lake. I could have rested for an hour and meditated. It was as if we were deep into the living breathing energy of nature. All my senses were alert. But I also perceived the children were a bit scared.

'C'mon lads,' I chirped, 'it's only a half a mile to the lake.' But the utter, complete quietness of it and the thought of meeting a bear slowed the pace to a tiptoe.

'Why do they want you to sign in?' Deirdre asked as if in an afterthought. She was beginning to piece it together herself. The penny was dropping.

'I guess they want to know when people spot wildlife so they can track them, but also,' I added in lower pitch, 'I suppose, they also want to keep track of hikers.'

'What did you say? Keep track of hikers or keep track of bears?' Joseph asked timorously.

Imagination got the better of us, I'm afraid, and after some more minutes we stopped, we listened, we stood there in the middle of nowhere with imaginary bears in every black shadow ahead, and at last we turned back. It wasn't fair to frighten Joseph and Deirdre. I had wanted to give them a feeling of being deep in the wilderness which, apparently, I had succeeded in doing. Deirdre wrote in the book on our way out:

12.37 p.m. Too scared, turned back. No sign of bear.

~

During the night it had snowed in Yellowstone. Mt Washburn was blanketed in white and the road was closed. We had been hoping to return to the mountain because bears had been spotted there the day before. Instead, we had to turn around and head back to Mammoth Springs. It was beginning to look like we weren't going to see bear up close after all. Plenty of bison and elk in large herds grazed the meadows and crossed the roads we travelled, but no moose and no bear. We all agreed that, considering what we had seen and experienced already in the sheer immensity of the wide-open landscape and natural beauty, we were far from disappointed. Viewing a bear would only be icing on the cake. Halfway back, however, we came upon a line of cars pulled to the side of the road. Aha! What was all the fuss about? In the way of these things, you begin to know without asking what is happening. I gave the thumbs-up gesture to a man in a baseball cap, camera swinging from his neck, and he indicated back to me with a nod and a knowing smile that 'Yup, there's a bear here!' The kids were excited. I was excited. Whoa! We were officially in a bear jam! Niall pulled over straight away, lucky to find the last space. Travellers behind us had to move on because there was no more room. An extraordinarily beautiful-looking park ranger, like Bo Derek on the beach in the movie *10*, appeared out of nowhere and kept the traffic moving. It was like everything was swiftly in soft focus. We were cued to wait. Suddenly the cameras started rolling. The star was a bear that appeared twenty-five yards away from the edge of the wood in the meadow that lay below the road. A bear we could officially see without telescopic help!

It was an odd scene. Twenty-five to thirty of us tourists, some regular bear watchers, some novices, with all kinds of equipment, from the Kodak instamatic to the Leica. There were people with serious hiking boots and an aging couple in white sneakers who climbed out of a white Cadillac. 'How,' I wondered, 'did the park ranger get there so quickly?' It seemed to be an integral part of her job to track bear and this spot was obviously along the bear's route. It was thrilling to watch the small black bear making its way between the trees, threading around the underbrush and rock outcroppings, disappearing up into the woods. The show had lasted about fifteen minutes. We were content and hopped back in the car completely happy that we had seen a bear with our own eyes. We shoved off the lay-by. The park ranger, whom I had christened 'Beauty', waved us to slow down. Niall stopped the car before her and we waited as she had indicated. Within seconds, the black bear that we had been watching jumped out of the woods only a few feet before us, scrambled in front of the car and bounded across the road to the other side.

'Can you believe it?' Joseph yelped, like an excited puppy.

'Cool!' responded Deirdre, still peering out the window to watch the bear disappear down the ravine. We were like a hive of honeybees.

'Thank you for waiting,' Beauty said to us with a smile that deserved to be on television for the world to see.

'No, thank you!' I think we all said simultaneously.

She reached into a pocket in her uniform saying, 'Here, I hope I have enough of these,' and handed us four official Yellowstone National Park 'I've seen a bear' pins. The heart-warming thing for me was how genuinely Beauty shared our enthusiasm for participating in the bear jam. Okay, it mightn't be as exciting as your first kiss, but surely seeing your first bear in the wilderness ranks among the top-ten thrilling firsts. Now we were truly satisfied. Two bears in one afternoon. Baby bear and mama bear. We headed off towards the grassy lawns at Mammoth Springs where the giant elk graze. We were filled with a kind of natural wonder and each of us glowed with a sense of reward, aware that here was one of the prizes of a journey like this, the unexpected marvels of the world.

One thing about Yellowstone is that you find yourself doing a lot of driving. You can spend the whole day driving the loops, and although there are plenty of small hiking tracks along the way, you also see plenty of 'Beware of Bear' signs. You can therefore spend a lot of time participating in wildlife viewing from inside your car. I think this is what the nature purists particularly find insufferable, but at the end of the day, there are no right or wrong ways. There are as many ways to appreciate beauty as there are people.

We were heading back to our family room at the Best Western just before twilight, preparing in our minds for our long drive to Sun Valley in the morning, when suddenly there was Beauty again, directing traffic in a completely different area of the park. *How do these guys and gals do it?* We found our spot to pull in off the road and scrambled out of the car towards the heaviest concentration of people. This time the serious photographers were there carrying equipment larger than children. This wasn't just a little black bear frolicking between sunshine and shadow they were intent on. No, a great grizzly bear was causing all the commotion. Huge telephoto lenses settled on tripods. I stood beside a weatherworn woman with long hair and a woodsy smell who was wearing hikers and a wax vest. She said to her companion while looking through her binoculars, 'She's probably going to head around back to Norris.'

He nodded knowingly in response. I was trying to place Norris on the map in my head.

I butted in. 'She?' I asked. 'How do you know she's a she?' I presumed they were referring to the great grizzly clambering on all fours fifty yards into the meadow and not to an absent companion who was getting the tea ready for supper somewhere in Norris.

'Because she's tagged,' came the monotone reply, revealing a weariness that suggested the great divide between the purists and us, the tourists.

'Oh, I see. Does *she* have a name?' I said persistently, watching the bear disappear into a thicket of young trees.

'248,' they responded again, without enthusiasm, their minimalist dialogue in stark contrast with the fever around them. I sensed they resented my intrusion and left them alone and reported back to the kids.

248 reappeared at the edge of a meadow's pool. Urgent whispered shouts of 'There she is!' alerted us. Cameras ready, eyes back on the telescope, we watched her slope in and out of the trees. Her massive size, even at the distance from which we watched, was, quite frankly, awe-inspiring. The 'sighting' lasted about five minutes and ended as 248 lumbered back off across the meadow and out of sight, back to Norris I presume. It was, quite simply, thrilling. We had come to Yellowstone to see wildlife. The Trail of the Great Bear had been rewarded. I personally was on cloud nine and felt the world wasn't in such a dismal state if a group of total strangers can share an experience like this and go back to their lives enriched by the result.

～

Flurries fell from a grey sky, clouding the landscape and veiling the Grand Tetons that we were hoping to view in the distance on our drive to Idaho. We learned that if you allow just one day to visit a place, you have to be prepared for the possibility that the weather might not cooperate. And if you're visiting a place just to see what it looks like then you'll be shit out of luck if rain descends. Long, straight Idahoian two-laned highways bordered with wide flat fields echoed what the Belton Chalet waiter had said. And, there were *no* potatoes. Not a single potato in sight. We had mistakenly left West Yellowstone without a picnic, expecting that we would stop for lunch along the way. But what we were slowly coming to realise was that the West was not dotted like New England with quaint little cafés in quaint little towns. Far from it. I was having one of those *New Yorker* cartoon-type moments. You know the one where you imagine that New York is not only the epicentre of the world, but larger than life and bigger than anything, and that places like Idaho are just a dot beyond like the yellowing eye of a potato.

We had downloaded from www.trip.com a suggested itinerary from West Yellowstone to Sun Valley which we followed easily until we hit Route 33. We were still hoping to stop for lunch, but each signpost that indicated fast food required a detour off the road into a town. We chose to wait for a nice little diner further on. Surely, there'd be one. We weren't tempted by Pizza Hut or McDonald's. We quickly realised that there was not a hope in hell of us finding a café. Miles and miles of flat, dead-looking landscape with nothing but sage bush stretching flatly for acres. It looked like a nuclear wasteland and in fact one long tract turned out to be a nuclear testing site. They don't tell you that on www.trip.com! Nor do they tell you it's a 'bring-your-own' affair. On and on we drove past the black lunar landscape of the National Park Craters of the Moon where the US astronauts trained, or, according to some, carried out the faked moon landing. Idaho, so far, was dramatically different from Montana and nobody in the car seemed to like it.

'Like I told you,' I cheerily said to the kids, 'it's a once-in-a-lifetime trip!'

'Yes,' said Niall in his somewhat cynical manner, reserved for just these occasions, 'and you'll never have to come back here again.'

For the fun of it I put the 'O Brother, Where Art Thou' CD on in the car, which seemed appropriate, and we sang, 'As I went down to the river to pray, studying about them good ol' ways and who shall wear the starry crown, Good Lord, show me the way!' We sang all the way to Sun Valley, starving and praying, arriving by sundown.

Out of the bleak and desolate inhospitableness, the Idaho landscape transformed as we neared Sun Valley. In the town of Ketchum, there were designer shops and restaurants and quaint cafés and galleries. Here was something familiar and comforting because of its contrast with barrenness and lack. Here was wealth. And I'll admit that after the desolate landscape we felt at ease with it. So here was something else I was learning about myself. I could travel *through* a given landscape from the comfort of the car, but when it was empty of the trappings of life or scenic beauty, was I able to appreciate it for itself? Did I want to eat there? Did I want to sleep there? Certainly not. Atmosphere is vital to me. I have to face it,

I'm a three-star and higher hotel girl. I wasn't altogether sure I liked this about myself.

Once we settled in our room at The Sun Valley Lodge, we scouted out the impressive hotel where we hoped to rendezvous with two of my brothers – residents of Seattle – Stephen and Sean, who had arranged for business there with the express purpose of being with us. Just outside the dining room and within the shelter of the mountains was the hotel's outdoor skating rink. There was also an outdoor, heated pool which beckoned to Joseph, and a beauty saloon where we made an immediate appointment for Deirdre to have her long hair washed and coiffed. There was even a bowling alley downstairs and activities of every sort available, ranging from tennis to cycling, from roller-blading to fly-fishing.

My brothers arrived late, but we caught up with them at breakfast. I hadn't seen them for over a year and it was a delight for us to meet them in Sun Valley, especially for Deirdre and Joseph. We'd be travelling to Seattle in a few days anyway to stay with Sean, my youngest sibling, but the novelty of sharing part of our adventure with them was exciting. Neither of my brothers had been to Yellowstone or Glacier, so there was plenty to tell them.

'What did you think of Montana, Joseph?' Stephen asked.

'It's fine, but there's too much of it!' We all laughed. My brothers are tall, handsome men in their forties and command attention whereever they go, so when our table of six started laughing, the room stilled. Young waitresses in Swiss smocks from international locations edged by to see if we needed more coffee. Having been cooped up in the car for days, Joseph let loose. We relayed other stories to them of our trip so far, like the time we watched two men in their seventies standing chest to chest, ready to charge each other on the beach in Amagansett over a dog and woman and a bit of kicked sand. We told them about the storm in Ditch Plains and how our brother Joe tempted fate in the howling surf. We told them about our escapade in Kennedy Airport and Joseph's retelling of the coca scene became funnier and funnier. For me it confirmed that the trip ahead had many more experiences, memories were being made here and there would be many such moments. It pleased me to think how much my mother would have liked to have been at our table and that maybe she was watching over us from her place somewhere up above.

Later that day, Sean arranged for all of us to go fly-fishing. Suffice to say that only Sean had ever done it before. We rented as much gear as we could afford and headed out to the river. The image of Stephen – all 6'3"of him, in his blue cashmere jacket, jeans and white shirt – walking sock-less in his tasselled loafers up to a car load of capped and wax-vested sportsman and asking them for directions to the river was priceless. They took one look at him and at us and pointed the way. Sean had bought about fifteen flies. We lost all of them, caught not a single fish and wrapped ourselves more than once in our lines. But the dusk was settling along the river that rippled across river stones, aspens were yellowing against the bluest of skies and I was in harmony with my brothers, my husband and my children. Nothing was missing.

Sun Valley seemed to us in the short time we were there to have been singled out like a spotlight from heaven. Yellow hills rising up to a blue sky. Cabins and million-dollar homesteads nestled in-between the rivers and trees. And while one could easily resent the inequality of wealth in a place like this, compared with Browning, Montana, for example, you couldn't dispute the fact that it was very beautiful. Do the rich have all the beautiful places in the world? Joseph tells me that all the Republicans from California have moved here. It was the place Hollywood movie stars and winter sports stars used to come to. Their photos line the hotel hallways. There was Errol Flynn, Ernest Hemingway, Peggy Fleming. Two nights was all we could afford, but we enjoyed every moment. Our lasting memory, apart from the fly-fishing, saw Niall sitting and drinking a coffee on the edge of the skating rink while we skated on the empty ice under a cerulean sky. Our skating on the large rink was a combination of slips and slides, of moments of grace and panic. As we pushed off, making soft clacks of the blades on the ice, the public address system was switched on and there was Fred Astaire's voice clear and loud with its easy romance and gaiety singing – 'I'm in Heaven'.

And so we were.

Pacific Coast

What was becoming abundantly clear on our journey was that each of us viewed the landscape differently, and our individual abilities to appreciate it varied greatly. Paramount to a successful day's touring was less time spent in the car – more than four hours of driving a day was definitely too much for Deirdre and Joseph. Anything after that was explosive! After six or seven hours, raw nerves began to jangle. My desire to see and experience as much as I could was at great variance with what Niall was interested in. I wanted to use as many senses as possible, taking in the landscape, making a mental record of it, walking along the streets and *being* where I was by exploring the territory and seeing what was available in terms of natural attractions. Niall seemed to be able to close his eyes and soak up the atmosphere as if that alone could convey all he needed to know. Deirdre was interested in where she could have a vegetarian lunch, where she could shop and where would the sun be shining next, Mum? She took selective photographs of the landscape but didn't linger. She quickly observed and moved on. She was quite like Niall in that way. The landscape of Montana will undoubtedly leave an impression of hours spent driving in the car, but the sense of vastness and beauty will also remain.

Deirdre got a kick out of driving into Canada and she was keen to spot that we left Montana from the edge of West Yellowstone and entered Wyoming at the start and close of everyday. She was sending postcards home to her transition-year class. The art teacher was making a world map and attaching them under the heading: 'Where's Deirdre?' She was keeping a journal as well and by mid-October had written sixty pages. She was collecting samples of bags and kept everything from ticket stubs to napkins for our scrapbook. A kind of 'been there, done that, got the T-shirt' approach. Joseph, our armchair traveller, wanted to know where on the map we were and any facts we knew about the place we were in. Also, he wanted to swim – anywhere and everywhere – whether it was in a fountain, a stream, an ocean, or a pool. And he wanted a space to call his own in which to watch television and draw. Joseph quickly nested wherever he was, whether it was in the car or hotel room and, unlike Deirdre, he was able to read in the car. Niall was less expressive about his personal experience and more laid back about accumulating impressions. All through Montana, Wyoming and Idaho, he was lost somewhere in memories of his childhood, when he envisioned from his small room in Kilmacud what America would have been like in those days of native Americans and western cowboys and buffalo and horses. He was also working on his novel, the book he had begun many months before.

'How's it going?' we would ask him.

'Slowly,' he'd say. Or, 'I'm at a difficult part.'

And we'd nod as if we knew. But in fact we could only guess what extra baggage he was carrying in his imagination on this trip, what characters he kept with him in the middle of their plot. For here he was in very different landscapes, each of them stunning in their own way, and all the time he was also in the imagined locales of the novel in his head. So, for the most part, travelling with a novelist meant allowing for the extra dimension, the silent, secret workings of the imagination. The landscapes we passed through were entering Niall, I knew, but perhaps wouldn't appear in his work for years.

I was twelve years old when I travelled for the first time, visiting relatives in Belgium and Holland. Collected images of La Grand Place, the Peeing Boy and the canals of Amsterdam flicker in my memory, but also I remember running through a famous Balinese restaurant in Amsterdam with my cousin, shouting, 'Look, we found American toilet paper!' I still have the menu we all signed, something for which my uncle is remembered fondly. Along with postcards and museum exhibition posters, signed menus from special occasions were his signatures. The special mint candies that I was able to buy when my aunt let me walk down to the corner shop stand out and also the bread of Belgium which was so different from the bread of America in the mid-1960s. The landscape in Brussels takes the shape of a sunken park with a high bank of green trees. A child's memory is like a treasure: whatever it was that my children were experiencing on this trip, it was as valuable as what I was experiencing. Searching for bear and watching the herds of elk and bison in Yellowstone made the landscape come alive for Niall. Skating in Sun Valley was magical for Deirdre and me. Seeing the mud pots, the blue pools and sulphur hot springs was a highlight for Joseph and although sitting, watching and waiting for Old Faithful to erupt was disappointing for him – he had been looking forward to it since we left Ireland – it will turn up thirty years from now as a fond memory. And he'll probably chuckle at the child he was then when we remind him that he shouted amidst the busload of Japanese tourists, 'I've seen better pictures of this in *National Geographic*!' So it is, we are all travellers gathering the moments of our lives.

~

We landed in Seattle and hailed a taxi to Stephen's stylish two-bedroom apartment which had large windows for viewing the sunsets over Puget Sound and a view of Mount Rainier which peaked above the cloud line to the east like a Japanese painting. The Pike Street market was a stone's throw away. After nearly two weeks of driving, we were happy to settle in Seattle for some rest and relaxation, some good food and the city's ubiquitous coffee. So we headed straight to Starbucks for a *latte grande* and a double-whipped brownie mocha frappachino. It was always a part of the plan that we would visit with my brothers in Seattle even before they arranged to rendezvous with us in Sun Valley. It felt like we had had dessert before dinner. They had arranged time off and had offered to put us up between them for four nights. Stephen is my daughter's godfather, so we arranged for them to spend the first night together while Sean and his wife Kim brought the rest of us back to their house in the suburbs. Joseph was delighted to play with their son Conor, an elf-like three-year-old who ran everywhere after him, and to investigate a house in the suburbs of Seattle. Keenly interested in people's homes, Joseph seemed to file the ranch-style layout somewhere in his memory for use later in his drawings. Deirdre and Joseph were happy to visit with family again. Living over 6,000 miles away across a few time zones, a continent, and an ocean, it was unlikely that these kinds of family visits would be an annual event. In fact, Stephen hadn't been to Ireland in the seventeen years since we moved there. Sean had been a few times in the early years, but his last visit to Kiltumper was a decade ago. It was doubtful that we would be back soon ourselves. So, it was with some heartache that I watched as Joseph held Conor on his lap, playing robots. As I was learning, it was a moment to savour and not a moment to waste bemoaning that it wouldn't come again. You can spend valuable energy on a moment that doesn't exist and end up eclipsing the one you are in. I decided to be where I was and fully experience this time with my youngest brother and his wife in their home beneath the tall trees of their garden, content in the knowledge that Sean was doing well and was happy in his life. Conor was born after my mother died, but I knew that she would have adored him and would have seen in him her own youngest child. Family moments like this were a bonus on the trip, but they were part of the reason for coming to America and spending the time where we did. For when I had asked myself what *I* would want from a year away, family was one of the answers. It was a response largely out of the isolation I had sometimes felt living for seventeen years away from my own country in the west of Ireland. And I was aware that after we left San Francisco for Central America, none of us would be seeing family or friends – not a single familiar face – for the following seven months.

Seattle is a city I could call home. It's got a west-coast American laid-back feeling but without the attitude of California. It bustles to its own pace. It's well known that more coffee is drunk in Seattle, home of Starbucks, than anywhere else in America, and the inhabitants buy more pairs of sunglasses than anyone else in the world, which Sean says is because the sun keeps coming out after the rain. Sounds like optimism to me and my kind of place. Wearing my sunglasses, which I never go anywhere without, and sipping a latte as I strolled though the Pike Street market, I felt at ease. We watched as the fishmongers, famous for their selling style, played catch with a giant sea bass that Stephen had ordered fresh for our dinner. Red chilli peppers hung like clothes on a line strung between two stalls. Flowers of late summer like Day-Glo flash-lights flanked the passages. We bought a punnet of raspberries and a block of Parmesan cheese, stopping to listen to a jazz quintet of voices with a harmonica. Five ageing African Americans in dark clothes and hats entertained a crowd. The sun was lowering in the sky and we ambled as if it was always meant to be like this.

~

The anti-war rally in Seattle on 6 October drew a much larger crowd than the organisers, Not in Our Name, were expecting. Nearly 10,000 people, many of them first-time protesters, walked peacefully from the Capitol's Volunteer Park down to Seattle's Westlake Centre. Deirdre and I had taken Stephen's advice and gone shopping, unaware of the demonstrations until we arrived. We manouevred ourselves past a long line of parked police motor-cycles. Policemen in black sunglasses and knee-high black leather boots stood beside their cars and cycles. It was like a walled garden of police on the outside and protestors on the inside where giant papier-mâché puppets, costumed and masked men on stilts, along with mothers and fathers pushing baby strollers, demonstrated peacefully. Deirdre had an idea of what the rally was about but I explained further. It was certainly the first time she had seen anything like this except on Sky News or CNN, if at all, from the safety of Kiltumper.

'Mum, is there really going to be a war?' she asked. We stood on

63

the corner beyond the police and took photographs of what looked to be more than a hundred police motorcycles.

'Not if these people have anything to do about it,' I replied, nodding towards the crowds in the street. 'But I don't know, Dee, maybe. It's early days yet. And the United Nations will have something to say about it if the US government continues in this direction.' (Well, that's what I truly believed at the time.) If we had read between the lines, we would have understood that the big guns in Washington were polishing their weapons while more than half of its citizens, largely removed from the consequences of a war thousands of miles from their shopping-centre malls, were unsuspecting. Perhaps because we had stepped onto the global transit, in a manner of speaking, we were more aware than we would have been at home in Ireland, but the anti-war rally left us feeling alert and oddly disempowered. We watched the protestors and the police uneasily sharing the streets around the Westlake Centre like a chess game in its early stages. Although it was peaceful and orderly, you couldn't help but feel there might be trouble ahead. With a little heightened anxiety, we came away.

～

Impressed with the fullness of Seattle, we left to continue our travels. We had scheduled seven days to explore the Pacific coast, and had chosen to drive down Highway 101 from the bottom of Washington State to San Francisco. With Sean's help we had booked accommodation all the way, beginning with two nights in Canon Beach, a sea town at the northernmost point of Oregon. We settled into a range-rover type vehicle, packed all our gear in the back, and set off like modern-day explorers for a tour of the Pacific Coast of North America.

Once we crossed the Washington State border, it was a scenic drive along the Columbia River across the top corner of Oregon. Something about Oregon being between Washington and California had made me think of a forgotten land of green, a place I had always wanted to visit. In no time at all we arrived at Canon Beach and, as we approached our rented cottage, The White Heron, it was with growing excitement as we soon realised it was directly on the water. Acres of a wide blond sandy beach stretched in front of the holiday cottage. Here was a beach of a thousand herons. The windows of the apartment framed the scene like a triptych painting. We knew immediately we could have stayed here a week, just looking out. It was our first time this trip to see the Pacific, and no sooner were we in the door than we were out the door to the water. Rows and rows of breakers rolled into the shore. The kids ran forward, hundreds of sea birds scattering into the air above them calling to each other rather inharmoniously. It was the biggest beach we had ever walked along. No wonder it had been recently named as one of the ten best beachcombing beaches in America. It was big enough to land a plane on, which apparently had been done before. Canon Beach is home to the world's third largest monolith, fondly known as the Haystack. It rises on the edge of the water like one of Monet's haystacks coloured by swirls of misty haze circling it, obscuring its base. While we were there it was silhouetted against an expansive blue sky and a rolling carpet of sea. Every manner of beach activity was happening, from kite flying to sand surfing. It was heaven for beach lovers like us.

The town, like a transported slice of New England, misled us into thinking that this is what we would encounter further down Highway 101. Quaint shops and cafés, half of which close down for the winter season, were still vibrant in mid-October. It was peaceful, and just what I wanted small-town America to be like. It was like a perfect, clapboard-grey shingled town. Home to a community theatre and a bookshop, more than half a dozen artists' galleries (peopled by painters who actually lived there), a library, a fire house, and even an old-time candy shop, painted pink with a long white porch. Saltwater taffy was made each morning by old-fashioned machines whose gooey arms turned and stretched and mixed the soft taffy while passers-by watched.

'It's a long way from Browning, Montana,' Niall mused as we walked the length of the street looking for the grocery shop.

'Yeah, it is that,' I replied, feeling myself falling into an 'I could live here' daze. 'I wonder what the real estate taxes are? Probably too high for middle-income wage earners, like ourselves, hey?'

Niall gave me a sideways glance and took my hand.

'Well, considering I'm tax-free as an Irish writer living in Ireland, I think you could safely say that,' he laughed.

It was quickly turning into an upscale seaside resort for Seattleites and Portlanders, but for all that it still had some down-to-earth charm.

'It's an auspicious start,' Niall said.

'How come, Dad?' Joseph asked.

We were having a dinner of macaroni and cheese while watching the herons and the breakers.

'Because we are on a journey that will see us on the shores of the Pacific Ocean from Seattle to San Diego in North America, from Manuel Antonio in Central America, to the bottom of South America all the way to the Straits of Magellan.'

'The Straits of Ma-who-llin?' Deirdre asked, giving one of her endearing smiles that means she is wondering if this is something she should know.

'That's it, Dee. You have it there. Straight Mawhollin! Yes, if ever there was a crooked man it was him, Straight Mawhollin of Gellan.'

'Dad! Leave me alone,' she barked.

'Don't be mean,' Joseph laughed.

'Now,' I said continuing the fun, 'might he be the half-brother of Houliwho?'

I knew that it was for times like this that I had put so much energy into organising the trip – innocent times of togetherness. While living in the moment is fine and what we are aiming for in the end of the day, there's something to be said for a happy memory that lives on in its own world inside you, like time-released food for the soul.

'Houliwho and Straight Mawhoolin, a desperate pair, indeed they were,' continued Niall, unable to resist the possibility of a story, 'walked all the crooked way from Cork to Chile.'

'Eh Dad,' Joseph cut in, too attached to real geography to take this leap.

'All right, they took a crooked boat part of the way.'

'I see,' Deirdre said, tidying away her plate with the kind of indulgent smile she reserves for her parents. 'Joseph, this is what our entertainment is going to be like on the trip.'

'O God,' he groaned.

~

We left Canon Beach following signs for Highway 101. What we had envisioned was a coastal drive along the mighty Pacific, a rural road dipping in and out of the landscape onto to the shoreline like you see in the movie sets in California. The guidebook we bought for the Pacific Coast Highway told of travelling one of the most beautiful highways in the world, a region of friendly towns and secluded coves with 1,800 miles of winding, scenic roadway. However, instead of friendly towns we found sprawling shopping malls on both sides of the streets where fast-food joints were king and fresh food a pauper. The secluded coves were so well hidden beneath acres of forests that you couldn't see them. When the landscape did open up, revealing the Pacific Ocean, it was too fleeting. It was not what we were expecting and we were greatly disappointed. As it turned out, only one fifth of the guidebook was dedicated to Oregon and Washington states, so we quickly dispensed with the author's advice and made our own way down to San Francisco. We stuck to our original plan and stayed on Highway 101, first passing Lincoln City in a maze of malls and taco stops. Dismaying enough to all of us in the car was the fact that there wasn't a Starbucks-type coffee dock in sight. 'Must be some law against it,' Joseph remarked.

Over or under-fried chips, undercooked or greasy grilled cheese sandwiches and limp lettuce salads were the fare wherever we stopped. Finding that golden nugget in the sand was too much work, so we settled into the car to continue on, driving to Florence, Oregon. Breathtaking scenery around Hecata Head and a visit to the Sea Lion Caves nearby broke the mall maze and the pine-tree parade that lined the so-called scenic road. At Hecata Head there was, finally, the kind of dramatic scenery that we had envisioned. A magnificent view of one of America's most photographed lighthouses perched on a cliff edge, with nothing but the Pacific all around. The children went down to the caves, but unfortunately the sea lions were out and about and not to be seen. I fussed about with the fancy camera Stephen had given to Deirdre, reading the manual and pushing buttons and photographing the lighthouse in buffeting wind. Niall, meanwhile, was happy to be out of the car. Not a cave-goer, he bought a soda from the machine and looked out across the Pacific. I wondered to myself in private if he was happy to be doing this. Sometimes I thought that the material world meant nothing to him. A good cup of tea with two heaped spoonfuls of sugar and a biscuit was all he needed. Besides us, his family, the company of words and music were the cornerstones of his world. Sometimes I felt that I was pushing him around the globe. 'Ah sure,' I consoled myself, 'it'll be good for him.'

The B&B in Florence had advertised a full kitchen and after we cooked some pasta and vegetables for ourselves, we followed the owner's directions to the sand dunes that are renowned along the southern coast of Oregon. They stretch for miles and are rightly legendary. After braving the fierce wind, we nestled down among the reed grasses and the dune ridges, soaking up the stored warmth of the sand from the day's sun. We took photographs of Deirdre as a beach bunny, her long hair falling perfectly for the camera. We could have been somewhere else. Long-bleached tree limbs piled like discarded soup bones gave the place a desolate, yet beautiful, feel. The roar of the ocean echoed against the wind-sculpted dunes, which seemed to form before your eyes. There wasn't another soul around, making me realise how little advantage people sometimes take of their natural landscape. It wasn't the first time I thought about how easily we are seduced by our own man-made malls and marketplaces when we should be tuning ourselves into the energy of the world beyond our making. After the cobwebs that had encircled us during the day's driving had been well and truly ripped from us, and we had been renewed with fresh ocean air, we slept happily in Mrs Drake's B&B.

The food wasn't bad all the time. The next day we found a good café with homemade scones and pastries and had brunch in Brandon-by-the-Sea, a charming enough little town below Florence. We drove along the recommended Beach Loop Drive which at first we couldn't find, not realising we were actually on it! So much for the scenic. We got as far as Brookings that day, near the Oregon/California border, watching the temperature in the car rise by ten degrees as we approached 'banana belt' territory, known for its Californian-type year-round, pleasant weather. Joseph was amazed and convinced us that he was telepathically making the temperature rise.

It's a sobering thing, meeting one's own expectations, but what I was finding on the drive down the Pacific Coast Highway was America the Convenient where I was hoping to find America the Charming. The food was particularly disarming. Bed and breakfast establishments seemed also to have lost that 'homespun' quality, apart from those that charge triple figures for a bed. The B&B in Brookings took the cake as far as breakfasts go, however. When we arrived in late afternoon, the proprietor, a lady named Betty who introduced herself to us three or four times before we reached the door of our rooms, quickly brought us around the back of her house. She showed us to rooms which, while pleasant enough, had a little too much of that plastic-coated touch. There on the table in the kitchenette-cum-bedroom-cum-sitting room was our breakfast for the next day. Saran-wrapped muffins double baking in the dying sun. Tiny plastic tubs of UVH milk warmed in a basket near the automatic coffee maker. We had paid by credit card and, once Betty showed us where to leave the key in the morning, it was the last we saw of her.

~

'Don't merely visit one of California's historical landmarks, stay in one!' The Eureka Inn is a listed 'National Historic Place' and supposedly one of the finest hostelries in Northern California. According to their brochure, it has served as host to numerous dignitaries and celebrities, such as Sir Winston Churchill, Presidents Hoover, Ford and Reagan, John Barrymore, Shirley Temple, Laurel and Hardy, and Truman Capote and Herman Wouk. We had tried the charming B&B approach and now sought the charming inn approach.

Eureka, said to be one of America's 'prettiest painted places', is nestled on Humboldt Bay and surrounded by redwood forests. Stately Victorian houses sit along the waterfront and reflect a time of prosperity, many still retaining their original elegance and splendour. There are more Victorian houses here per capita than in any other city in California. The best part of Eureka is along the waterfront where the old town is being carefully and beautifully restored inch by painted inch. And if we hadn't ventured beyond the Eureka Inn, which clearly had seen better days, we would have missed one of the highlights of our road trip down the Pacific.

The following morning was a Sunday. Deirdre and I got up early and walked around the morning streets with their strong echoes of 1950s architecture as if we were on assignment for a photo-essay. Here was a curious mix of Victorian elegance on one side of town, a kind of '50s and '60s retro style east of Highway 101, and a dozen painted building murals in between. Merle Haggard was headlining the Eureka Palladium. Inside the Coffee Bean on the corner of the north side of the old town we saw advertisements for everything from farmers' markets to vegan take-outs to all-women string quartets. Patchouli oil sweetly scented the air. Our thirty-six hours in Eureka impressed me and made me think we may have been missing other equally engaging places along the way. Or was it simply that we had arrived in California – not only a State, as they say, but a state of mind?

Leaving the historic seaport city in the heart of the Redwood empire, we were surrounded by one of the ancient wonders of the natural world, the Sequoia sempervirens – the world's tallest trees, which remain from the days of the dinosaur. By nightfall we would arrive in Mendocino, staying for two final nights, before at last arriving in San Francisco and our own rented Victorian house – well, according to the plan that was. Just south of Leggett, there is the original 'drive-thru' tree. And just when we thought we had seen enough trees, Joseph announced he wanted to see it.

'C'mon guys,' he pleaded, 'just a little detour, pleeeease?' Not usually game for these kinds of tourist attractions, Niall agreed.

'All right, all right,' he said. 'We'll find the drive-thru tree for you. Dee can take a picture and send it home to your class. Will that do you?' Joseph was excited. Except for the picnic in the middle of the Redwoods, he and Deirdre were getting more and more unimpressed.

'What do you think of it, Deirdre?' I was referring to the scenic drive we had been on for five days.

'Boring,' she sighed.

'How's that?' asked Niall.

'Nothing to look at. You can't see the sea. Too many trees.' It was true. Often the sea was only just behind a thin corridor of trees bordering the highway, but we couldn't see it. It made me realise what islanders we are, living in Ireland, and that our natural habitat is coastal. We all really missed the sight of the open horizon and the sense of the sea.

The Redwood Highway through the Benbow Valley was stunning and, if we had orchestrated our trip differently, who knows, we might have been converts to valleys and mountains and lakes. After Leggett, the highway turns back toward the coast and screws down in astonishingly tight bends through the forest into descending mist and fog. At no more than ten miles an hour, it seemed to take a stomach-twisting forever.

'This looks exactly like the last hair-turn bend!' Deirdre groaned.

Finally we emerged at the bottom and out of the woods onto a highway that skirted the ocean. The landscape was desolate in the grey cloud, and startlingly tree-less. We didn't stop for any Kodak moments and arrived at the Mendocino Hotel on Main Street in brilliant sunshine by mid-afternoon. *You have arrived in a familiar place* something inside me seemed to say. I got out of the car and breathed a sigh of relief. Our rooms at the hotel were quaintly Victorian, and quaintly musty. Both children hated it. I, on the other hand, was easily charmed by the antique lace and iron bed stands and heritage-coloured walls. Our rooms were across the garden from each other behind the main hotel. I surrendered to the surroundings in a greedy sort of way while my Irish compatriots sniffed at the hippy-like atmosphere with some reserve. Was that marijuana they caught wind of? I liked the odd blend of grey-haired pony-tailed blue-eyed Californians, barefoot, New Age hippies, and purveyors of modern commerce.

Mendocino is inescapably New England-like in its Main Street shop-frontage, sitting on the edge of a rocky cove. A white church spire completes the scene. What I saw was the kind of town that I liked. A town on the edge of the sea where you could get fresh vegetables, fresh bread, good coffee and browse in a bookshop or gallery and not feel like you should be dressed by a designer. We hadn't known at the time of booking the hotel that it was the town where *Murder She Wrote* was partially filmed – news which thrilled Joseph, an admirer of Angela Lansbury since *Bedknobs and Broomsticks* and *Beauty and the Beast* as well as an occasional viewer of the television series. So we spent an afternoon looking out for scenes from the show while measuring the small-town, homey feeling of the television series with reality. I found Mendocino to be the kind of place that I liked. But I was alone in that.

On our first evening, I sat alone by the fire in the lobby of the hotel typing some notes while Niall was settling the kids. The air was thick with the scent of wood smoke and the spirit of other artists and writers. An old man stood beside me in a blue beret and brown tweed coat. His buttoned-up dark green shirt bore the tiniest hole near the pocket. Walking back and forth in front of the fire, he finally decided to put a log on. He turned to look at me and took a flower from his worn lapel and offered it.

'It's from my garden,' he said.

'Thank you.' I took the flower and held it.

'I don't work here,' he said. 'I just come by to check on the fire.' Blue eyes looked straight at me as if he thought I had spoken.

'I live on Main Street.'

'It's a nice place to live,' I replied, not sure if this old gentleman was the full shilling or not.

'I grow flowers in my garden and paint.'

I nodded. He watched the log on the fire safely settle. We didn't say anything more. I stopped what I was doing on my laptop and joined him in watching the fire. If I were to speak, I'm not sure he could have heard me anyway. Earlier in the day, at the Mendocino Café, another grey-haired man was passing around small books of his poetry for visitors to buy. Mendocino is peopled by older poets and artists and young photographers. Side by side are the chic boutique and the organic muffin shop. Maybe too many shopkeepers were trading in quaintness, but the diehards stay on through the wind and rain that affects this part of the Northern Californian coastline and provide the backbone of the town. They say the weather in winter is not for the faint-hearted; mists sometimes taking days to clear. My feeling was that it was not just another pretty painted town. But maybe I am too easily seduced. The gentleman fire-tender didn't appear to be looking for something from me. It was just what he did, this stopping by the hotel on an evening to see if the fire needed minding.

'Do you like it here?' I asked, attempting to make polite conversation.

He turned slowly towards me, gathering his words, discerning whether I was the sincere sort or the nosy sort. He was a man of few, slow, soft-spoken words.

'A friend of mine moved here. She told me about it. I followed her.' He paused, as if considering this, then added, 'That was over thirty years ago.' His pale blue eyes were still, serene. I think he was composing something in his head but he didn't share it with me. After a few minutes, he left. He smiled and walked backwards away from me and disappeared. I wondered if he were a vision or the real thing.

Passing the desk on the way to the room later that evening, I asked about him. The receptionist said his name was Jim and he came every evening for a brandy.

'He always has just one brandy. He changes a twenty in the morning and I think that's all he spends in the day.'

'He said he's a painter and lives on Main Street.'

'I don't know if he's a painter, but he does live down the road. I've never been to his house,' she said, not exactly interested.

Browsing the next day in the Gallery Bookshop and Bookwinkle, I was leafing through the section on Mendocino and came across a book entitled *Mendocino Artists: A Dying Breed*. I flicked through it until I recognised a photograph. There he was, Jim Bertram. He grew up in Detroit and was a World War II navy veteran. He had been 'making pictures' for more than three decades. He specialised in a form of non-verbal calligraphy the book said. 'The alphabet is made of dancing lines and dots saying *love* primarily.' And I realised that in just this casual encounter I had found something of what I needed and most enjoyed on the trip, and for which a place like Mendocino seemed made.

California

Our Internet contact in LA, Jeffrey, who was helping us organise the trip to China, called it a San Francisco hiccup. It was definitely that, the hiccup that lasted five days. When we were in the planning stages, I wanted somewhere on the trip to have a 'city experience'. San Francisco, I decided, would be perfect. Only I forgot to insert in my wish, city experience as in a *neighbourhood*, like Noe Valley. The 'flat' we had rented, and paid for in full, turned out, in short, to be not what we were expecting. I had been in San Francisco twice before and, in my mind, I was imagining accommodation something similar to what I had previously experienced. No such luck. I had seen a few photos on the Internet of the 'flat' in the Mission District and we had corresponded several times with the owners – writers, like ourselves. Like ourselves, or so we presumed... I should have listened to the faint voice in my head that whispered, *danger*. Presumption is often the first step towards disappointment, as we were to find out shortly.

As we neared the street that our furnished rental was on, still driving the SUV that we had had for the past week, that odd mixture of silence and dismay that speaks too loudly grew in the car. We were tired from the drive from Mendocino and of having been on the road for a week. We were more than ready to settle into what was to be our home away from home for the next three and a half weeks. (In hindsight, I can admit that I had talked about San Francisco too much to the kids. During the long drives through

Montana and Wyoming and Idaho and down the Pacific Coast, I had said to them in response to various questions they asked:

'Just wait till *we get to San Francisco*.'

'We can do that when *we get to San Francisco*.'

'Deirdre might even get to rent a cello when *we get to San Francisco*.')

Joseph had anticipated from his research an abundance of Victorian houses. He imagined we'd be staying in one. I imagined we'd be staying in one, too. A nice, tidy one. As we drove nearer, we realised that the apartment was *in* the Mission District and I could see straight off that while it was a kind of happening place, it wasn't appealing to the kids. We were withholding judgment till we landed inside. The Mission was a hive of activity as we drove along Mission Street, turning up onto the intersecting street that was ours.

'It could be very nice inside, you know,' I said to Joseph as we climbed the steps up to the rather stale-looking grey door. He looked at me askance. The windows looked as if they hadn't been washed in years. Turning the key in the lock, I said a little prayer: *May it be something like what we had hoped for.* Inside we were greeted with what can only be described as absolute clutter: Books, papers, magazines and post from weeks of the owners' absence. The sofa, which we had been told was also a pull-out bed for two, was entirely covered with mail. There was tons of mail on the floor and covering a nearby table.

'And, where am *I* supposed to sleep?' Deirdre demanded. Joseph stood in the centre of the room with disappointment so clearly apparent on his face that for once he was lost for words. I tried to keep a smile. Quietly, I was assessing how much work it would take to make the apartment feel livable for us. Niall was still outside trying to manouevre on the steep hill for a parking space. We had hoped to greet him at the door with smiles galore and show him the territory. Instead, Niall arrived and studied the carpet with a silence that revealed his displeasure.

We didn't know where to start. I checked for the bed linen to see if we could make the sofa bed into a cosy space for Deirdre and Joseph and, after much searching, finally discovered a suitcase behind the grey couch containing two pre-war-style pillows, mismatched sheets and dusty blankets. The pillows were as brown as stale tea. I was more than happy to buy new pillows, if that was what it was going to take, but the penny wasn't long in dropping. That would only be the beginning. This just wasn't going to work!

The owners had not seen the need to make space for us. There was no place for the kids to put down their things. Every corner and shelf was jammed. No place to make a nest for themselves, which is what we needed to do. Every inch of the place was packed with stuff. I was reminded of George Carlin's routine: 'Even their stuff had stuff!' It was like *Green Eggs and Ham* and the more I looked the more I realised that it was going to be too much to tidy. Dust rose from the sofa when we cleared away the papers. I was imagining that Joseph's vulnerability to dust and mites would trigger trouble within hours. In short, doom and gloom settled upon us and we were stuck in it. I rang my sister, in part to get some advice, but more so that I could hide my intense disappointment from the kids. If I broke down, it was going to make matters worse, surely. Luckily she was home. The kids followed me as I walked the length of the apartment, back and forth, trying to whisper to her. It was then that I discovered that the back door was open, fully open. Perhaps a neighbourly oversight on behalf of the dweller downstairs, but it didn't bode well with me. Deirdre, my sister, an angel, allowed herself to be the recipient of all our grief and each of us in turn vented to her. Joseph then exploded and began to cry. We had waited so long for this. It was to be one of the American highlights of our trip. We had foregone seeing much in New York City because we had saved our city experience for here. Nights on the road we had slept four to a room in two double beds and were side by side in the car for long hours stuffed among our belongings waiting for San Francisco. It was like we were half undressing on our way from Mendocino. In over-zealous anticipation we had walked into the apartment ready to jump in to the cooling atmosphere of space and settlement. It felt like we had been caught with our pants down, so to speak, and we had to quickly pull our tired selves together and hold out a little longer. But hold out for what? What were we going to do next? It was already five o'clock in the afternoon.

After several more attempts at clearing spaces for ourselves and, failing miserably, we decided that we weren't going to stay there that night. We'd come back in the morning with fresh eyes and decide our next move. It was then that Joseph said, 'Call Justin, Mum.'

'Justin?' I said half considering, half hesitating. 'I don't know if that's a good idea. He said to phone when we got here. But I don't think he meant the minute we landed.'

'Yeah, call Justin, Mum,' Deirdre joined in. Suddenly there was possibility in their voices where minutes before there had been despair.

Justin Cheen was Jeffrey's son who lived in San Francisco. Initially, we had met both via the Internet. In fact, we had invited Justin to stay with us in Ireland during the previous late summer when he flew through. It was, quite literally, a flying visit. He drove down from Dublin, spent the night with us, and followed our directions back to Dublin the next day, taking in the Cliffs of Moher, Lahinch, Doolin and a bit of the Burren before departing for Spain for some surfing and Spanish. Oh, to have some of that energy now. He had made quite an impression on the kids. A very likeable and personable young man, thirty years old, single, with the Irish gift of the gab.

So be it, we listened to the voice of reason from our children, and sat eavesdropping on Niall's call.

'Hello, Justin? This is Niall Williams.'

'Yes, we're here. Just arrived in fact.'

'Ah huh, well we're having some trouble with the apartment that we've rented and...' And within minutes, Justin was inviting us over to his apartment for a bit of reconnaissance and strategy. We returned the rental car and arrived by taxi just after eight in the evening. Once Justin understood our dilemma he welcomed us into his apartment and suggested we stay the night.

Justin's apartment was in a section of San Francisco called Soma, South of Market, where the dot.comers came when the city revitalised the warehouse section along the Embarcadero. It overlooked the Bay Bridge, stunning by night, when the bay would shimmer in the near full moonlight. It was clean and tidy, with huge windows that let in full daylight. It made our pre-paid rental seem even more like a dump – not to put too fine a point on it. By morning we were no closer to having the energy required to make the rented flat work for us. We made an executive decision, there and then, perhaps with some haste, but with plenty of support from the children and encouragement from Justin. We decided to forfeit the full fee (and car that came with the apartment) and instead search for another accommodation. Justin was sure this would be easy with so many dot.comers out of work and with the economy still in a downturn. He drove us over on our first morning in San Francisco – to the home away from home that was not meant to be – and helped us get our luggage. He wholeheartedly agreed with us, after a quick perusal of the Mission Street apartment, that we had made the right decision.

In actual fact, however, we were still on the road as it were. Still living out of suitcases. The last time we had unpacked was nearly three weeks earlier. Nice as Justin's apartment was, it was also a tight squeeze and totally unexpected on behalf of his girlfriend, Sarah, who kindly put up with us for three nights. (We left in the middle of our stay for a Union Street Hotel to ease the overwhelming impact we three homeless Irish bodies and one pissed-off American were having on her.) Niall phoned the owners of the rental and they expressed surprise and disappointment that we had decided to leave, but unfortunately could reimburse us only about 40 per cent. With $1,000 dollars on the way, we felt some satisfaction. However, the hard lesson was being learned: *Never pay in full, no matter what.* But more importantly, the message we were giving ourselves and Deirdre and Joseph was that if you make a mistake you can usually rectify it with a good decision and that money isn't the golden rule. The trip so far was turning out to be more expensive than we had planned and the bad news was that we had already anticipated that it was going to be an expensive adventure! Ah well. As an uncle of mine used to say, 'Onward, Hail and Ole.'

Luckily for us we *did* find a place but it didn't turn out to be easy. Finding furnished, short-term accommodation in San Francisco was like finding gold dust after the gold rush had come and gone. And, considering the week that was in it (the World Series was in San Francisco for the first time in forty-eight years), we had given ourselves quite a hard task. But the luck of the Irish works both ways and a suitable one-bedroom was available downstairs in Justin's building for the time we needed. His knowing us made the transition easy.

Interestingly for us, given that it was not the neighbourhood we were hoping for, it was in a neighbourhood all its own just the same, and the loft-like apartment was adjacent to the new ball park, Pac Bell. It was a great location, you might say, especially if you were young and worked in the financial district. It was definitely going to be a city experience. There wasn't a Victorian house in sight.

We moved into the apartment, owned by Wendy and Stephan Chin, two thirty-something Chinese-Americans, just before midnight on a Saturday – five days after arriving in San Francisco. Five days in which we roamed around the Embarcadero, walking from there to Union Square up through the financial district under the enormous Bay Bridge and feeling like we were smack in the middle of a city with fumes from buses and taxis and dwarfed by tall buildings. Five days where, not able to unpack, we couldn't liberally summon the freedom of exploration. We'd return from our outings in the same clothes as the day before, eager to hear if there were any solutions to our accommodation dilemma. Justin and his girlfriend Sarah had gone on eBay to see what was available, but nothing was turning up. Suffice to say it was the hardest five days of the trip so far, feeling homeless in San Francisco.

Once we were finally settled in Wendy's loft-like space on the second floor of Justin's building, it felt like the previous five days had been stolen from us and we had to beckon the energy to treat our arrival in the loft with renewed enthusiasm for the city of St Francis. Meanwhile, the San Francisco Giants were tied one game apiece in the World Series with the Anaheim Angels. There was a buzz on the streets and it helped. Fireworks coloured the sky over the Ferry Building on the night the Giants returned from Anaheim to face into game three. The third, fourth and fifth games were being played in Pac Bell Stadium. With tickets costing over $500, admission was out of our league, but we'd planned to watch game three on TV and open the window when the Giants scored. The excitement gave us the jump-start that we needed. Baseball was completely foreign to Niall. I had fun trying to explain the difference between balls and strikes and fouls. We learned about Barry Bonds, with the crucifix-studded earring, and watched as the Angels 'walked' him nearly every time he came to bat, which Joseph thought was entirely unjust. It was an excitement that we certainly weren't anticipating and it gave us a real slice of American life – where baseball is king and the World Series more exciting than the Super Bowl.

We had paid upfront, once we were actually standing in the apartment, for fifteen days. The one-bedroom apartment with its wall-to-wall white carpet and white walls was like an oasis. Deirdre was in desperate need of her own space, so we gave her the double bed while Niall and Joseph and I slept on a futon on the floor. We set up our laptops and organised a drawing space for Joseph. Our portable Sony speakers, which we attached to the CD drive of my laptop, were fixed on the kitchen table and we listened to the music we had been carrying around with us since leaving Ireland: Martin Hayes's fiddle playing on *The Lonesome Touch* and Ella Fitzgerald, whom Joseph adored.

It was too late in our stay in San Francisco to organise a rented cello for Deirdre, a relationship for which she was feeling lonesome, and instead she practised her flute in the mornings. On our walks up to Union Square we passed a 24-hour gym and, after some negotiating, we bought two three-week passes, fulfilling a promise to Deirdre that when we *got to San Francisco* she'd have the opportunity to try out a gym. She went nearly every day, and I accompanied her when she dragged me along, looking every inch the middle-aged mother I was feeling in Joseph's sweatpants and my new sneakers that didn't fit. Deirdre on the other hand fit right in with the other young women in headphones and ponytails with shapely arms and flat abdomens. Long gone were the days when I conducted a Jane Fonda-like aerobics class down in our village in the community centre. I chose not to lock into any image of myself except the one I was experiencing as a mother admiring her daughter, although it was a bonus that I was also getting some much needed exercise on the treadmill. Deirdre might say that I was too much of a force in her life – well she would, wouldn't she? I wouldn't expect any less from a teenage daughter. But it felt to me like I was a shepherdess guiding one of my flock to the fields, standing off and watching her until it was time to go home. Call me Little Bo Peep, but I was acknowledging to myself the gratitude I felt for this unique opportunity. There she was, my daughter, away from friends and home and even the familiarites of school and routine, and absolutely thriving. Sometimes I allowed myself a smile.

~

Joseph thought there were a lot of homeless people in San Francisco. We passed many of them sitting against the buildings down near Folsom station. One guy had a family of cats with him. I told Joseph that I thought it wasn't necessarily because San Francisco was a poor city, but just that the weather was such that homeless people could live more easily out of doors. I couldn't explain it otherwise, although the economic climate was certainly not vibrant in the wake of the collapse of the tech industry. But when I considered that the cost of housing in the Bay Area was one of the highest in the world, it made sense. It didn't have anything to do with the weather. How naïve am I? Joseph was right, there were a lot of people living homeless. A recent survey listed California as the 'meanest' state to live in in terms of the attempted criminal-isation of 'panhandling' and the lack of subsidised welfare housing. San Francisco was even higher than New York City on the list of ten meanest places to live in America, a fact that greatly surprised me. It wouldn't be the first time we encountered the contradictions that make up the United States. The best and the worst of everything. And it wouldn't be the first time that Joseph's keenly sensitive barometer of social injustice would veer into the red zone. I was proud of him. It also made me realise that I couldn't dismiss his astute observations and was once again grateful. His questions were a constant reminder to live life more consciously.

There was so much to do in San Francisco, but we found it hard to summon the energy. Niall was content to stay put and write. He was struggling with his novel and engaged in one of those bouts of faith that none of us could help him with. 'I'm not sure it's any good,' was all he would say. Deirdre wanted to visit the shops and Joseph wanted to draw. I felt like we were missing something if we didn't get out and explore. We settled on writing down on paper the things people wanted to do and then prioritise. Joseph wanted to go the TransAm Building and the Exploratorium, and also to see the Victorian houses on Steiner Street. Deirdre wanted to go to Whole Foods on Nob Hill that Justin and Sarah had told us about so she could get some proper vegetarian food staples. I voted for Noe Valley. I also wanted to go to Muir Woods and Big Sur, but without a car it was looking doubtful. When I expressed my disappointment to Niall he said that San Francisco would always be here and we could always come again. It wasn't a once-in-a-lifetime experience, whereas the actual day-to-day living as a family on the road for nine months was. He was of the opinion that we could take a slice of the pie and know a part of the whole. I was reminded of the expression that you can tell an elephant even if you just see the tail and its ears.

So we went to the Exploratorium and revelled in it. The TransAm observation deck was closed since September 11 and we kept missing Steiner Street on our sojourns around the city. Sarah took us to Whole Foods and we spent, like San Franciscans, the equivalent of a whole paycheck on the purchases. We did take a taxi one day to the top of Noe Valley at the corner of Sanchez and Hill Streets and stood looking down across the city to the bay. We ogled the houses on the hills and planned how next time we would get a monthly rental in one of them. The mixture of Victorian architecture and small gardens on a slant was inspiring to the gardener in me and to the budding architect in Joseph. We walked along Dolores Street and over to Castro Street where Niall got his hair cut by a flamboyant barber in leather pants in a moment that made us giggle.

A nice surprise for us was the Crossroads Café on Delancy Street, and the more we investigated this part of the city the more we settled into the neighbourhood of Soma. At the Crossroads Café we were able to get morning lattes and muffins for breakfast, paninis and salads for lunch and afternoon tea. It was established as a rehab for people recovering from substance abuse, allowing them to work in a safe environment and return to the community. It was light and cosy with many windows opening onto a small garden and a quiet street. There was no time limit for sitting at the tables, so occasionally I brought my laptop and sat for a few hours and wrote while others nestled in armchairs deeply involved in conversations or playing chess. Magazines and books and ecologically friendly gifts were for sale as well as some quirky artwork and funky items. It was never overcrowded. Also in the same neighbourhood, around the corner on Bannan Street, was a gourmet restaurant called the Slanted Door, which served Vietnamese food based around organic produce from the Bay area. Some of the best food we've ever tasted. There was nothing exclusive about it except the endeavour to bring good food to the table in a relaxed setting. Deirdre was chuffed that the waiter remembered her the second time we had a meal there. Such was the atmosphere. Such was the neighbourhood we eventually came to know. From the top of our building we had seen the fireworks for the World Series and had watched the cars and trucks coming from the Oakland side of the Bay Bridge, appearing dramatically through a mist that half covered the bridge. We had watched as the full moon rose over the cargo ships temporarily on strike in the bay. We had walked along the Embarcadero, where one night we passed an elderly lady in a pale blue evening dress and blond wig talking to herself, and several homeless men stretched out beside their shopping carts, to the farmers' market where we rubbed shoulders with the cool, suave city dwellers and bought too much of everything. It was late October in San Francisco with the weather perfectly autumnal. It was the week before Hallowe'en and Deirdre and Joseph insisted we decorate the window so we bought two pumpkins and carving tools and a banner. Deirdre made some black cut-out witches and we strung them across the window and lit our pumpkins by night. It was an eye-opener at times how much we needed to make a nest for ourselves. In the rhythm of our lives for this year I understood the importance of it and allowed for it as often as possible. For several days, in the white apartment on the corner of Byrant and Delancy, we cooked regular meals and ate at the wooden table by candlelit pumpkins. We were in a kind of oasis and I secretly wondered if we shouldn't just stay where we were. But at the same time, the feeling of isolation that can befall you in a city eventually caught up with us. We felt the lack of belonging to anything. The longer we stayed put in one place, the more obvious was our dislocation. Although I definitely felt the comfort of being among fellow Americans, its temporariness unnerved me. It felt as if I were continually having to ask myself *would I prefer to be living in America*? Sometimes the answer was a resounding yes, but yet I couldn't allow myself to entertain those thoughts. It was much easier when the answer was a resounding no.

Yet, as an American living abroad, I believe I am fortunate in having another perspective, because I no longer view the world through America's vision. Watching the evening television news, I found myself grateful for that vantage point. It was a new experience for us to see the screen divided up into window-like sections running different informational segments simultaneously. Only in America can you get the weather around the country, the sports news, and the CNN headline news all at once in little side bars around the main picture as well as *The New York Times* bestsellers list popping up under the evening's main story. On this night, 26 October 2002, the headlines were about the DC sniper.

In between the news were commercials for drugs advertising that bi-polar disorder is *not* depression, and for politicians whose negative campaigning had reached quite libellous proportions. The effect of this bombardment of information reminded me of that wonderful little theatre group called the Reduced Shakespeare Company where they perform all of Shakespeare on stage in one evening. Whereas the Reduced Shakespeare Company is clever and entertaining, the Reduced Television News is not. Somebody seems to have got it wrong. Television news now attempts to be entertainment. It's part of the whole hype, though, like the AT&T ad says, 'Your mobile life made better.' The fast-food way of life has given birth to fast television, and it's just as indigestible. Too much information coming too quickly. Television news competing with print news competing with Internet news has turned it into a twenty-four-hour 7/11, all-you-can-eat smorgasbord.

Inter-galactic visitors would find on this day in time a society where the country's leading cosy home guru and household icon, Martha Stewart, was being questioned for insider trading. Where 12 per cent of teenagers have taken a dangerous, mood-altering drug whose name means happiness. Where the cost of sending your kid to college in the US is three times more than what the average yearly wage is in mainland China. Where so-called representatives of the people, grown-up men and women, slander each other in the name of democracy. And where the people of the greater Washington DC area are afraid to get in their cars for fear of being gunned down by a sniper. All this in a world where children die in bus bombs, where tourists die in a nightclub in a holiday resort, where nuclear armament is a global issue. Modern life is moving dangerously faster than a speeding bullet. Maybe with a bit of multi-tasking I could train myself to read the headlines while listening to the broadcaster and download the important bits – much like running several programmes on Windows at the same time. But would I want to? I think I'm already too numbed by the whole experience. Nearly all the news of that evening should have set off alarm bells, but the piece that made us really stop and listen was the news of the bombing in the Kuta nightclub where nearly 200 people were killed. In five months we planned to be in Bali and had already sent our deposit for the villa rental. I wondered would it be the first time that our plans would have to be re-arranged for our wellbeing and safety?

~

We had originally expected that we would fly to Los Angeles and rent an RV and drive out to the Grand Canyon for a few days. My brother Joe had moved to LA and, together with his daughter Meghan who lived in Culver City, was going to join us for the week. But what looked good on paper, what looked do-able according to www.roadtrip.com, made the kids go ballistic. Especially Joseph. No way was he driving that far, he said. The northern rim of the canyon was closed this time of year anyway and we understood that we couldn't 'do' the Grand Canyon in two days. It was a destination in itself. For our needs at the moment, an uneasy stroke of the pen crossed the Grand Canyon off our itinerary. Instead, we decided to fly to LA, rent a car, drive to San Diego, and stay at the Hotel Del Coronado for a last few days in America.

The Del, as it is fondly known, is one of those grand hotels listed as a national treasure. The peninsula of Coronado is connected to the mainland by only a narrow stretch of sand known as the Silver Strand and only accessed by a two-mile bridge. The hotel opened in 1888 and retains much of its Victorian charm. The white, wooden hotel sits on the edge of the beach like a giant cruise ship with a red roof. One of its many claims to fame is that it was the location of the movie *Some Like It Hot* and was frequented by Frank Baum, the creator of *The Wizard of Oz*. Its high red cone sits like a crown majestically overlooking the ocean. Its beach features highly in those Best Beaches of America lists. Inside, the corridors are wide, the ceilings high, and great attention paid to preserving its Victorian detail. We booked two family rooms in the Victorian section of the hotel across the hall from each other and were pleased with them. I won't go so far as to say that we were somewhere over the rainbow, but the sunken enclosure of white wooden railings and turrets around the pool made me think of the emerald city.

My niece and godchild, Meghan, is a tall slim redheaded beauty. Watching her and Deirdre get ready for dinner, which I did discreetly, was special for me. We hadn't seen Meghan for several years and, while I knew that she and Deirdre wouldn't become kissing cousins overnight, I felt I was doing something towards laying a foundation for the future, whatever form it may take. Again I felt here was the trip giving us an opportunity for family. I enjoyed the company of my brother Joe and was happy to share these final days in North America with him and Meghan.

On the first afternoon at the hotel, Joe told me he had taken a walk down the far end of the beach until he could go no further because he was stopped by US naval personnel. We discovered that the Naval Base Coronado was at the far end of the beach – a hub for naval amphibious operations, including training and special warfare, and headquarters for America's elite US Navy SEALs. NAB Coronado is known as the premier conference site on the West Coast and a major shore command. The Naval Air Station on the North Island, a small city in itself, with a population of 30,000 navy personnel, is part of the largest aerospace industrial complex in the US Navy, bracketing the city of Coronado from the entrance of San Diego Bay to the Mexican border. It explained why so many naval aircraft were flying through the skies above our heads. Niall and Joe were convinced that no one was in the water not because it was cold but because it was clearly SEAL territory and everyone but us somehow knew this. Trenches and banks of sand were sculpted on the beach. We imagined this was for manouevres, although in reality the Navy probably had its own beach for that. However, we did spot one lone swimmer who was crawling, arm over arm, steadily through the cold water, and Niall speculated that he was probably under disciplinary orders. We spent three nights at Del Coronado in luxury. Niall bought Deirdre and Meghan a three-day pass to the spa and they went everyday while the rest of us hung out between the beach and the swimming pool and wandered about the hotel fantasising about the golden days of Hollywood when the movie stars used to come. The large, bug-like navy planes that flew in low above us were like a hive of bees in the quickly advancing preparations for possible war in Iraq. And though the hotel was lovely and the days warm and pleasant, one couldn't but be reminded of the Wicked Witch of the West circling on her broom with black smoke pluming out behind her above the peaceful inhabitants of the Emerald City in the merry old land of Oz.

Costa Rica

There seemed to be no getting around it. It was our fifth flight on our Oneworld Explorer ticket and the fifth time we had been 'randomly' searched. Joseph was furious. He was sure that anyone who was not American was being double-checked. It was pointless to argue with an observant eleven-year-old. In reality, it was more likely that we had been tagged at the start of our journey as non-American. We were going to be searched no matter what, in the United States at least. It was no use telling the security people or the check-in personnel, because they all said the same thing in response.

'Sorry, madam, but it is done randomly by our computer.'

They have the knack of saying this without looking you in the eye.

We came to recognise ourselves as 'Group Two' and were well practised, unlacing our Timberlands before we joined the line. Some officials were more thorough than others. Nothing, however – no way, no how – matched our experience flying from JFK to Seattle. In contrast, the security check at the gate from San Francisco to Dallas was cursorily performed, and it was the first time that we were not the last on the plane.

Once we were seated, there was that limbo time inviting us to contemplate what was in fact happening. This extra time was dangerous because it gave pause for hindsight and second-guessing. We were leaving North America. We wouldn't see anybody we knew for the next six months – if all went well and according to our itinerary. That was the scary part: leaving the comfort and familiarity of the United States. The imminent foreignness of it was unveiling rapidly. The trip had been planned with North America as our first destination where we would be in known territory, where we would see family now and again and where we would settle into this experience of travelling extendedly away from home. It had worked pretty well. Nearly two and half months on the road and not one of us had suffered with a tummy bug or cold and not too much homesickness. There were half a dozen times when Joseph, particularly, felt lonesome for his home in Ireland, but on the whole he threw in with the rest of us. We were getting used to living together without separation and learning to accept the rhythms of each other's moods. But there was always the familiar to distract us when it was paramount. There was English-language television for Joseph. There was shopping for Deirdre. There was family for all of us. However, ahead of us were two weeks in Costa Rica, and although it was indeed a holiday, it wasn't a holiday, we'd be returning from after the two weeks. No, we'd be moving further south down the continent. Next stop after Central America was South America.

In Costa Rica, we had arranged to rent a house, again through the Internet, on the Central Pacific coast. Of all the countries in Central America, we chose Costa Rica as the one that would give us a good impression of that part of the world while enabling us to travel in safety and comfort. It would be the closest we would get to experiencing the jungle as, having decided against the Amazon River Basin in Peru because of the threat of yellow fever and malaria, and having also decided against Brazil for further reasons medical and security-wise. It was our opinion that the Amazon was a trip for more seasoned travellers. Not for us at this juncture. We had seen many photographs on the Internet of the villa and felt fairly confident that we wouldn't have a repeat of our arrival in San

Francisco. In fact, Niall had rung Sandi, the owner of the Costa Rican villa, to be sure.

'I can tell you that you are going to love it,' she said from her home in San José, Costa Rica. The beach house was her holiday home which she rarely rented out, but my persistence had paid off this time. It was a two-bedroom with everything we'd need, she said. In fact, having learned a bit about reducing our expectations, we were ready for anything. Sandi hadn't even asked for as much as deposit for her house (definitely more approachable than our previous rental experience). It had all the right vibrations. In a day we would be there.

The airline captain on American AA 131 was loquacious, interjecting humour into his announcements from the cockpit, which was pleasantly distracting. It eased us into the two-plane journey: first to Dallas, then a connecting flight down to San José. Everything went smoothly and we arrived on schedule, got our bags, went through Customs without a hitch and located a Marriott courtesy van to take us to the hotel. It was one of the smoothest transitions ever, of which Niall and I were grateful because we were anxious about how the children were going to react. Having travelled previously to European capitals and America, Costa Rica loomed large in Deirdre and Joseph's imagination as really foreign. I had talked with some American students on the plane who had been injected against hepatitis A and typhoid and who had all been taking anti-malarial tablets, revealing to me a perception that it was a semi-hostile environment at least in terms of disease. I didn't share this information with the kids or Niall and kept it to myself. I had made the right decisions for my family in this regard, hadn't I? The question as to whether to vaccinate or not had plagued me for months prior to our departure. In the end I believed that the threat of diseases like cholera, typhoid, and hepatitis were minimal and that vaccines would do nothing but harm our immune systems which we would need to keep healthy during what would sometimes be a stressful trip.

~

The kids didn't want to leave San Francisco. Neither did I. We were just getting used to Wendy's apartment and to our new neighbourhood around Delancy Street. There were many things we didn't get to do. No theatre or concerts. No sailing trips on the bay except the ferry to Tiberon and back. And, most disappointing of all, we didn't get down to Big Sur. Niall assured me that this meant we were definitely coming back. There were things we forgot to buy for the two-month stay in Central and South America, like extra film, DVDs, sketching pad, vegetarian gravy mix. And what about all those chic restaurants we didn't eat at? Since we had got off to a bad start, it felt unsatisfying in some ways. It felt that we were leaving prematurely. But I guess that's the way to do it: leave wanting more. I felt a bit constrained by my own agenda and itinerary, but we couldn't stay – the house in Costa Rica was already booked as well as the tour in Peru and Bolivia, and we had to get to Fundo Chacaipulli in time for Christmas. It would be interesting to see what flexibility lay ahead in terms of timekeeping and scheduling.

~

When travel goes smoothly, it underscores not only the notion of how small the world can be, but also how diverse it is. In half a day you can be transported to an entirely different reality, half the world away. The Marriott near the airport was ideal for our needs and gave us our first feel not only of the heat, which was exhausting and sticky, but also of how so much life in a hot climate is lived outdoors – an experience we would become fully acquainted with in Manuel Antonio, our final destination in Costa Rica. Our shirts clung to our backs. My jeans were like snake skin against my legs as we waited to check into our rooms. The staff members of the hotel were helpful and friendly, anticipating our requests. Too hot to eat, we went straight to bed. I could hear Joseph in the next room flicking through the Spanish channels which he soon tired of and fell asleep looking forward to a morning's swim in the pool. We turned the air conditioning up high and slept peacefully in wonderfully attired, old-world style rooms with auburn-coloured tiles.

At breakfast, it was time to try out my Spanish, prompting the kids to laugh when I ordered coffee.

'*Con leche, Señora?*'

'*Si, con leche, por favor. Muchas gracias.*'

'Try it in English, Mum. They'll understand you better!' Joseph laughed, shrugging up his shoulders and giggling.

Deirdre, a girl of few words, just said, 'Show off!'

So much for making conversation. We had intended to listen to Spanish tapes while driving around Yellowstone and down the Northern Pacific Coast but it was too much anticipating. We opted instead to live in the moment, as they say.

But picture it, us sitting among the elk or in a bison jam in Yellowstone:

'*De donde eres?*'

'*Soy de Irlanda.*'

'*Hablas Español?*'

'*Si, un poco.*'

Or, as the Florentine taxi driver said to us in Italy when questioned if he spoke English, 'No, but I speak Italian very well!'

It had turned out to be too much to learn Spanish while travelling in North America. So, as a result, we were unprepared to speak with the 'Ticos' except for basic greetings and thank yous and to order coffee with milk. I'd have to make do on my high school Spanish, albeit with my children laughing at me.

The business centre at the Marriott had arranged a Toyota Rav 4 for our two-week stay and, after the kids had a long dip in the pool, we stuffed the car with our luggage and set off for Manuel Antonio, a three- to four-hour drive over the mountains on a two-lane road where overtaking was next to impossible. Being caught behind a lorry could extend the journey greatly. The roads are not really signposted and the route numbers are not evident, so finding our way from the hotel was a bit of a guessing game. There was an inordinate amount of people in the middle of the road selling sweepstake or Lotto tickets, long streams of cardboard cards dangling from their arms. Others, gazing into each car for customers, were selling a kind of round pancake-like bread in plastic bags. Eventually, after a few false starts, we hit upon the right road.

As the guidebooks say, 'driving in a developing country can be a challenge…. Keep in mind that mountains and poor road conditions make most trips longer than you'd normally expect.' (*Fodor's*, 2002) Straight off we realised that an overnight to the Caribbean coast was not going to be an option. We would be a day getting there and a day getting back on these roads. What we had here in our family was a split: one of us was game for road journeys, no matter what the length; two of us hated long drives in the car; and one of us went either way. With some long drives behind us in the US and more ahead of us in Chile and Peru, we voted democratically and agreed to stay put once we reached Manuel Antonio.

When the guidebook cautions, 'conditions on the road are lamentable: you'll run into plenty of potholes and long stretches with no pavement at all', it isn't until you actually find yourself there that you can fully appreciate this. The children were *gob-smacked*, to borrow one of their own expressions. We were used to small, narrow pot-holed roads in Ireland, but what startled us most was the poor-looking condition of the houses and the barefoot people along the roadside. But poor by whose standards? Houses were partially sided with corrugated iron and enclosed by walls and gates. Everything was small and earthy with little evidence of kept gardens or fresh paint. I was affronted by my own middle class-ness too. I also thought it was poor. I explained to the kids that while it might *appear* that Costa Rica was poor, in fact, by Central American standards it was not. There were many reasons why the people lived as they did and it was partly for this understanding of world cultures that we had decided to take this trip in the first place.

Like any developing country, infrastructure is weak. One gets the sense that it is a feat of Sisyphean dimensions to maintain the existing roads when torrential rains bucket down during the rainy season. It's quite like Ireland in that respect, no sooner has a pothole been repaired then the rain comes and washes the filling away. Money is distributed to health and education, with some of what remains going towards improving infrastructure for the massively growing tourist industry. Like Ireland, tourism has become the leading source of income, replacing agriculture. However, also like many tourists coming to Ireland who are dismayed by the roadside clutter, we found ourselves grumbling a bit as we passed roadside waste. The view of stagnant water with floating rubbish was disturbing too. In these circumstances I have to pull myself up short and ask: Is it a *designer* developing nation you want? No. I don't want to be like the tourist flying into San José, arriving at my four-star hotel, holidaying in lush surroundings and flying out after a week or two, experiencing the countryside by being picked up and returned to the hotel by one of the several dozen tour companies in Costa Rica that offer complete door-to-door adventure trips. It's easy to be seduced into one of these holidays. But we wanted something else.

Winding in and out of the mountains, with thick, jungle-like vegetation bordering all sides of the road, we drove down along the coast. Sometimes the road wound so tightly in on itself we travelled at ten miles an hour. Sometimes the road became nothing but rocks, sometimes it was two lines of timber crossing a brown river, a rattling unnerving bridge when you looked down and thought you glimpsed crocodiles below. Eventually we arrived on the outskirts of the town of Quepos, not one of the jewels of the Central Pacific coast, it has to be said. Once a thriving banana port, Quepos is still slowly recovering from the death of the banana industry. Palm oil has replaced the banana plantations and rows of palm trees line the roadsides for miles. A maze of green-fronded umbrellas. The seeds of the palm tree's flowers have to be harvested every six weeks, a torturous job as poisonous snakes often nest at the base of the trees. With this kind of rapid production, the palm tree exhausts itself and dies after a few years, leaving in its wake a tall, dead, blackened stump, like a giant extinguished torch. The new undergrowth is freshly green with emerging palm trees, but the result is eerie and does nothing to lessen a rather devastating-looking landscape.

It was raining when we arrived. The townspeople of Quepos were making their way home on foot along the main road. The rain showered down upon them, clothes and skin and all. A vested man on a bicycle rode along holding an umbrella with one hand and carrying a machete on his waist. Children walked barefoot in shorts and thin shirts, unperturbed by the rain. Women walked beside them with shopping bags, not hurrying in the downpour.

One of the most interesting things we learned about Costa Rica was that it abandoned its army in 1948 and the Ticos have carved out a character of social peace that is paramount to their identity. For the thirteenth consecutive time, Costa Rica has lived through an electoral process in peace.

One of the guidebooks we read said that the road from Quepos to Manuel Antonio had been overdeveloped with hotels and that it was a pity that the government hadn't kept a check on it. Before long it would resemble Cancun. We were expecting a hilly landscape crowded with buildings, tourist shops, cafés – all the trappings of a beach destination. In fact, there are hotels along the narrow windy road, but the lush vegetation hides them from view. (The handful of five-star hotels is well hidden down private roads, chained and guarded.) But contrary to what the guidebooks say, there is not a plethora of shops. Hardly even a grocer's shop, and no pharmacy. We turned off the main road, the road that comes to an end at Manuel Antonio National Park, and followed the directions to the house. We turned at the yellow-painted Café Milagro.

Sandi, the owner of the beach house, said that Bismark and Gloria, the caretakers, would greet our arrival, but to be aware that they spoke very little English. As the directions indicated, we pulled up in front of a concrete wall with steps and a green railing. The noise of our car doors opening and closing alerted Bismark who appeared, bare-chested in his shorts and gold neck chain, midway up the long steep slope of a garden.

'*Hola.*'

'*Hola. Bismark?*' We shouted up to him.

'*Si, si yo estoy Bismark,*' he said, smiling, his small frame climbing down the steps blithely. It was after four in the afternoon and very hot. What followed was typical of when two groups of people meet who don't speak each other's languages. Interchanges of smiles, silences and nods mixed with known words.

'*Es muy calor,*' I said.

'*Si,*' Bismark responded and continued in Spanish that I couldn't follow. We all nodded. Meanwhile, we unloaded all our bags, including our winter coats that we'd been hanging onto for Patagonia in a few weeks. Bismark laughed.

'*Es muy calor, Señora. No neccisito un ropa,*' he laughed, holding my black winter jacket. We all laughed then and loaded the bags onto a rudimentary cable lift and began the steep ascent up to the house, navigating the erratic steps that stretched ever upwards. We were unprepared for the heat and by the time we arrived at the front door, having climbed more than 120 steps, we were like panting dogs.

Red hibiscus flowers dangled everywhere from shrubs that lined the paths.

'*Es muy bonita aqui,*' I said to Bismark.

And he replied in sentences that I imagine indicated for me to wait until we were inside, where it was just as beautiful.

He beamed as he let us in and immediately began opening the windows and doors – windows and doors that mostly had no screens, I quickly noted. Maybe we should have taken anti-malarial tablets after all, I thought to myself. The children went upstairs along narrow concrete steps along the length of the picture window that halled one side of the house to survey the bedrooms and came back happy. There were just two bedrooms upstairs – one for us and one for them, and a bathroom.

'But Mum,' Deirdre whispered to me, 'there's something moving on the wall.'

I murmured, 'I'll check it out in a minute. Okay?'

She nodded. But I could see her looking around her for similar moving creatures.

On the first level, entirely floored with oiled teakwood, a balcony opened over a canopy of jungle trees to reveal the world's largest ocean which unfolded a few hundred yards below. From the windows and open doors the ocean was *everywhere*, a mesmerising panoramic view. From three sides of the house, no matter where you looked, you could see the water and the shoreline of white beaches. It was like we were in a tree house at the top of the tree with just the birds and the sky above us. From this perch we surveyed for miles. It was the kind of view that can be described legitimately as breathtaking. But it was also so hot and humid that if we could have busted out some walls to let in more air, we would have done so. We were boiling. Niall was drenched in perspiration. After telling us through sign language and broken English where we could eat dinner, where the shop was and how late it stayed open, Bismark disappeared down into his jungle paradise.

'*Hasta luego*,' we shouted down to him as he went. He turned and beamed a smile at us. '*Si, si*,' he said and vanished into his own house midway down the path.

~

We were then left with just the four of us. The long journey to Manuel Antonio was over and, similar to other journeys, we had the weird feeling of *now what*? Now that we have arrived, what do we do? The long anticipated arrival is completed in a flash once you actually get there. It's always a bit of an anti-climax. Journeys can be measured this way. Many little journeys strung out over the course of the trip. Even the walk from the car to the house was a little journey, climbing past scents unknown to us, past flowers and a sea of green. The sun was setting. We were standing on the balcony, the sun colouring the sky a deep pink over hushed palm trees and flowering treetops, hearing only the sounds of nature. Waves were breaking in the distance while birds called to each other. *Now what do we do?* We unpacked and went upstairs to discover that the moving thing on the children's bedroom wall was a charming little gecko.

The first night was disconcerting for Joseph. The foreignness firstly, then of course no television, no radio. Just peace and quiet, surrounded by scented darkness of Central America. It was too much for him. On the flight down I was reading in *Newsweek* magazine an article on whether TV was good or bad for kids. We had just visited with friends in Tiberon, California, whose children attend the Steiner school system and who have never watched television, and I was embarrassed to reveal that we as a family did watch a good bit of television. We call it our down-time. It's true that we are too plugged into it. Here was evidence that the daily drug once withdrawn was having its effect. Another opportunity for me to coax Joseph in the direction I wanted him to travel on this journey, at least a little bit. So we sat outside and counted the number of sounds we could hear. Was that a three-fingered tree sloth making growling noises? (The three-fingered sloth travels about only at night.) Sounds of insects buzzing. The rustle of the tall trees against each other. The waves below crashing on the sand. A jungle symphony. We sat watching the clouds move across the stars as the lights of fishing boats lit up the horizon.

I could make the argument that because we live in rural Ireland we get our fill of peace and quiet and that television is our way of connecting to the world. It's a weak argument, perhaps, but television helps quell the loneliness that can descend on a winter's day when the only sound is the sound of rain. Perhaps we are too absorbed into digital life, and have lost our ability to focus within. In some small way, then, for a couple of weeks here and there over the course of this trip, we would get to experience a sense of the unplugged-in life. We went to sleep with the windows open and the ceiling fans on, naked except for cotton sheets, and succumbed to the night jungle.

~

The next morning I awoke early not expecting to find blue skies, it being the rainy season, or the 'green' season as it is known in Costa Rica, but when I opened the balcony doors to a blue morning, there was a group of squirrel monkeys, just a few feet away, staring back at me. Tiny, orange monkeys with long tails scrambled over the treetops, disappearing quickly in the thick green awning of vegetation below. I wasn't expecting them and they weren't expecting me. Each subsequent morning we saw two toucans watching. We saw many yellow-breasted birds feeding from the treetops of the palm trees, flittering back and forth from the red seeds that hung like grapes. Vultures circled and scanned the skies. Each morning we were treated to this vista of wildlife and weather. It was a constant visual delight.

It rained more at night but the days were sprinkled with showers whose aftermath yielded up to us the scents of the flowers in Bismark's garden. On several nights, the sky lit up completely with lightning, like a giant flashbulb, illuminating everything as brightly as day. Sometimes it rained all night, making us feel like we were sleeping in a cloud, as if the cloud itself were moving through the house. By morning everything was damp, including ourselves, except for the clothes sheltered inside the teak closets. When the sun appeared in the daytime, everything dried. It was suffocating for us to close all the windows against the rain because of the heat and humidity. Our Irish-conditioned bodies welcomed any bit of breeze that blew in off the ocean, even a wet one.

That we were free to leave the windows and doors open all day and night amazed us no end. There were no biting insects and, except for an army of ants that paraded whenever a crumb or two escaped being wiped away, we felt the freedom of living half indoors and half out in a house above the treetops. Eating our lunch at the round table, we looked through opened windows with green-blue shutters angled against the house where the hibiscus flowers dangled within an arm's reach. The fact that there were no mosquitoes at night was enormously comforting. The mosquito net that we bought in London lay in its nylon bag at the bottom of my suitcase.

The beach house, as Sandi named it, was a mile from Manuel Antonio National Park – the most popular park in the country. A hilly evergreen forest with natural shade from the tropical trees was lined by two curved, white sand beaches, sloping to a warm, gentle surf. Trails lead through dense jungle to hidden sandy coves. The mountains literally meet the sea and the eco-system was teeming with land, sea and air species. White-faced monkeys, two and three-toed sloths, coatis, pacas, brilliantly coloured land crabs, butterflies, and insects. The endangered squirrel monkeys, the ones I had seen my first morning, are often spotted in Manuel Antonio. Over 100 species of animal, and nearly 200 species of birds have been identified in the park whose access is curiously unmarked. To enter, you just follow the steady stream of people. When the tide is in, you walk through the water nearly waist deep or get a ride a distance of twenty yards in a rowboat pulled by the Ticos. (Any opportunity to make a few *colones* seemed to be a hallmark of the Costa Ricans we encountered, from parking your car at the beach with a chap to mind it all day for 5,000 *colones* to a boat trip of a few yards for 1,000 *colones*.) On our first trip to the park, Niall had to jump out of the small boat and push us and a half dozen other passengers who didn't want to wade waist-deep across the tide when the boat got stuck in the sandbar. And of course we still paid our boatman for the service.

The beaches inside the park are below the tree-lined coves, and wide but not very deep. Visiting them is not quite like visiting any other beach I have been to. Between the trees and the very warm water lies a band of sand so soft it feels like cashmere to the skin but, because of the humidity, it sticks. The palm trees provide a bit of shade for animals and humans alike. An iguana rested inches from our blanket where we too were seeking shelter from the hot sun. Hermit crabs, scrambling all over the place, gave Joseph quite a surprise. Now they were moving, now they were not, as you edged closer to them. They look like bits of rock at first glance until they suddenly move, crab fingers scrawling rapidly to a new place inches away, like a multitude of children playing 'Red Light, Green Light'. Half a dozen white-faced monkeys appeared in the trees closest to the beach and began inspecting the towels and clothes left hanging on the branches while their owners took a dip. One elderly woman chased a monkey along the interior path because it had taken her blouse. Living side by side with teeming wildlife is a special, endearing feature of life in Costa Rica, a country that contains 6 per cent of the world's biodiversity, making it one of the most eco-friendly holiday destinations.

Deirdre and I arranged for a tour of the park and asked Henry, our guide, about the apparent lack of mosquitoes.

'I think you will remember that it is the birds that take the insects,' he said, immaculately dressed in white tennis shirt and long khakis, sweating across his forehead.

'Ah ha!' we responded. 'Of course, that's it!'

'It is because of the balance. In Manuel Antonio it is just right, I think.'

We nodded.

'You agree?'

Henry, laden with a telescope and tripod, his bag and guidebook, led us through the national park with beads of perspiration forming along the margins of his hairline. We were in string tops and shorts, but it was still too hot. First he showed us a boa constrictor high in a tree just inside the entrance that we never would have spotted ourselves. In fact, everything Henry pointed out to us we would have missed on our own. From the Jesus Christ Lizard, which moves so fast it looks like it walks along the water, to the beautiful orange land crabs like sitting ducks on the forest floor, easy prey for monkeys and birds. The land crabs that look like beacons in the dark forest floor are the same flamingo colour of the bird-of-paradise flowers that grow wild everywhere. We saw dozens of crabs only because Henry knew to look. We were treated to an acrobatic performance par excellence of a two-toed sloth climbing from the top of one tree to another with amazing dexterity. The tour lasted about two hours during which we conversed with Henry in his thickly accented English.

'You will remember along the *roothe* you will see many, many animals.'

'Sorry, Henry, what did you say? Along the what?'

'*Roothe, roothe*.'

'*Route*, Mum,' Deirdre whispered. 'He's saying *route*.'

'Is right? Is better word?'

'Well, you could say *path*, maybe.' I replied.

'*Pathe*? Pathe, yes it is easier. Thank you very, very much.'

In the end I don't think pathe was any easier for him to say than roothe but we welcomed it anyway, giggling to ourselves.

'*De nada*, Henry.'

He was an exceptionally earnest guy and was wearing his professionalism as a guide a bit uneasily. Maybe it was the outfit. In trying to be professional, he was also sweating to death.

'Henry?'

'*Si?*'

'Is that a popular Costa Rican name?' I asked knowing full well that it wasn't.

'My mother, she has eleven children. When I come to be born, she was listening on the radio. She hear Henry Kissinger and think what a nice name for new baby. So she name me Henry.'

We all laughed because it was funny. Henry thought so too and began to recite some of the names of his siblings. There was Marilyn, after Miss Monroe, and Leo and Damian, and Lady and Giovanni. All children from a farming family in the mountains of Costa Rica. It was the kind of innocence that lingered in the air of the peaceful Ticos.

We spent most of our days in Manuel Antonio going to the beach. The water was warm, but at times it was too warm. Niall and Deirdre and Joseph loved it. The sand bar stretched far enough out so that Joseph felt safe swimming and every day pushed himself to go out farther and farther, but it also meant there was a steady roll of waves breaking for body surfing, which Deirdre and I loved. We were too hot sitting on the beach, even under an umbrella, so spent much of the time in the water. It was true relaxation, the kind where you *really* feel you shouldn't be doing anything else. It's the best a holiday can be: idling on the beach, taking long walks through the water's edge, swimming when you get too hot. We didn't feel the need to do, or go anywhere. And the best part was that when our time at the beach house was over, we weren't headed back home to jobs and school and the routine of the business of living. We were going on, somewhere else. We were spoiling ourselves rotten.

~

Our quiet evenings in Costa Rica were passed playing cards together. Someone had given us a card game called Wizard and we had tournaments every night as the sun went down. The ceiling fan above us whirred in the nightscape. No television to sedate us, we relied on each other for entertainment, or else we read. Joseph took out his pencils and drawing pad. Deirdre wrote in her journal. She was preparing an article about travelling the world for a teen magazine in Ireland. Sometimes the children played their instruments. To hear Joseph playing Irish fiddle tunes on his viola in an exotic destination like Costa Rica was entertaining. Deirdre, meanwhile, played classical pieces on her silver flute, the notes floating down to Bismark and Gloria who wondered where we had got a radio. (Deirdre and Joseph were preparing for a Christmas concert in Chile at the farm we were due to stay at.) In truth, not much practising got done, but just enough to keep their fingers limber. Some evenings Niall would write, although he was usually too relaxed by then, preferring the morning hours for completing his novel. It was a curious thing and we were all conscious that each time we moved Niall became unsettled with what he had written in the previous place. We'd watch him sitting over his laptop, murmuring words to himself as he typed two-fingered on one hand, three-finger on the other. Some days he was happy with what he wrote, other days he simply was not. I think it was difficult for him not to have the consistency of a sense of place that is so important in his work. His schedule of having the novel finished by Christmas had to be renegotiated. Yet I continued to believe that the time away would enrich his future work in a hundred ways.

With the help of Bismark and Gloria, we felt completely at home in the beach house. Gloria, a petite woman in her early thirties, worked for one of the five-star hotels which we could just about see from our treetop balcony. They had a swimming pool that we were dying to test out but, like many of the luxury hotels that allow you to use the pool if you buy lunch, they had an age limit. No one under sixteen was allowed. Gloria seemed to work long hours and we rarely saw her. On two occasions, however, we asked her to wash our clothes as she had a washing machine and they came back a day later, neatly ironed and folded. She even mended one of Deirdre's shirts that had holes in the underarm seams without telling us. We thanked her days later when Deirdre discovered it.

Bismark was prompted to appear one night with a bouquet of greeny white flowers on a stem after I had asked him about a delicious scent I smelled after the rain showers a few days earlier.

'*Aqui es ylang-ylang,*' he said delighted with himself and he took my hand and motioned me to follow him down the path. Just below his house was a ylang-ylang tree.

'Christian Dior, he come to get the ylang-ylang,' he said in English.

'Really?' I asked.

'*Si*, for the perfume,' he smiled.

'Yes, I understand. It's very beautiful.' And I thanked him for showing me and vowed that whenever we returned to the beach house, which we were sure we would, I would get my Spanish in better working order. We were definitely getting a feel for what it was like to live in Costa Rica through participating indirectly with Bismark's family. We learned that his children walked a couple of miles to school and back every day. No one except the rich has cars. They were taught a bit of English in school, but were too shy to speak with us. Rice and beans were their main food staples. The grocery shop was nearly devoid of vegetables and fruit consisted of pineapples, papayas and odd-looking bananas. No meat to speak of except packages of bacon and what was frozen white in the small freezer whose door seemed to be constantly ajar anytime I was shopping. We survived on tomato sauce and pasta and tinned tuna. Even the larger grocery shop in Quepos had little in the way of vegetables.

Our craving for some familiar food was answered every morning with a trip up the steep road to Café Milagro, a small open-air café on the side of the road, owned by two Americans who served food with a slightly American twist. BLATS (bacon, lettuce, avocado and tomatoes on toast) served with banana chips were a favourite, along with a large glass of vanilla chilla, a vanilla-iced coffee. By the time we got up the hill, we were already half drenched, so when the children were awake in time they joined us and we took the car instead. Café Milagro was a bonus and we visited nearly every day, striking up a conversation with a friendly waiter from Columbia who was biding his time until he could apply for an American visa. He had to wait another two years just to apply because he was a Columbian. It seemed to me that Americans were quickly buying up Costa Rica, a rather disarming fact. I hoped the government was keeping a check on it. I was faced once again with the contradiction of feeling at ease in the American-owned café – which to its credit did not speak loudly of its North Americanism and sold Costa Rican coffee as well as fine-crafted local products – and uncomfortable with signs elsewhere that read 'American-owned', as if that guaranteed superiority. And here was this Columbian who had fled his country in search of a better life which a life in America represented, but was being denied. There was no way to get it right, I decided.

~

No trip to Costa Rica is complete without some sort of adventure experience. We sorted through the brochures on offer at the café and decided on a Canopy Safari, a trip through jungle trees on high wires like Tarzan and Jane. Niall and Joseph opted out, leaving Deirdre and me ready at 6.30 a.m. at the base of the road awaiting our pick-up. We arrived at the office in Quepos and boarded a large, red, open-air truck with giant-sized wheels. Nine others joined us – two couples from Canada in their early sixties, three Californians wearing Triathlon T-shirts who had done this sort of thing before, and two newlyweds.

Our guide was a handsome Costa Rican with shark-blue eyes and curly hair who looked more like a Roman God than anything else. He had played soccer on the national youth team. His English was perfect and he chatted up the females in our group with just the right amount of finesse, eyeing Deirdre in particular, who seemed oblivious to his attentions. The journey to the starting point of the safari was an hour's drive away and we were blessed with blue skies. We held on to the overhead frame as the truck jaunted bumpily along pot-holed roads that disappeared altogether under running streams of large gravel. It was spring and the green grass on the hills looked neon in their newness against the sky. Flame trees with huge orange blossoms on dark leaves glowed on the hillsides. Jorge, our guide, instructed the driver to stop and he jumped out of the truck, grabbed a few leaves, jumped back in and balanced himself as the truck sped off. He rubbed the green leaves between his hands and explained while he was doing so that these were the leaves of the henna. There was no stopping him and he adorned our faces one by one with red paint squeezed from the leaves. (Days later we would still be washing it off!)

Breakfast was included in the adventure and we arrived to a roof-covered wooden building with no walls in the middle of the tropical jungle. Tables were set for us. Rice and beans and tortillas were on offer with eggs and ghastly cheese and a special tea that we sipped sceptically before harnessing up for the start of our adventure in the tree tops. I didn't know what I was letting myself in for. Usually game for just about anything, I bring myself along to these experiences and start to think about it only when it's too late. Deirdre was keen to partake and I was granting her wishes. If Niall hadn't a healthy fear of heights I would have insisted that he go. Let me say at this point that if I had it to do over again, I'd decline with a loud, leaping, 'Not A Chance!'

Harnessed up, looking like babies with black tight nappies, we climbed red-earthed pathways that wound up a mountainside covered with every kind of vegetation, passing tiny green tree frogs and leaf-cutter ants. The trees were deadly tall-looking to me. Deirdre followed behind wordlessly. She may have been humming to herself for all I know. Eventually we reached stairs to a wooden platform where our little party of nine and two guides jumbled together midway around an enormous tree trunk. Midway up a tree that was easily a hundred feet high! No edges to the platform. One slip and you were gone. Suddenly I was thinking: *Are we insured for this kind of thing?* One by one, in turn, we were hooked onto a wire that stretched across the open air to another tree. We were instructed not to hold on to the wire. The message was that we would be likely to burn the bejesus out of our hands if we did. The zip line was stretched between two trees. There were trees below us and all around us. There was a drop of 100 feet and the wire stretched about 75 feet. If we were brave enough, we could go free-handed, not take hold of the hanging bit. It didn't make any difference to our safety, just our sanity. And if we were *super* brave we could turn upside down. One guide would send us off while the other guide would grab us when we landed at the other side. I wanted to close my eyes. I held on for dear life. My heart thrumming. Zip! There I flew. Instants that seemed brief and forever at the same time, a blur of green trees and space and a perspective only birds know.

When it was Deirdre's turn, I watched back with my heart in my mouth. *What if?* It didn't bear thinking about, I told myself but my body has its own mind and suddenly my nerves were raw and gaping. Then there she came, a look halfway between astonishment and giggles on her face. With each zip line we climbed higher and higher until at one point we were near the very top of the tree canopy, making the descent below mighty deep. Huddled on a platform not expansive enough for a single other person, I hugged the tree and steered my eyes into its bark – the view below me was too frightening. *Crikey, what had I been thinking?* Deirdre on the other hand got braver and braver as we zoomed along. I had to marvel at her. She was right up there with the Californians, zipping along upside down now, free-handed. I on the other hand was pathetic, and worst of all I couldn't stop my fear. There was no way out. I had to go through with it and finish.

'Good thing Dad and Joe stayed at home, hey Mum?' Deirdre smiled.

'Yeah. I wish I had done the same!' I chattered.

'You'll be fine, Mum. Don't worry. Look at them – if they can do it you can.' She indicated the lovely grey-haired ladies in shorts and white sneakers beside me.

This adventure had been constructed by the Safari company literally in the middle of the Costa Rican jungle. There wasn't a sign of habitation anywhere. There were eight trips in all including two rappels that had us dropping 200 feet and saw Deirdre and the Californians going upside down, head first. Deirdre got a nasty burn on her leg from the wire but was pumped along with her own adrenalin and ready for anything. She took the burn in her stride. I could see it was blistering right up, but right then she didn't care a bit. The Canopy Safari was to be the highlight of her trip to Costa Rica, and while this mother could have done without quite so much of the adrenalin rush and the fear that attended it, I wouldn't have missed for anything the chance to be here with my daughter, high in the jungle, seeing her flying through the air, free as a bird, without fear, trusting in the power of human adventure and reaping the benefits.

By the time we left Costa Rica, we all knew that it had been much more than we imagined it to be. We vowed to come back again. We had a small farewell with Bismark and Gloria and their children, giving them some Irish souvenirs we had brought for just such a time, Niall passing Bismark his Irish soccer jersey, which he took with great pleasure and pride.

'Ireland,' he said, 'yes, good football.' His full face smiled. He made a thumbs-up gesture. They were, I think, as sad to see us go, as we were to leave them. But leave-taking is something we have to become used to on a journey like this. We waved goodbye, midway down the steep flora-covered hillside, among the tangled scents and the birdsong, saying we would be in touch again someday. And we meant it.

'*Adios, mi amigos. Bueno suerte.*'

Peru

In the arrivals lounge of Lima Airport, a lady appeared with a sign: 'Niall Williams'. She spoke in Spanish only and navigated us to a mini-van, flashing a gold-tooth as she kissed Niall on both cheeks. 'Hmmm,' I thought, 'friendly people.' We hopped on board with all our bags and were driven the twenty minutes to our hotel through the sprawling city of Lima. It was grey and flat and smoky and poor. We had booked a two-week organised tour of Peru and Bolivia with a travel company based in Cusco and this was the start of it. Hmmm….

More than one guidebook writes of Lima that it is the saddest city in the world and what emerged as we crept through the crowded streets where no lights controlled the traffic, where no street signs indicated direction, and where the honking horn was omnipresent, was that Lima is clearly a poor, sad place populated by millions and millions. Buildings were square and flat and faceless.

'Joseph,' I whispered in the backseat, 'notice anything about the cars?'

'Uh huh,' he replied, semi-disturbed, 'there aren't any new ones.'

In fact, it looked like the cars were pre-'80s. We never saw so many VW beetles – and I mean the old kind. Diesel fumes puffed chaotically from the backsides of buses, making it uncomfortable for us to breathe. Passengers stared from windows at Deirdre and Joseph. It still remains a mystery how anyone gets around in Lima. We were glad we had paid for a tour, because it was clear that we couldn't have navigated on our own. Our escort landed us at the hotel and disappeared. No itinerary, no mention of further contact. Just a kiss goodbye and *adios*. Now what? We looked back and forth at each other. We left Manuel Antonio for this? Disbelief and disappointment. Another journey over. Another destination arrived at. Here the journey had been nicer than our arrival. Our initial encounter with Lima propelled us to reconsider our stay there. We simultaneously and immediately agreed before we had even unpacked our bags that three nights was too much. Here, first impressions would likely be lasting ones. We went to sleep in brown and mud-green rooms in a kind of quarantine feeling of isolation and foreignness. Below our broken window, a constant hoot of cars punctuated the night.

Deirdre was adjusting well, even after finding some hair baked into her bread at breakfast, but Joseph was distinctly disturbed by the complete change of atmosphere from Costa Rica to Peru. It was everything he was afraid it was going to be: foreign in all its presentations to him. Worst of all was the language barrier. Joseph is enthusiastic about language and likes to communicate. After two weeks in Spanish-speaking Central America he was ready to talk to someone not only his own age but in English. He insisted on staying in his room, drawing, while the three of us walked outside. We were told that Miraflores, meaning look at the flowers, was the nicest part of the city so we went in search of it only to discover that we were in fact *in* Miraflores. Yikes, I thought to myself. And where had all the flowers gone?

'Yuck,' Deirdre blurted indiscreetly. We didn't stay out long and returned to our brown rooms after buying a guidebook on Peru with a section on Lima, looking for inspiration. We were definitely missing something, but to discover it would probably take more than a guidebook. It would take a local person and we had not a single contact in Lima except the kissing lady who had met us at the airport, and she had vanished into a din of car horns and grey light. I don't like to say that Lima felt unfriendly to us, but it did. The staff members of the hotel were not too welcoming either. It seemed that they made no effort to enquire of our needs as foreign travellers, and travellers with children at that. We waited to hear from the travel agency, hoping this was not the beginning of a disaster, another paid-in-advance debacle. Was the Internet going to fail me? Were all those testimonials on the company's web page false? A woman from the agency finally appeared in the late afternoon. She didn't ask why we wanted to leave Lima a day early and we didn't say. She came with changed tickets for the flight to Cusco up in the Andes, which she had arranged quite easily, and an itinerary and a balance invoice. It was beginning to look promising. Maybe we just needed to get out of Lima. (In my opinion, Lima suffers from an inferiority complex – it knows it is just a stopover for the tourists who are all on their way to Cusco and Machu Picchu and the Nazca Lines – and turns a cold shoulder to the visitor.)

The following morning we stayed in our rooms till noon and came downstairs to ask at the front desk where to eat lunch. The taxi driver who had been called to take us suggested a different restaurant from the one the hotel had and, pleased that we agreed with him, drove us and waited the hour and a half till we finished. He was very obliging, happy to be practising his English and to be escorting us. He showed us a small bit of Miraflores which had some promising sections, but nothing you might expect from a capital city that had been home to so much Inca heritage. Eight million people have made Lima their home and more arrive every day from the countryside. It is spilling with people. It was a grey misty day, typical of the weather for this time of year. It wasn't pretty.

They say that tourists often miss the jewels of Lima. (What else are they going to say?) But this time around, on this adventure, we weren't prepared to go on a treasure hunt. We departed readily the next day for Cusco, leaving behind a hooting, crowded, diesel-fumed sprawl of a flat city, the population of which constituted the whole of Bolivia!

But before we could leave, a rather amazing thing happened as we attempted to clear airport security in Lima Airport.

'Is this your bag, sir?' the security personnel enquired of Niall.

'Yes, this is mine. It's a laptop computer.'

'Yes, sir, but it also has a knife in it.'

'No, I don't think so,' Niall replied, looking around at us and wondering what was happening.

'Yes, sir. It's a Swiss Army knife,' insisted the security man, steadfastly and very politely.

'Really?' Niall rejoined, very surprised, opening his bag and showing the security man its contents.

'Ah, ha,' Joseph responded.

'So there it is!' I laughed, rather inappropriately. It had fallen down and hidden beneath some netting in his bag. It was indeed a Swiss Army knife – the very knife that Niall was sure he had lost back in Amagansett – the Swiss Army knife that had been given to him by the staff of St Michael's in Kilmihil village – the knife, it must be said, that had escaped every double scrutiny preformed by US airport security! We were astonished and, believing that we wouldn't be allowed to continue to carry it – however well hidden it could be – gladly tried to hand it over to the security man.

'No, no,' he professed. 'Wait. I will see what I can do.'

And he disappeared. The airport security police were astounded themselves and a little proud that they had detected it when the Americans – the North Americans – hadn't. In the end, after a few paper-signing agreements, we were allowed to keep the knife and, not only that, but we were allowed to keep it in our hand luggage.

'Just don't kill any of my pilots,' the security lady said, smiling at Deirdre, whose knife we had claimed it was.

It made a bit of a farce of the somewhat over-the-top security checks we had encountered for two months in North America. Joseph was feeling vindicated after all his complaining. In reality, our Swiss Army knife could have single-handedly brought down an entire aircraft with its thirty plus arms! It was a nice ending to a rather dismal introduction to Peru. Without further shenanigans, we boarded an aircraft for the eleventh time in less than three months, and headed for the great Andes.

~

Cloud-cover obscured the view of the mountains until we were close to Cusco. The thrill of suddenly seeing these tremendous peaks, 50 million years old, was simply awesome. Joseph and I were sitting beside each other, and looked back and forth at one another and out the window in wonder.

'We're really here, Joseph,' I whispered. It was nearly too fantastic. Miles and miles of green mountains, like folded blankets draped upward, stretching to the sky and folding back over as if their weight had become insurmountable. Huge crevices and grey-black gorges and small villages of red-topped roofs appeared below us. The Andes Mountains conjure up mystery, immensity, and remoteness and here we were about to land in the heart of them in Cusco, sacred city of the Incas.

As if on cue, a Peruvian band dressed in traditional costume was beating a drum and blowing on wooden flutes the minute we landed and appeared in the arrivals hall. Our bags came quickly. I looked around for a placard with 'Niall Williams', in a light-headed haze, suddenly feeling dizzy, while Niall loaded the bags onto a trolley. Deirdre and Joseph stood watching the band of browned-skinned middle-aged Indian musicians dressed in colourful hats and skirts, tooting and drumming with blank staring faces as if mesmerised. Were they for real, or for show? Almost at once I began to notice that my breathing was shallow. It felt as though my lungs had ceased operating on all cylinders. The altitude was going to be an issue for me, I could tell. But I would give it some time to see if I could acclimatise myself. Nothing can prepare you for the lack of oxygen that hits – or starves you rather – in the high altitude until you experience it for yourself. You can understand its symptoms and read about its various effects, but experience is everything. Not everybody suffers, however; and I was hoping that at least the children would manage. For the moment, I would say nothing and see if I could make the adjustment. I had the coca I had snatched from the airport security man in JFK, just in case.

When we had booked the tour, we had specifically asked for the Monestario Hotel in Cusco and it was to there that the mini-van with all our bags, our driver and our escort transferred us in near total silence as we measured the city against what we had already seen in Lima. It was colourful, not dismal. Cusco was more prosperous, with small, red adobe brick houses climbing up into the steep hills in all directions. Here we saw people dressed not in dark, cosmopolitan dress as in Lima but in flaming pink and red, even turquoise skirts. Wide-skirted women in round rimmed black hats and layers and layers of shawls walked along the streets or stood on corners. Only their brown legs showing from their knees down and their brown faces framed by black braided hair were visible. Others in high-topped white hats carried babies in blankets that hung around their backs and tied at their necks. These were postcard images. Indians walking with llamas down the street. A woman holding a baby lamb in her arms against the large Inca stones waiting with an empty stare for tourists to take a picture in return for one *sol*.

Mestizos, the race of half-Indian, half-Inca, populate most of the city of Cusco, the city of the Incas which the Spanish conquered in the fifteenth century. A mix of Inca stone and Spanish ornate architecture blends oddly. It would take time before we would begin to understand this interesting mixture of proud Cusconians, if ever. The notion that they were at the navel of the world still permeated through the narrow and cobbled streets. Side by side were luxury shops selling gold jewellery, while Indian men and women stood in tiny doorways that led to darkened shops. Many buildings along the streets were lined with Inca stone. It was bustling with tourists and Indians alike. Cars darted hither and thither. Tour buses waited in traffic while white-gloved policemen motioned them forward. The great square, the Plaza de Armas, was like a parade of commerce, people, policemen, students and colour. Side by side are Internet cafés, historic buildings, Irish pubs, churches, Indian stalls, hotels of every description and small shops selling water bottles and Kodak film and everything else you'd possibly need, while up in the mountains, the white statue of Christ overlooks it all.

When we arrived at the hotel, the deep, imposing yellow chairs we sat in embraced us while we took in our surroundings – tall, grey walls and a high, decoratively carved wooden ceiling. Our escort made the arrangements for our rooms. We were all feeling the effects of altitude sickness. I was suffering particularly. Deirdre and

Niall less so. Joseph was experiencing breathlessness. Cusco is 3,600 metres above sea level with 30 per cent less oxygen in the air. My heart was palpitating. We were offered the greenish coca tea immediately and instructed to sip slowly.

'Just tastes like one of your herbal teas, Mum,' said Deirdre, who seemed to be handling it the best. (Admittedly, Deirdre had been prescribed a good constitutional remedy a few weeks earlier by an MD homeopath, and after a steady regimen of vitamins and supplements, she was reaping the benefits.)

Joseph baulked at the tea and asked for a coke instead. While he had enough energy to complain, I knew it would be all right.

Since we had arrived a day earlier than planned, we had a free afternoon before us and, after moving into our somewhat monastic cell-like rooms, with small wooden shuttered windows and high white ceilings, we went for lunch and then rested for the afternoon, attempting to acclimatise to the atmosphere. During lunch, Deirdre remarked to me bemusedly, 'Mum? Are you feeling all right? Your lips are blue.'

And so they were. Fewer red blood cells were carrying oxygen to my extremities and I was literally turning a bit blue. All I could do was watch and wait.

～

The Monestario, as the name suggests, was formerly an old monastery and lies in the heart of the city. It was built in the late 1500s on the site of the Inca Amaru Qhala Palace and was given the royal seal of approval in 1692. It wasn't turned into a hotel until the mid-1990s. The sound of monks singing softly reverberates in the air. The Chapel of San Antonio Abad with its ornate gold altar is open daily and Gregorian chants echo from the great stone corridors out into the courtyard. The hotel is sheltered behind ancient walls, like so many prosperous houses in the old cities. An oasis-like atmosphere, distinct from the bustle and hum of Cusco, welcomes the guests who in one degree or another are here because of the Incas. Four stone walls surround a courtyard with a stone fountain in the centre and diagonally divided flower gardens with short clipped grass. Open-arched walls enclose the square. It feels like a sanctuary, especially once you've tasted the hectic life outside.

The Mayor of Cusco announced to its citizens that *touristos estara nuestros amigos* and the people are very friendly. Unfortunately, however, they can also be a bit like hounds after a bone. And it is next to impossible to walk the streets without being accosted by tens of children and women asking you to buy postcards, blankets, earrings, paintings, gloves, hats, and souvenirs of every kind. The Cusconians have a very clever tactic, which was new to my experience of travel. They ask you your name, 'Please Mrs, what is your name?' If you make the mistake of answering, which feels rude to refuse, then they shout your name in the street whenever they see you again. When you depart from your bus after a half-day city tour or a day's visit further afield, they are there, waiting for you. In fact, every time you leave your hotel they are there. They tell you their names as well. There was Julio, Alicia, Jorge… They travel in groups, mostly with their families, and when they spot you they shout:

'Mrs Christine, remember me?'

'You promised, Mrs Christine, to buy my postcards…'

It takes a special kind of hardness to ignore them and one which we were incapable of, especially Joseph. Deirdre was game for it because she loves to experience shopping on all levels. Mostly, there was no way out for us. We had made the mistake of making a connection by giving our names and had to pay the fiddler. We were too many feet from the sanctuary of the hotel. Only a little closer and the hotel staff would whisk us in. I think they rather enjoyed watching tourists engaged in the web of Cusconian marketing. You end up forced to buy more postcards, or earrings, or woven water carriers – items that you didn't need more of – simply to get away. But the more you buy, the more they expect you to buy. It is a vicious circle and the single worst thing about Cusco. Joseph couldn't stand it. He couldn't stand the swarming like bees around honey when we appeared on the street. He couldn't stand the shouting in his ears. He couldn't bear to say 'no'. Mostly, he couldn't bear the idea that behind their nagging sales technique was poverty. So he stayed inside the refuge of the hotel except for the guided tours and, when we returned, we asked to be left at the door of the hotel so he could sneak in without the assault of the sellers.

~

Dear D,

We've made to the Andes! Spectacular and stunning. But I can't sleep. Can't breathe. Wouldn't you know that I'd be the one to suffer from the altitude? Taking Coca 30 for relief and drinking coca tea. Joseph is holding up well considering he doesn't quite want to be here. It's like an assault on all his senses and he can't assimilate it. Deirdre is grand. Happy and able for everything, although feeding her is a bit tricky. Vegetarian food is not easily found. In two days we go to Machu Picchu! Tell D and J that we saw alpacas and vicuñas and llamas today.

Love C

~

Our tour took us around Cusco for half a day; to Sacsayhuaman, the Inca complex just outside of Cusco; to Ollantaytambo and Tambomachay; and a full day's tour of the Sacred Valley of the Urubamba River. Even the music of the place names begins to conjure up these images of extraordinary places. The imperial city, Cusco, meaning 'navel of the earth,' is believed to have been laid out in the form of a puma, the animal that symbolised the Inca dynasty. The belly of the puma was the main Plaza, the river Tullumayo formed its spine, and the hill of Sacsayhuaman its head. Cusco was the ceremonial nexus and the centre of the Inca cosmos. Only nobility were welcomed. (It felt a bit like that inside the Monasterio Hotel.) It is hard to imagine today the opulence that was once abundant in the Inca temples in Cusco and elsewhere in the Inca Empire. However, the oddly decorative and garish Spanish churches may give some idea as to the lavishness that once was Cusco. Even the statues are dressed in cloth, like dolls, in the cathedral in the square. The Coricancha, meaning the corral of gold, was dedicated primarily to the creator god and Inti, the Sun god, with smaller shrines to the Moon, Venus, the Pleiades, and various weather deities. Reports by the first Spanish who entered Cusco tell that ceremonies were conducted around the clock and that its opulence was fabulous beyond belief. The carved granite walls of the temple were covered with more than 700 sheets of pure gold, which the Spanish seized at the first opportunity and melted into coins and sent home to Spain. The spacious courtyard of the Coricancha was filled with life-size sculptures of animals and a field of corn, all fashioned from pure gold, and, facing the direction of the rising sun, was a giant golden image of the sun encrusted with emeralds and other precious stones. The sacred site in Cusco was also the centrepiece of a vast astronomical observatory and calendar device. Roads ran for miles, signifying the celestial points on the horizon as well as the equinox and solstice points, and different stars and constellations highly important to the Incas.

When the Spanish conquerors first arrived, they could not explain how the Peruvian Indians whom they considered ignorant and wild could have built such greatness as can be seen in Sacsayhuaman – considered one of the best monuments built by mankind on the earth – just outside the city of Cusco. The religious fervour of the conquistadors of the fifteenth century led them to believe that the construction of these stone sites was the work of demons or bad spirits. In fact, many believe that the ancient Quechuas were entirely unable, physically and intellectually, to create such wonders as are seen in the Peruvian Andes. Suggestions linger that beings of other worlds, extraterrestrials with superior technology, made it all possible. There are no other walls like these. They are different from Stonehenge, different from the Pyramids of the Egyptians and the Maya, different from any of the other ancient monolithic stone-works. Most of these walls are found around Cusco and the Urubamba River Valley in the Peruvian Andes. There are a few scattered examples elsewhere in the Andes, but almost nowhere else on earth. The structures are beyond under-standing. Modern man can neither explain nor duplicate them. The huge stones fit flawlessly. Not a single blade of grass can slide between them. Steel can barely pry them apart. There is no mortar. Connected in complex and irregular patterns, it looks like child's play, but would baffle a modern stonemason. At first all you see are these giant rocks lying like an interrupted game of children's Lego on a green playing field; it requires interest and imagination, otherwise it will be lost on you.

'Hey Joseph,' I shouted over to him, 'go stand there against the wall. I want to see you next to it.'

'Okay,' he said, 'but hurry up.' He was dwarfed against the grey stone. He splayed out his hands and touched its smooth surface, and just then I could see on his face an expression of sheer delight. He had read a lot about the Incas on the Andes, and across his face then you could see the knowledge and the realisation pass, as well as the sheer childlike fun of being in such a huge fantasy-land of stone and grass.

The walls or ramparts of Sacsayhuaman, the most impressive aspect that still survives, were built with enormous carved limestone boulders. Like all of the other rocks there, they had to have been be brought from a quarry 3 km away, a feat that defies belief considering it was constructed in the 1400s by a people who had no knowledge of the outside world. The boulders used for the first level are the biggest, 8.5 metres high and weighing about 140 metric tons. It has been speculated that the three walls of the complex represent the three levels of the Andean religious world: the bottom is the underworld, the earth is the middle, and heaven is on top. These levels are also identified with the three sacred animals, the Amaru (snake), the Puma (cougar or mountain lion), and the Kuntur (Andean condor).

Scientists speculate as to how the masonry process might have worked, from carving and tracing and suspending the enormous rocks to fit a jigsaw-like design. The surfaces of the rocks are as smooth as marble. It is said that they must have used finger-sized stones for sanding and hand-sized stones for sculpting. Not a single tool has surfaced that supplies an explanation. All is conjecture. Someone has even suggested that the precision-fit Inca walls were first softened by a technique that used the acid extracts of plants. Included in their ingenuity, these massive, multi-sided blocks were precisely fitted together in interlocking patterns in order to withstand the disastrous effects of earthquakes. There is neither adornment nor inscription, just sheer raw energy of spiritual dimensions.

Garcilaso de la Vega, a sixteenth-century chronicler, seems not to have had a clue as to how Sacsayhuaman was built. He wrote:

'...this fortress surpasses the constructions known as the Seven Wonders of the World. For in the case of a long broad wall like that of Babylon, or the colossus of Rhodes, or the pyramids of Egypt, or the other monuments, one can see clearly how they were executed...how, by summoning an immense body of workers and accumulating more and more material day by day and year by year, they overcame all difficulties by employing human effort over a long period. But it is indeed beyond the power of imagination to understand how these Indians, unacquainted with devices, engines, and implements, could have cut, dressed, raised, and lowered great rocks, more like lumps of hills than building stones, and set them so exactly in their places. For this reason, and because the Indians were so familiar with demons, the work is attributed to enchantment.'

And enchanted we were while there. Whether it was the altitude, the colour not only of the landscape with its rich green mountains and underlay of red earth, but of the women and children in pink and blues and browns – or the lingering belief that the Incas had that the earth influenced the heavens, I walked around in a kind of daze which seemed to settle on me the moment I arrived. Joseph was absorbing everything, his spirit replenished during the hours he had spent drawing in his room. (His pictures of buildings and houses now with a backdrop of mountains, red skies and blue suns.) Deirdre was in top form and not questioning a thing, just feeling the freedom that travel affords you away from your own life. She had well and truly stepped out of Kiltumper. I could see that Niall was constructing new creative territories in his mind. Every now and again a quietness came over him while he registered a person or a scent or a certain light. He was getting no time for writing his novel, but instead indexed the images before him as feelings that would later translate back into words in his work. For each of us the very air was intoxicating.

At the Pisac Market, bargaining is part of the buying, where in the narrow cobbled streets, on steps, in doorways, under plastic-sheeted coverings offering shade from the sun, everything is sold from potatoes to panpipes. Shirley, our Mestizo guide, told us clearly and

119

without equivocation to offer half the asking price, a strategy that didn't come easily to any of us. We ventured around for about two hours. The boys in one direction and Deirdre and I in another.

We eventually came away with some beautiful woollen crafts and a large rug featuring a colourful butterfly design that we had, after a fashion, 'bargained' down to an acceptable price for buyer and seller. The butterflies reminded us of Costa Rica. If we had had room for more, we would have bought three times as much. The prices were sinfully inexpensive. We felt uncomfortably greedy as it was and refrained from taking advantage of the marketplace. It felt awkward to buy handmade products so inexpensively, especially as I remembered well from my days at the Clare Craft and Design Shop in Ennis where I used to sell handpainted terracotta pots and watercolours of my 'Irish' garden to American tourists, how much work goes into handcrafted work. I know I resented not being well paid for it. I had to rationalise to myself that the Pisac market has been going on for a long time and it has become a way of life in the Peruvian Andes, providing a livelihood for many Indians there, a living they make from tourists like myself. Further, I convinced myself that Pisac would still be in business long after I left. At least I hoped it would and maybe our readiness to accept the prices they asked for might cue some of the artisans to maintain their prices rather than lower their value.

The journey to the hill village of Chinchero at 4,000 metres was one of the highlights of my passage in the Andes. We arrived just as the sun was setting. The snow-capped mountaintops and glaciers touch the sky there at 6,000 metres. As we drove over the winding road, it was like driving through a living tapestry of colour and landscape, like a motion picture that we were a part of. Mountains. Hilltops. Single lines of Eucalyptus trees. Red-tiled roofs, off pink-red adobe houses, made rose by the light of the setting sun. Women dotted the distant fields, their hats like white chimney tops. Their bent over bodies, toiling in the Peruvian soil – the abundant, red and pinky clay of the Andean earth – rich and vibrant, like Inca gold. I wish I could have got off the bus, and walked out into that landscape then, but the bus didn't stop. And in a way, I'm grateful. When you feel part of the living scene the memory of it is etched permanently inside you, somewhere. It is coupled with an immense peacefulness that cradles not only the landscape, but also your soul.

'Is the sky bluer here because we are closer to it?' Deirdre asked in an awestruck dream-like state.

'Yes, dear, I think so,' I replied dreamily too. Not knowing if it was just the landscape or the altitude that was making me so light-headed.

That ride high in the Peruvian highland with the sun setting and green hills turning bronze, copper and gold will be engraved in my mind forever. The peace on top of the Andes in November is a thing to be experienced. Miles from a city, from the Internet, from the Dow Jones, from CNN, from an impending war that loomed closer daily. The landscape was alive with farmers tending their acre by hand and hard work. We saw fewer than five tractors during our entire crossing through the highlands. In an odd way what I saw out of the window of the bus reminded me of Paul Henry's paintings of the potato farmers of Connemara one hundred years ago – bent over, hand tending the fields, also in vibrant, bold colours against skyscape and mountain top. Here, it was as if the clock had stopped for these people. A kind of Brigadoon-like atmosphere appeared in the twilight. Maybe it wasn't real at all. It felt privileged yet slightly voyeuristic to be a passenger through this landscape, with digital camera and expensive hiking boots, hoping the Andean scene that unfolded before me would be everlasting and would remain at least as untouched as it appeared then to be. The journey passed without another word. We watched like dreamers in a dream.

～

We noted that all our Peruvian guides expressed in as many ways as possible and with somewhat snide remarks how the Spanish conquistadores were villainous, robbing the Incas of their gold and culture, destroying their temples and causing the decline and extinction of the Incas. The Cusconians are especially proud of their Inca heritage, even though a large majority of them are Mestiso. The memory of the Spanish conquerors is long and still fresh. The Incas are mythical and lend their unique identity to all who walk their path.

Evenings saw us walking ceremonially around the square in Cusco, arm in arm, avoiding making any new acquaintances with hawkers. Deirdre was taking wonderfully composed photographs with the camera my brother Stephen had generously bestowed on her for the trip. We were learning how to avoid the sellers by smiling and walking on and saying, 'No, but thank you so much. How very kind of you to ask.'

We would have liked to have stayed longer in Cusco, but soon realised that we were on a tour designed for travellers who wanted to squeeze in as much as possible in as short a time as possible. There was too little time to soak it in. It felt a bit like taking mental snapshots for viewing at a later time. When you could sit down with maybe a Pisco sour, a traditional South American drink, and reminisce about the time you watched the golden lights of Cusco appear on the edge of the twilight as your train returned from Machu Picchu, where from your room at the opulent Monestario Hotel you felt at the navel of the earth.

The altitude, however, was making it difficult for me. In fact, one evening, I felt so wretched that I called room service and asked for some oxygen. Moments later, a smartly dressed porter in gold buttons arrived with a small tank as if it were champagne on a tray. Quietly he showed me the mask and the valves and then left. The kids laughed at me as I sat in our room with the tank beside me and half my face covered in a plastic mask. It felt wonderful to breathe again and I hated giving it up. It was like I was addicted to abundant air. We learned too late that the Monestario is the only hotel in the world that can oxygenate the guest rooms. You can order your air at the front desk. Or, we learned in time, but also learned that it was too costly. Anyway, I can't remember which – blame the altitude – it was going to my brain. I suppose the biggest laugh was on me who came prepared like superwoman for any eventuality, but couldn't stave off the *soroche*. Nothing in my bag of tricks was going to help, short of getting back in my balloon and flying back to Kansas. That said, I was the only one of the four of us who was really having a difficult time and I could put up with it. I wouldn't exchange a single moment.

~

The early-morning train from Cusco to Aguas Calientes, a four-hour journey, that departs at six in the morning, carries passengers whose sole intent is to visit Machu Picchu. A friend of ours, Allen Flynn, the owner of a charming hotel in Ennis, County Clare called The Old Ground, chastised us when he heard we weren't trekking the Inca Trail. In fact, you do feel a bit of a cheat when you take the train rather than the trail. If we were travelling without our children, we would probably have made an attempt, if not the whole five-day trek, at least from the 88 km mark, a starting point for the less hardy. Arriving by train and bus is what the purists would scoff at, but in my mind it's just a different way, not a better way. Another holiday perhaps will see me hiking the Inca trail, but not this time.

The train journey itself is stunning, passing rich fields of corn and potatoes. Like in Chinchero, the soil of the valley is red gold. School-age children ran to meet the train, waving to the passengers. Watching and waving back, Joseph especially seeming to connect with these children, we slowly sauntered on along a single-track line, shaking and jaunting into the mountains. In a green valley, a wild rose hedgerow suddenly appeared on the side of a riverbank. Flowers of the purple Peruvian potato plant stirred vibrantly in the morning light. (We learned at the Pisac market that there are over a hundred varieties of Peruvian potatoes, and some can keep for ten years!) Farming women in their traditional hats, and wide, colourful skirts, in muddy, barely sandalled feet, tended the acres. Men guided their oxen, ploughing a red earth field. The section of the Andes Mountains between Cusco and Machu Picchu is like the etched sides of a cradle guarding a precious valley. Multi-layered fields with sepia houses of red adobe bricks and fresh green growth of corn dotted with rural mountain villages unfolded with the early morning. We were finally on our way to one of the great wonders of the world, the Inca spiritual mountain site at Machu Picchu, 130 km from Cusco.

When we eventually arrived at Aguas Calientes, a half-dozen buses transferred us across a wooden bridge and through a sprawling chaotic market up along a steeply winding, zigzagging road to the entrance of Machu Picchu. Only serious backpackers and Inca trail hikers were unaccompanied; the rest of us were corralled by bilingual guides into groups, like herds of sheep on the mountainside. It's an industry, for certain, but one that respects the majesty of the site. Our guide, Roberto, instructed us to climb the hundreds of steps up, adding that he would meet us there. Walkers of all ages and nationalities joined together in ascending the steep, grass-tufted Inca steps.

One Dutch woman spoke to Joseph:

'I learned this in Nepal,' she began. 'If you go diagonally, it's not so hard on your legs.' So we crisscrossed our way up several hundred steps, stopping in the midmorning sun to take a breath and a drink from water bottles in woven carriers that Deirdre had bought on the street in Cusco. Machu Picchu is 1,000 metres lower than Cusco so the altitude wasn't as much of a factor or hindrance in our ascent. After what seemed thousands of steps, we arrived to join Roberto who opened his arms wide saying, 'Now, here for you is the postcard!'

Beyond his open arms and winning smile was indeed the picture from the postcard image of Machu Picchu that we had seen a dozen times. Camera shutters clicked like chirping birdsong. Exclamations in different languages sang across the terraces. The Incas were bestowing on us a graceful day of sunshine and cloudscape, enabling us to see their magical site. And it was just that.

Roberto pointed up even higher to the Intihuatana stone, the 'Hitching Post of the Sun', which has been shown to be a precise indicator of the date of the winter solstice and other significant celestial periods. It is a frequently climbed spot that every Inca trekker passes through. Every midwinter, the Incas held a ceremony at this stone, in which they 'tied the sun' to halt its northward movement in the sky. Shamanic legends say that when sensitive persons touch their foreheads to the stone, the Intihuatana opens their vision to the spirit world. We didn't make it up that far, but I wouldn't be surprised if my own aligned sensitivities to things spiritual and mystical were ignited. Or perhaps my touching of a similar stone inside the cathedral in Cusco opened a gateway to roaming deities or raving entities. Maybe that would explain the daze I was in.

Speculation still abounds about Machu Picchu. Even today, new information is unfolding. At first, Machu Picchu, not its original

Inca name, which is unknown, was considered a religious site for chosen beautiful women. The remains of 150 plus bodies were discovered, the majority of which were thought to be women. Now with new imaging advances, it turns out that half the remains are men. The virginal women theory vanishes and a new one arises. Little is really known of the social or religious use of the site except that it was a hidden sanctuary for Inca nobility, rediscovered in 1911. What is clear is that it was a sacred place for royal Incas. It is befitting of the mystical-ness of the pyramid-shaped mountain that its origins as a place of worship are shrouded in mystery. Invisible from below and completely self-contained, surrounded by agricultural terraces sufficient to feed the population, and watered by natural springs. Was Machu Picchu a secret Inca ceremonial city or a holiday home away from home for royalty? It sits like a capped fortress, 2,000 feet above the rumbling Urubamba River. Sometimes cloud-shrouded, sometimes sun-drenched, the ruins have palaces, baths, temples, storage rooms and some 150 houses, all in a remarkable state of preservation. Like the Inca sites elsewhere in this region, the structures are carved from the grey granite of the mountain. The blocks that make up the foundations of the buildings are sheer wonders. Here there are blocks weighing fifty tons or more. Hundreds of stone terraces transgress the mountainside in a multi-layered wedding-cake pyramid, tufts of grass and wildflowers spilling over their edges. Wild llamas roam. Birds nest in rocky crevices.

And in the way of these things, it becomes unimportant as to the why of it. Here, as in so few places else on earth, it is possible to be in the moment of extraordinary being-ness. A state of wonder that defies explanation and invites you to be fully in tune with the mystery of the universe. We lingered for the afternoon and gazed anew with each shaft of light that fell before us, excited to have made it this far into the continent of South America, to be witnessing one of the wonders of the world amid the throng of tourists who come to partake of the cycle of magic that occurs when mankind and the planet harmonise.

Bolivia

I t was bound to happen. Sometime, somewhere, someone was going to suffer gastroenteritis of some description. Reading in my *Homeopathy for World Travellers* manual, I browsed askance the classification of 'Travellers' Diarrhoea'. I didn't see my symptoms listed – not the way I was experiencing them. But whatever it was, it had me in a vice grip. Intense colitis-like cramps, unlike anything I have ever felt, in the dead centre of my navel. (The fact that I had just come from Cusco, the navel of the world, didn't occur to me until much later.) *Muchos flatus* with pain that extended up my ribcage to my shoulder blades plagued me for days. Diarrhoea would have been a blessing. You might say, it was inevitable; just get over it. And I'd normally agree, but in this case I found myself lying on a thin foam mattress in a bed that was less than three-foot wide in a room that was less than eight-foot wide in a Bolivian catamaran docked for the night on the north side of the Isla del Sol on Lake Titicaca in a rain storm. Where's James Bond when you need him, hey? It was a scene out of a surrealist movie. The boat didn't rock this baby to sleep, all night long. It was torture.

The twelve-hour journey on the Orient Express from Cusco to Puno that we had taken a few days earlier was sheer heaven compared with this. We had boarded the train at eight in the morning saying goodbye to Cusco and the Monasterio Hotel with some regret. I was just beginning to get a handle on the altitude, or so I thought. Following a hotel mix-up, we had been moved to de luxe rooms for our last night and saw for the first time on our tour what *luxury* class really meant. (Suffice to say that if we could ever afford it again, those are the rooms we'd book, complete with balcony, plush amber carpets, gold-framed oil paintings of Madonnas and drape-bordered bathtub.) But, as so often in this trip, just when we were beginning to feel that we had somehow made a home, it was time to move on.

The slow train to Puno, the rather grimy-looking city on the edge of Lake Titicaca, nearly ached as it delivered us across the high Andean plateau. Fortunately for us we were seated in first class, sitting in armchairs facing white linen-clothed tables bedecked with china and dainty little lamps with silk-tasselled shades. Miles and miles of Andean highlands emerged around every turn in the single-track rail-line and disappeared into a blur of blue sky, green mountain and red earth. Hour after hour we sat bewitched, watching from the open-backed, glass ceiling caboose; the landscape continually unfurling like a daydream, shifting with each bend into even more phantasmagoria as the train inched along, wobbling back and forth. It was one of the highlights thus far, especially for Joseph who ended up at his own table with his books and drawings spread before him. Deirdre and I took our cameras back into the caboose, the wood-panelled 'Panoramic car', but the bumpy ride made it too difficult to take photos. The cameras echoed the train's rocking movements and it was next to impossible to get a still shot. (I regretted that I hadn't got fully back into the swing of sketching.) When your camera fails, your mind clicks into overdrive and certain memories of quite awesome scenery can be recorded there, much like a virtual photo album.

The journey was a kind of still passage, like a portal to subconscious awareness of an energy beyond yourself. An invitation that bids you to enter into a realm of pure feeling. Only great luck would have captured this on film. In a trance, then, we passed the long lazy day between meals and card-playing and reading and looking out the window. By the time we arrived in Puno, twelve hours later, and 200 metres higher than when we were in Cusco, it was dark and cold and raining hard. We were hungry. An English-speaking escort met the train and helped get our bags into the van, and we were driven silently through the mud-puddled night streets. In the dark rain, Puno looked like a poverty-stricken city. It has been described as cold and uninviting even by the government-issued 'Peru Guide' that we received in Lima.

As if to mirror the disquiet we were already feeling, our van suddenly pulled up short in front of earth piled five feet high and covering the width of the street. The road we travelled was entirely impassable. Niall shot me a worried glance. Deirdre looked to me with silent appeal. But in the way of these things, it seemed a mere customary disturbance for the driver who found an alternative route by backing up and driving up on the broken paths and rubble and red bricks lying beside half-completed buildings. Apparently nothing to be alarmed about. I don't know what I was fearful of: maybe I was half-expecting terrorists to jump out and seize the van in the style of some recent movies set in South America. I had just finished reading *Bel Canto* by Ann Patchett, a story about a group of revolutionaries who kidnap a gathering of international guests at a residential mansion in a South American country. We arrived at the hotel nearly without a word spoken from the driver, the escort or ourselves. Discomforted and just a bit nervous of what we had got ourselves into this time, we found an invisible shield construct-ing itself within moments, It was a response that was evolving from months of travelling. My first worry was always for Deirdre and Joseph. *What have you dragged them into now?*

~

Dear D,

Hello from Puno on the shores of Lake Titicaca! Not the world's nicest city, I'm sorry to say. The lake here might be turquoise but I've literally turned blue from altitude sickness. Niall had an attack in the middle of the Andes Mountains on the train when we hit the highest point at 4,400 metres. His head sank to the table with dizziness and perspiration. It took a few moments to realise what was happening. Then I gave him coca 1M and he was right as rain half an hour later, thank God. (Wish homeopathy worked that well for me, hey?) Kids are doing okay. Joseph wants to go home, I think. I sometimes watch him struggle with foreignness like a low-grade fever. He hated Cusco but enjoyed Machu Picchu where he tried to make friends with a llama. Deirdre is doing terrifically. It's fun just to be with her and to watch her. Sometimes she catches me looking at her and says, 'What?' And I say, 'Nothing, I'm just watching you.' She looks back at me long enough to say, 'That's nice, Mum.' Anyway, we're off tomorrow to sail across the lake to the Island of the Sun. Won't be able to email again until La Paz – The Peace.

Love you to bits, C

~

Once we had left Cusco and the comfort of the Orient Express, it felt like we were in truly foreign territory. Our guide was not the guide we had been told to expect and the one who appeared didn't have an itinerary for us. He disappeared and said someone would be there to collect us in the morning. Tourists do make it this far, to the Peruvian shores of Lake Titicaca, but the hotel staff didn't seem particularly welcoming.

Our rooms in the Isla Estevez were plain and tiny, but on the bright side there was a tub and room service and we went to bed with good food and warmth, yet weary at the thought of getting up at six in the morning for another excursion. The previous three mornings had seen us waking between five and six. Niall and the children were sleeping well, although not enough. Insomnia is one of the common side effects of altitude sickness and I passed many nights in the Andes with just a few hours' sleep. I am not a good sleeper at the best of times, and with the altitude still playing havoc with my system, I slept poorly again.

Downstairs at half past six the next morning, we waited at the front door, and eventually were escorted by a non-English-speaking guide who dropped us at the small harbour. Above the green lake, the blue sky was mixed with clouds alighted with sunshine. We squeezed ourselves into the small motorboat with about twenty other tourists. We left the dock without fanfare or introductions from the Peruvian guide and sat wordlessly as we moved slowly through the reed-filled water in the inside harbour of the lake. We were headed towards the Floating Islands of the Uros. Another mood descended: a kind of sheltered togetherness rose around us. It was a mechanism of which I don't think we were fully aware, but which left us partially enclosed in an invisible safety net.

As every student of geography knows, Lake Titicaca is the highest navigable lake in the world and we were slowly sailing out upon it. Located 70 km west of the city of La Paz it is fed by 'meltwaters' from the glaciers in the Apolobamba and Royal or La Paz Cordilleras. The colossal peaks of the Bolivian Andes are covered with eternal snow and rise majestically near the northern bank of the Titicaca. It was thrilling, despite our tiredness and guardedness. The lake is about 8,500 sq km and is sometimes called the Bolivian Sea by the Bolivians since the Chileans stole theirs, or so the Bolivian history books say. It is bordered by the Andes Mountains and the Cordillera Real Bolivian glaciers. At times it really does feel like you are floating on top of the world. The people of Uros are said to have descended from one of the ancient peoples of the Americas – some say they are the true descendents of the Incas who first arrived, as legend has it, by rising out of Lake Titicaca in the form of *Manco Capac*, the first Inca, and his sister-consort, *Mama Ocllo*. Another myth states that the Sun God came from Lake Titicaca and He, in turn, created the people of the world. (The Bolivians say that the sun jumped from the Isla del Sol into the sky and that Manco Capac and Mama Ocllo were the children of that union.)

An hour later, we disembarked from the boat, arriving on one of the islands in a blaze of sunshine. Stepping from the boat in wonderment onto the cushioned island of reed – spongy, bouncy and soft – on such a blue day, impelled me to whisper to myself *Titicaca, Titicaca, Titicaca.* Like a mantra of exotic dimensions. An island made entirely of reeds, floating stationary on the lake of Titicaca, it was nearly unreal. It was one of those times where you have to pinch yourself. The island people had prepared a demonstration for us of how they use the reed, what they eat and what they make on the island. The people of Uros live permanently on these islands, made of totora reed, which extend to a depth of approximately twelve feet, literally floating on the surface of the lake. (Lately they have moved their sleeping quarters to another floating island that has raised beds because it was discovered too many islanders were suffering from rheumatism!) The diverse reed also serves as a food supplement, which we were offered by the islanders during their demonstration. It tasted like wet, soggy Styrofoam. Little blue-green eggs lay in a wooden bowl and small fish served to show us what else they ate. Potatoes grew in mounds of earth piled on top of the reeds. It was an altogether surreal scene with clicking cameras and a few blue-jeaned tourists standing in an inner circle while the Uros islanders sat in an outer semi-circle on their blankets, waiting expectantly. I'm never sure in these situations who is looking at whom. I expect English was as hard for them to learn to speak as Amari would have been for us. Only smiles were exchanged, sprinkled with well-practised phrases of: 'Please Mrs, buy from me this. Very nice.' Panpipes, miniature reed boats, cloth cushion covers with embroidered blue Inca symbols, necklaces bearing the sun and moon, all lay on the blankets in front of their brightly clothed bodies. Their brown skin, long black hair and strong white teeth against the amber reed-woven surface were as colourful as their skirts and hats and woollen products. With the sun shining, it was a symphony of visual enchantment.

It's difficult to know how much of what we saw on the islands of Uros was just for our benefit, the benefit of Western tourists. While it is true that up until very recently the islanders have survived on these floating reeds without the help of tourism and live an insulated and isolated life amongst themselves – still sailing between the closely situated islands on reed boats they make by hand – there was evidence that a shift was happening. The wares spread before them were for cash in hand. They awaited the exchange of money for goods, a transaction that seemed oddly vacant. Perhaps it was just the language barrier. But I had the uneasy feeling that I was watching an orchestrated show, designed so the tourist companies bringing us there could make a living. The islanders subjected themselves to my audience for a payoff – this small exchange of money that I traded for a set of panpipes for Deirdre, some reed boats that would look exotic on our Christmas tree, and cushion covers as gifts for friends. *What was I doing there?* So many questions I would have like to have asked: Do you guys know about satellite television? Or Harry Potter? Have you heard of a man named Saddam Hussein? What games do your children play? But that was one of the drawbacks about our chosen travel in Peru. We were travelling to so many places, and our guides changed so quickly, we had little time to make a connection.

Our next stop on Lake Titicaca was at the Island of Taquille, another two hours away across the green-grey water. Taquille and Uros are on the Peruvian side of the lake and are therefore treasured by the Peruvians. On Taquille, the culture has been 'preserved' to such an extent that its people still dress in traditional costume. Their handweaving and knitting is arguably the finest in Peru and is sold in the main square under the control of a cooperative. Taquille is a jewel of an island and, as we climbed higher and higher in the hot sun along well-trodden paths, we could see below us the terraced farming plots and flowers and shrubs. At every bend the sun and water met against the Andes. Apart from the glaciers you could see in the distance, it was reminiscent of a Greek isle. Here the men stand knitting woollen hats along the paths looking out at the lake or in the village square. Standing, knitting, speaking Amari, the ancient Indian language. In the sun-heavy noontime it felt like a time warp. We learned later, after noting the island houses were roofed properly and windows were covered not with plastic but glass, unlike so many dwellings we had seen on the train across the highlands, that several of the islanders were quite wealthy, owning several boats and even restaurants in Puno. They discard their traditional dress for baseball caps and sneakers when they travel to Puno for business. But that's a whole other discussion: the delicate balance between preserving heritage and making it profitable and sustaining at the same time.

By the time we re-boarded the boat, Joseph had made friends with some of our co-tourists. A lovely English gentleman engaged Joseph in conversation and listened politely to him. A few young Americans also found him quite entertaining and the three-hour journey back passed pleasantly. Our guide tried to teach us some Amari – and showed us examples of the different wools from the alpaca, llama and vicuña, demonstrating the fineness of vicuña and baby alpaca. No wonder the black scarf I wanted to buy Niall in

Cusco was priced at $400. Vicuña wool is incredibly soft – what you would expect angel hair to feel like. The fibres from the vicuña, who lives only above 4,000 metres, are extremely fine. It has to be felt to be believed.

The next morning was another early riser, but I promised the children it would be the last for a while. They could sleep in on the catamaran the next night I assured them, but first we had to board another mini-van and head out from Puno across the Bolivian border to Copacobana.

At the border, we disembarked from the van and passed through customs in a small hut-like house with a customs officer who was not in uniform. We then marked our entrance into Bolivia by walking out through an archway that covered the road. On the ground at our feet was a plaque showing the line: Peru–Bolivia. We stepped across. We were in Bolivia. At first between the two countries nothing was different. But we were in Bolivia! The land-locked country I had been looking forward to visiting for ages, since I was twelve years old, when Mrs Fitzgerald, the fifth-grade teacher, had showed us photographs of Indian women in bowler hats. Since then I always fantasised about going to Bolivia. I would even go so far as to speculate that my desire to go to Bolivia arose from a geography quiz she gave us around that same time. A question came up that required the correct answer to be *plateau* to which I had written, using my lateral thinking skills because I didn't know the correct answer, *flat toe*. Mrs Fitzgerald gave me extra marks for my ingenuity and singled me out in class. I was chuffed. Her praise came at a time when I was in great need of self-esteem. That moment in memory is as sharp today as if it was yesterday and now here I was, thirty-six years later, stepping into Bolivia, past women in bowler hats, as we approached the edge of the enormous plateau.

~

Our guide from Puno delivered us to the main square of Copacabana, which lies in a bay graced by the Sanctuary of Our Lady of Copacabana. We were now in the hands of a Bolivian called Ruben, who was to be our guide for the next few days. Very little fanfare, very little leisure time, just enough to walk into the cathedral and see the Statue of the Black Madonna. It is said that in 1580, the Virgin of Copacabana appeared in a dream to Tito Yupanqui. He was so taken by this vision that he set out to Potosí (then one of the most important art centres in the world) to learn to sculpt. With his new skill, he hand-carved the Virgin from the wood of a maguey cactus. He travelled on by foot with the statue from Potosí to Copacabana (a journey of more than 400 miles), where she was placed in an adobe chapel in 1583. Immediately afterwards, the crops of those who doubted her power were mysteriously destroyed. For others, miracles spontaneously occurred and it is believed by the faithful that they still do. The Spanish, smitten with the Virgin, completed this Moorish-style cathedral for her in 1617. The Virgin stands in a majestic mechanical altar. On weekends, the priests rotate the Virgin so that she faces the main chapel; on weekdays, when there are fewer pilgrims, they spin her around so that she looks over a smaller chapel on the other side. The silver ship at the bottom of the altar represents the moon, while the gold statue above the Virgin's head is believed to symbolise the power of the sun. Believers have bestowed millions of dollars worth of gifts upon the Virgin.

There was an energy about the cathedral that is hard to describe. It was more of a *felt* sense than an intellectual understanding, like the kind of *body* feeling that happens during meditation when you experience the flow of energy that arises when the mind is relaxed. Being an initiate in the art of meditation myself and having experienced the flow of energy, I recognised it when it was happening to me in the cathedral. Perhaps it was the assembled power of prayer from the thousands of pilgrims who visit, I don't know, but I do know that I didn't want to leave the cathedral. I felt the sanctuary of it. I learned much later that much has been written about the spiritual dimensions of the cathedral and the power of the Black Madonna. Had I known what was to befall us in a few short hours, I would have cancelled our trip and booked rooms in Copacobana. Looking back, I think I underwent some kind of healing, or initiation, and interrupted the process by departing too soon.

We followed Ruben out past old women in black sitting against the warm white walls of the cathedral, begging. We walked straight into the van, led perfunctorily it seemed to me by our guide, which took us to the port where a very large catamaran was waiting for us. In our little group were two French women, ourselves and Ruben. We awaited the arrival of other guests, expecting a good crowd considering the size of the boat, but to our intense surprise discovered that it was only the seven of us plus the manager, three short Bolivian waiters in tuxedos and bow ties, each with a shock of jet black hair and speaking not a word of English, and the crew, whom we never saw. The upper deck of the catamaran could have easily sat sixty people. Another one of those occasions where we sat wordlessly, half-smiling at each other, waiting and wondering. *Now what?* After a while, it became clear that this huge boat was to carry only us out on Lake Titicaca for the next two days. The engine started. Copacabana slid away, and we sat there in a line in the lounge, Deirdre, Joseph, Niall and I, studied from across the empty room by the inscrutable Bolivians.

There are journeys within journeys and sometimes the journey is within yourself. Lessons unfold. Truths are revealed. For me the experience on the Island of the Sun brought home an awareness of my over-engaging with a myth, for one. The energy of the Copacobana Cathedral had been real, I believe. The energy of the myth, however – the spiritual importance of the Island of the Sun – was seductive and untrustworthy and would play havoc with us in the twenty-four hours to come.

An hour after leaving the port of Copacobana we arrived on the south side of the Isla del Sol. It was paradisiacal. Ancient waterways guarded the Inca steps that rose to a fountain of spring water. Flowering shrubs bordered the steps. The sun was shining. Lake Titicaca looked surreal with the Cordillera Real rising on the western edge. I was excited to be there despite my initial hesitation on board the boat. It was like walking into an episode of *The Twilight Zone*.

I'd seen a kind of tourism in Ireland, especially around ten years ago, where the Irish manufactured an *experience* for Americans that wasn't genuine and, after much complaining on the side of the

'Yanks', the Irish learned to take a step back and present a picture of what is *was* like all those years ago rather than masquerading the thing as real in present time. (Niall's first play, *The Murphy Initiative*, explores this idea humorously when a village counsellor decides to 'manufacture' a local 'Murphy roots' industry to which the Yanks, in their innocence and in a sincere bid to find their Irish roots, flock like bees to honey. The play went on in the Abbey Theatre in 1991.) On the Isla del Sol we were being presented with something that felt bizarrely out of tune with reality. Here was the Bolivian national tourist board's rendition of what felt like a miniature theme park. In hindsight, it may have been the poor quality of our guide's performance, but to this day I'm not sure what we were looking at. There was a beautiful terraced garden of medicinal herbs and flowers and other plants which were not specifically related to Inca history or pre-Inca history. I had many of them in my own garden. There were a few llamas and alpacas, freely roaming, and some vicuñas in bamboo cages.

To cap it off, there was an 'initiation ceremony' with a type of high priest who was burning bits and bobs (literally bits of candy and bobs of yarn and coca leaves and the like) over a fire, tossing an unspecified liquid into the bowl, which resulted in ashes which he then sprinkled on our heads. It was a field day for a sceptic. I attempted to take it seriously, but no matter how I tried to put my intellect aside, somehow it didn't feel quite genuine. I had to hold back my impulse to stand up and say, 'Hang on here, what's all this hocus pocus?' Perhaps it was just the lack of explanation. The single most disturbing thing was the absence of contact, or involvement. For what was apparently intended as an offering and a type of 'clearing' to prepare the way for us to enter the sacred Inca site, there was no sense of intimacy. Disappointment loomed inside me as I endeavoured to make it real for myself. My cottage in Ireland houses a small collection of sun symbols and moons, and Bolivia and Lake Titicaca had always been one of the anticipated highlights of my own itinerary. Had I placed too much importance on destination? Had I missed the importance of the journey itself? As the late Harry Chapin sings in one of his old songs, 'It's the going there, not the getting there....'

During our excursion, Ruben spoke rarely and, when he did, his spoken English seemed better than his understanding. It was as if he had learnt all his English for speaking to groups, but in fact understood nothing spoken to him. It was as if he was deaf to us. The plan for the afternoon emerged after we lunched on the boat. After a catamaran ride to the north side of the island, we would take another short boat ride to the Temple of the Sun and the pre-Inca ruins. Unpleasant thoughts crossed my mind during our lunch, which I attempted to dismiss, trusting the preparation of the food was suitable for non-Bolivian tummies. However, it was a bizarre scene. The three waiters, although sitting in a row at a comfortable distance, seemed to be staring directly at us. The manager stood behind the bar, reading a paperback, exuding a non-committal role. It was unnerving to say the least. The long table was set out for a buffet and decorated with bits of hanging glossy metallic decorations in green and red. But it was a setting for sixty or more tourists, not just the six of us tourists. We ate our meals and who knows what else.

We disembarked after lunch into the blazing sunshine. An unmelodious music, which seemed to come from the square, filled the air. There we came upon an extraordinary scene, a crowd of villagers, men and women, playing wooden whistles and banging on a drum and dancing. It was straight out of a Fellini film. Some of the villagers danced in the centre of the musicians who followed each other round in a circle, heads looking downward and bending back and forth from the waist in an unsteady rhythm of mistimed beats. In the dead centre were brown bottles, presumably of liquor, which the men occasionally drank from between tunes, tunes which all sounded identical. There were no words. There wasn't even a crowd, just the dancing musicians and us the tourists. Now this wasn't for show. There wasn't meant to be an audience. There was no exchange of money. This was how it was. It was an astonishing scene, this mid-afternoon party of discordant music and wheeling villagers in the little square on the Island of the Sun. We stood around the edge shyly and watched. It was like a wedding but there seemed to be no bride, no guests.

'Ruben? Is there a special occasion?' Niall asked.

Ruben shrugged. 'It is for a saint. They always celebrate the saints,' he replied, half-smiling, half-mockingly, and turned on his heel, directing us onward away from the square along sandy paths and small concrete half-built buildings. We continued like this along the beach in single file, the music from the square like a rising vapour hanging above us until we reached a small dock where two wooden rowboats awaited us. A shoeless, thin man in a white shirt and a fedora hat, who looked quite similar to one of the dancing men in the square, helped the four of us onto his boat. The others boarded the second boat. As we pushed away from the dock, I noted with some dismay that the other boat had two rowers. We had a man in a fedora! Joseph and I sat at the stern with Niall and Deirdre at the prow. Our boatman was in the centre. It hadn't exactly been explained to us that we would be boarding a rowboat or how long the journey would take and we made the mistake of presuming that it would be short. Naturally. How far could we get in a rowboat?

As we rounded our first stony point, I started to become uneasy and clutched tightly to the camera bag that sat on my lap. We had been on the boat for fifteen minutes already and there was no port or dock in sight. The second boat had pulled away a good bit from us, powering ahead with four strong arms instead of two. Deirdre and Niall seemed content at the front. Joseph was enjoying himself. I said nothing. Another fifteen minutes passed, fear mounting inside me as I watched the straining sweat dripping in rivulets from our boatman's sideburns. I started to say goodbye to $2,000 worth of cameras, and hoped the Titicaca water wasn't too cold. The boatman had his back to Niall, who was oblivious of our Bolivian rower's slackening power.

'*Mira*!' I shouted suddenly and pointed.

The boatman turned to his right and saw what I was alerting him to. We were within twelve feet of the craggy shore. More than once I needed to tell him to mind the rocks, which we were in danger of crashing into. Still no dock in sight. The sun on the horizon was slipping behind grey clouds. I practised my Spanish in my head and finally blurted,

'*Usted quieres mi hombre ayudar*?' Which translates into *You want my man to help*? I couldn't remember the word for husband.

'*Si*,' the boatman replied but didn't stop rowing.

Did he misunderstand me? Had I said, *Isn't it a nice day*?

'*Ayudar? Si*?' I questioned again. *To help, yes*?

'*Si*,' he said and slowed. We were dangerously close to the shoreline again. Niall moved unsteadily beside the boatman. But it was useless. First Niall stood and nearly capsized us. He was unskilled at rowing and in a bit of a panic now himself, and his efforts failed. He and fedora couldn't communicate. Body language wasn't working either. A quick lesson in English on rowing in a Bolivian rowboat in the middle of Lake Titicaca would have been helpful at this point. I wondered was this kind of thing covered in the 'Worst-Case Scenario' Series? Back in position, fedora had had at least a breather. On he struggled. He smiled uneasily at me and said nothing. While I had tried to make things easier, it seemed I had made things worse, for Joseph in particular. We were at fear factor 8 and climbing. The lake water slapped like a sea. The boat dipped and swayed dangerously. We were making no progress at all, or none I could judge right then. Worse, angry clouds were coming up behind us.

'Crikey!' I said under my breath.

'*Aye carumba*!' I said in Spanish, hoping to communicate with our boatman and gauge his level of stamina by his response at my feeble attempt at humour. He only grinned back. This didn't make me feel any easier. Perhaps he had fallen into a drunken stupor. The water of Lake Titicaca was freezing. Four hundred yards of water. Stroke after stroke. Our progress was slow, our boatman exhausted. I was thinking how naïve I had been, assuming that the people to whom we had entrusted our lives were in fact capable. Doubt and fear are a terrible combination. I was caught in both, as well as guilt and anger, and a whole lot more.

When at last we arrived at the little dock, Joseph alighted in an absolute fury. He screamed obscenities and burst into tears. The others, who had arrived a good bit ahead of us, were at a loss to understand what the disturbance was about. I said to Ruben, 'That was dangerous. We nearly didn't make it!'

Ruben looked blankly at me. Did he not understand me, or was this his idea of handling the situation? Plead total ignorance. Instead of waiting for his response, I followed Joseph. And on rolled the camera of the surrealist movie in which we had become characters, the script out of control. Joseph stormed past the two French ladies, who spoke not a word of English, just some Spanish. I asked Niall to explain briefly in French what Joseph was on about. Ruben looked into the distance, twiddling with a piece of shrubbery. Joseph was shouting for us to go away. He was too upset to be talked to; we had nearly let him die as far as he was concerned. He had encountered real fear out there on Titicaca and you could read it now on every aspect of his face and body.

The landscape was made up of barren and sandy rock that sloped up to a height of about 500 yards to the site said to be the birthplace of the sun. Talk about disappointment. I wanted to shout 'Cut. Retake. Do over. Rain check. Beam me up Scotty!'

But this was just one in a string of situations that made up our travels. I had to take a step back. Here were our four heroes climbing in a fair Bolivian afternoon, our family journeying together – through thick and thin, rain or shine, on land and on sea. It was just a moment in time, part of the continuum but not the whole. The fact that we were on the Island of the Sun did not impress Joseph in the least. He was living in the moment and fully expressing himself. *Well done, Joseph,* I was silently thinking in between wishes for his speedy recovery. I admired that about him actually and thought I could learn a thing or two about self-expression from him as I followed steadily behind him, dodging his curses. He took a good while to calm down. Deirdre, meanwhile, was thoroughly disgusted with him, as any older teenage sister might be, and tagged along in the straggling line of trekkers that we had now become. Joseph in the lead; me behind, softly telling him it would be all right; Niall and Deirdre, following, climbing word-lessly; the two French ladies who were listening to Ruben discourse on God knows what; and an extra chap who seemed to appear out of nowhere, who hung back and said nothing. (It wasn't until later that I could see he carried an oxygen tank.)

It was a scene I would like to have edited but we were stuck in it and the only way out was through it. Niall was relieved to learn that we didn't have to take the rowboats back, rather, there was a roundabout walking track to the village about an hour away. He caught up with Joseph and together they rambled back to the village of merrymakers, not stopping to observe the sacrificial altar or the brass Bolivian National Tourist plaque that marked the birthplace of the sun. It meant nothing at this point to any of us. Deirdre and I attempted to explore the pre-Inca ruins in good humour. But in keeping with the energy that had gone awry, into its own orbit, I left her camera behind. Desperate for a pee and only finding a sheltered spot inside the ruins, I pleaded, 'What do you think, Dee? Can I go here?'

We looked about us and in between the dried sheep dung and rabbit droppings decided it was acceptable, a kind of offering. I had heard from a friend of mine that the earth was hungry for what we had to give. I hoped so.

'Go quickly,' she said, 'I have to go too!'

I remembered afterwards leaving the camera sitting on a window ledge, but only realised it halfway back to the village. Our man in the rear with the oxygen tank agreed to accompany us back to find it. I had to stop midway and let Deirdre and O_2 man continue when Deirdre said, 'Mum, you have a big blue circle on your check! I think you'd better wait here.'

The altitude was too much for me. Over 13,000 feet above sea level. As she had demonstrated already, Deirdre sailed through. It was as if she were walking up the back hills of Tumper behind our cottage in Clare. Not a bother on her, except for the fact that I had lost her camera. Off she ambled wordlessly with the non-English-speaking boy about her age. Half an hour back to the spot, they discovered the camera was gone. Taken by the sheep farmers we had passed along the way? Offered up to the Incas? Penance for our sins? Who knows? My brother Sean in Seattle, the youngest of my five siblings, is fond of saying 'this isn't how I thought it was going to be'. And I echoed that loudly up there on top of the Island of the Sun, alone on the barren hilltop, sitting on a rock, praying that I had not entrusted my daughter to a dangerous escort, hoping my son had recovered sufficiently and wondering how the hell we were going to get through it. The whole bizarre thing was too much and, as I sat there contemplating it all, I could find no answers. I was confused and wondered how the energy of the thing had gone so wrong. I can only surmise that I had relied too heavily on reaching the Island of the Sun as a destination, as if some wonderful transformative experience were awaiting me there and I only had to appear to receive it. Nothing could have been further from the truth. I had imbued the mythical birthplace of the sun with an overlay of my own desires and hopes it was incapable of giving, or else what it had to give was not vibrating well with me. A malevolent vortex swirled around me and I still had yet to walk through it to the other side. Back on the catamaran, Deirdre and I passed the night in fits of cramps and sleeplessness and an explosion of black liquid. By morning, both of us were really ill. And I mean really. The ride back to Copacabana across rough swells exacerbated our illness and we stepped from the catamaran into pouring cold rain and then into a freezing van without an ounce of sympathy or succour from Ruben. It was a long four-hour drive to La Paz, the city of Peace.

We had arrived in La Paz, having survived the crossing of the Strait of Tiquina in an open-topped twenty-foot boat in the pouring rain, with nothing to protect us but our raincoats. Women with babies hidden in wrapped blankets on their backs stood alongside us, others with small animals. Nothing to hold on to except each other. Rain falling freely down upon us all. Reaching the other side, we waited in the open while our bus, with everything we owned inside it, crossed slowly behind us in a wooden barge that took in water as it crossed. This trip was going from bad to worse. And we had paid for it.

~

The whole sorry affair of the Bolivian Sea finally over, I found myself sitting on a six-foot wide bed on the tenth floor of the Presidente Hotel in the centre of the bustling city of La Paz, suffering with Bolivian Belly and fasting for the third day in a row. It was a strange reality, the kind you do not think of when you plan your trip of a lifetime. The Presidente is a four-star hotel, but still the lights flickered and the power failed briefly. On our first evening, there was an overwhelming smell of petrol coming through the air-conditioning. But when Niall called to enquire about it, a thickly built dark-suited Bolivian came up through the corridor with a torch, sniffed the powerful scent, looked at Niall standing there in his pyjamas, shook his head, and disappeared. Too ill to move to another room or face the thought of finding another hotel in La Paz, I tried to sleep with the pillow over my head to keep out the fumes, and hoped we would all be alive in the morning.

Deirdre had recovered enough to be able to eat and, although pale and weak, said she could take a city tour of La Paz with Niall. Joseph was in the next room drawing quietly and watching television. For myself, I wondered how I was going to get through. By not eating I was sure it was only a matter of days. Besides the occasional cracker, I had nothing but cups of tea and plenty of water. As in Lima, the honks of the cars reached me in a constant din of movement and sound. The window was wide open. I could lean and fall out. The voices from the taxis shouting the names of the streets they'd be travelling along blended with traffic, creating a cacophony. I found some peace writing on my laptop, watching Spanish-speaking American television shows with English subtitles, waiting for the advancing hours that would soon see me back at sea level. We would be in Chile in a few days, where I would probably need to go to a clinic as dosing myself with homeo-pathic remedies was providing only temporary relief. (I have never been much good at prescribing for myself and was probably not taking enough of any one remedy to make headway on the vile disturbance.) Cramps continued to strangle my intestines in clutch-ing waves, accompanied by violent rumblings. Whether I had picked up some nasty parasite on the catamaran, or whether it was the impious vestiges of the Isla del Sol; whether it was a spell cast by Ruben with the jet-black, coiffed hair and black, round snake eyes, who could tell. Still worse was the knowledge that maybe I had been my own worst enemy. Maybe it had to do with my ignorant retrieval of a piece of toilet tissue from a Bolivian toilet a few days earlier. Yes, I had done that. As if I hadn't enough to contend with, I was guilty of being stupid in an attempt to adhere to the plumbing requirements of the primitive conditions. The wash closets have little plastic buckets for tissues and stuff and I had let my used tissue slip into the toilet bowl. (Surely a bowel movement would have clogged up the toilet more than the few pieces of tissue

I had let drop.) *What was I thinking?* You may well ask, but I couldn't possibly tell you except to say that I did it automatically, in a rush not to make a mistake. I didn't want to be the one responsible for clogging up the Bolivian system. (Like I could have single-handedly done that!) This frame of mind I sometimes suffer from is called in homeopathy a *delusion*. In this case I reacted *as if guilty of a crime.* I had thoroughly washed my hands in the tap water afterwards, but perhaps it wasn't enough. *What the blazes had I been thinking?*

~

We stayed in La Paz for three days and nights, cancelling one extra day so we could get to Chile sooner. I mostly watched the city from my hotel room, taking small walks with Deirdre up the hilly market streets to buy presents for family and friends for Christmas. We snaked our way up the hill streets, which were vibrant with native markets. It looked a very interesting city, medieval in many ways with cobbled streets and old wizened faces sitting beside stalls selling every imaginable thing. It was quite unlike the atmosphere we had encountered thus far. There was a kind of eerie quiet that descended after the parades died down. At night, it was like we were sitting in the bottom of a bowl of fairy lights as the houses, piled on top of each other, lit up like fireflies when the sun sank behind the mountains circling the city. La Paz is the highest city in the world. It felt like we were as close to the sun as we were ever going to get. I wished I had been feeling better. I wished I had a chance to explore La Paz, a city of noise and music, of colour and shadows. Joseph was turned off Bolivia at this point and stayed in his semi-comfortable hotel room, watching television, drawing houses and buildings, now with mountains behind them.

Deirdre and Niall took the city tour with Ruben, who seemed a bit more engaging now that he was back in the city of his birth. Later they described the city they had seen as a place of narrow streets with the most colourful and extraordinary markets. Streets with whole sections devoted to one particular thing. First a street of poultry sellers – yellowing chickens and chicken parts stacked in an unsteady mound on a cloth alongside a toothless, hatted woman; a collection of meat, similarly stacked, with flies buzzing all round;

and yet another street selling the black patent leather shoes all the women wore – hundreds of shoes on a stand, each nearly identical, but with a different coloured bow at the instep. Next to this, a stand of hard, black bowler hats. What struck Deirdre was that the hats themselves looked so glamorous, but their sellers wore a collection of brown rags. Sellers of fruit and vegetables – not the smooth perfectly shaped fruits of supermarkets in the Western world, but rather collections of the bruised, the knobbled, and the unripe – spread basking all day on cloths in the sun. Potatoes, black and pink and yellow. Stalls of socks, of balls of alpaca wool, of workshirts, woven blankets, and leather belts and bags. No seller had more than one item. While the sun boiled down out of the blue sky, men and women sat on the ground in the street and ate bowlfuls of a kind of stew from plastic containers. Turn a corner and you came upon a street of shops selling costumes – nothing but costumes. Next to a shop with full outfits was another specialising just in costume accessories. Beaded belts glittered in the windows, along with Amazonian headdresses and feathered footwear. It was like a street in a fantasy. These, Ruben had explained, were for the city's many parades and festivals. The best parades in the world, Ruben, told Niall who remarked when they came back to the hotel, 'It's as much a city of parades as it is of protests.'

'Yeah, and it's hard to tell the difference,' Deirdre commented. They had come out of the markets and had run directly into the Bolivian police marching six abreast down the Avenida de la Paz. At first they mistook them for the army because of their green uniforms and rifles, but when Niall asked Ruben what was happening, he simply shrugged and said there were often marches, and many protests. Within minutes of turning away from the marching police, they came upon a protest with beating drums and horns and giant puppet figures protesting against the lack of hospital rooms for disabled people. As representative of the official state tourism agency, Ruben took them to see the state buildings and the guards at the monument to Simon Bolivar, insisting that Deirdre take photos. But what interested her the most were not the official sites of this bubbling city, but something they came upon almost by accident as they headed back to the hotel.

'What's down there?' Deirdre asked, looking down a narrow cobbled street with colourful goods outside old stone buildings.

'The witches' market,' Ruben said unenthusiastically.

'Can we go there?' she had asked him hesitantly, as if it were perhaps forbidden to non-witches.

He did not answer her, but made the kind of sour smile he made only with his lips that barely masked his scorn which, whether for us, for all tourists, for the witches, or for himself, it was impossible to say.

The witches' market turned out to be a series of stalls in a shady street where you could buy yourself a spell or a cure from one of the old ladies sitting on stools. There were spells for wealth, for health, and, most particularly, for love. There were spells and cures made up on order from the selection of what looked like sweets and pills and strands of hair and pieces of bone and feathers and such things. You simply told the 'witch' what you needed and she made it up for you in a vial, small or large depending on what was required. Once home, you are meant to burn the vial or burn candles beside it – the directions for use or cure being unclear. Next to the smaller items in the trays were stacks of what Ruben said were llama fetuses which were burnt as an offering. This final stall lessened Deirdre's interest considerably. She said the smell was overpowering, like the rotting animal part it was. In any case, they spent a full day around the city and said it was certainly one of the most remarkable cities they had visited. Deirdre gave me a tiny vial with a gold-capped lid, containing coloured yarn and liquid and tiny things I could only wonder at. She had bought it for me from the witches' market.

'Here, Mum,' she said sweetly, rolling her eyes and smiling. 'This will make you better.'

Chile

We left La Paz and returned to sea level. I could breathe again. Standing in the airport arrivals lounge in Santiago, I sucked air deep into my being. Well deep yes, but sidetracking the pain in the pit of belly that was still rifling me like a machine gun. My innerscape expanded and I took bottomless breaths. An enormous ease spread over me like a breeze of fresh air. I had never got used to the altitude of the Andes and, much as I fantasised about returning to the Monasterio Hotel and trekking the Inca Trail, it'll probably never happen unless I can climb with an oxygen tank strapped to my back.

Santiago was blue and summery when we arrived. We had two days to spend there before heading down to Patagonia. A frail old gentleman named Ian Williamson, a British ex-pat who was formerly a pilot, had arranged a hotel for us in an area of Santiago known as Las Condes, named after two rich aristocratic Chilean sisters, and it was to there we headed, stuffed in two cars. Ian was one of those who, despite having lived a long time away from England, retained the air of the Englishman still confounded by the inefficiencies of the locals. Though he spoke fluent Spanish, and fired off a few curt phrases to dismiss the taxi men clustered around arrivals, he was soon telling us in thin-lipped asides that the bloody place was in chaos, that half the streets were dug up, that others were closed for a parade. And all of this as we made our way out into the warm Chilean afternoon. Hotel Montebianco, a small, reasonably priced hotel, was centrally located in the new city of Las Condes. Stunning modern architecture reveals the recent wealth of a country that had been led by a military dictator who had successfully lured foreign investment. There were two faces of the city of Santiago: old and new. Where Las Condes was affluent and chic, the old city was not nearly as prosperous. Inner-city poverty, although improved certainly by South American standards, is widespread. Las Condes felt modern and European. It is where the moneyed elite live and is home to the country's largest shopping mall, Altos Las Condes, which claims to be the biggest shopping mall in South America. Quite a change from La Paz and Lima. Having been in Costa Rica, Peru and Bolivia for the previous six weeks, I found the urban sophistication of Las Condes striking familiar chords inside me that sang of comfort and safety and, at that point in time, was welcomed.

One guidebook described Hotel Montebianco as a smart motel, but it was more than that. The staff members were very friendly and the rooms while small were tidy, overlooking a bustling avenue below, on which a flood of American-style eateries overflowed onto the sidewalks. TGIFriday's and little restaurants ranging from Italian to Vietnamese called to me. I felt deprived. I was craving western-style food, but my abdomen was warning me against it. As it turned out, the hotel was owned by a Chilean doctor, who while not there upon our arrival, sent word to phone if I worsened during the night. Otherwise they suggested I go to the German clinic the next day. I had been sick in La Paz for three days and counting. It was time to do something.

Although we had decided against immunisations for typhoid and cholera, and hepatitis A (the only one we *had* considered), we had been pragmatic enough to change our health insurance, at a substantially increased charge, to a global policy that covered every possible emergency, including repatriation home if necessary. So we felt pretty well covered. I was fairly certain that whatever I had picked up in Bolivia wouldn't have been avoided by immunisation;

however, it needed to be addressed. I stayed in the hotel room while Niall and the kids went out for a meal, but decided in the morning to find the clinic.

The hotel ordered a taxi for us and Niall and I set off for the clinic, said to be one of the best in Santiago. Without much delay, a tall, sandy-haired MD, who spoke an eclectic mixture of English, German and Spanish, showed me into his examination room. I think he was trying to be charming. He demanded that I speak to him in my fledgling Spanish, and we made humorous progress as to what was wrong with me, but in my mind I was thinking *what a hell of a time for a language lesson*. His first name was Spanish and his second name was German, something like Roberto Heinmann. I had the feeling that he had seen my symptoms before. He quickly diagnosed some kind of nasty intestinal 'bug', laughing knowingly when I said we had just been in Bolivia.

He advised me to eat nothing for another twenty-four hours and then to resume taking food gently and as blandly as possible. He presented me with a diet for the next five days and prescribed a hefty dose of Cipro, the antibiotic of choice for anthrax poisoning.When I said we were headed to Patagonia in two days, he laughed again and said, *'No es doctores en Patagonia. Bueno suerte Señora.'*

I told him if I continued poorly past Christmas I'd be back again before we headed from Santiago to New Zealand at the start of the New Year. He smiled and shook our hands and mildly chuckled to himself, saying, poor Gringos, I'm sure. I only half believed that medical intervention would make me better, but felt that yielding to Cipro was the best thing I could do for myself in the circumstances. If it had been Niall or Deirdre or Joseph, I wouldn't have delayed taking them to a medical physician. The fact that homeopathy hadn't been curative was not an issue for me, as most homeopaths are hopeless self-prescribers. I felt that I was strong enough to withstand the side effects of the antibiotic. It was bad timing to be heading to the bottom of the world when I felt like the bottom of the cesspool, but there was too much at stake to shift the next few weeks' schedule. The trip to Patagonia had been booked months in advance and, likewise, the trip to Northern Patagonia and Parque

Pumalin. I didn't want to forfeit either of them. Fundo Chacaipulli, our destination for Christmas, where we would settle for ten days straight, was solidly benchmarked. There was nothing else to do but continue.

The next day we had a serendipitous moment when we spotted a Spanish copy of one of Niall's novels in a bookshop on the Plaza Republica del Peru, where on weekends an antiques market lined the boulevard. It felt good to be in Santiago. So good, in fact, that we decided to scratch off the four days we had earmarked for Valparaíso on the coast after Christmas and rebooked the Montebianco instead. In a strange way we felt comfort knowing that we had a reason to come back.

~

Three hours after boarding a plane in Santiago, we arrived at the southernmost part of our journey around the world. We had come a very long way. I was picturing Deirdre, my sister in New York, threading the red string around the pin that marked our spot at the furthest point in Chile.

'This is where my sister Chris and her family are this week,' I could hear her say to her friend Linda, who often stops over for a cup of tea in the morning once the children have gone to school. My nephew Daniel was sharing our itinerary with his class and they seemed to be enjoying our destinations in geography lessons. In the airport in Punta Arenas we bought printed certificates declaring the bearer had undeniably and certifiably reached the most southern city in the world. Some say that Ushuaia in Argentina is really the southernmost city in the world. Whether the discrepancy is due to the rivalry in that part of the world that still exists between Chile and Argentina, or whether Ushuaia itself doesn't really qualify as a city, who knows? But one thing was indisputable for us – it was the closest we were probably ever going to get to the bottom of the world. When we landed and collected our bags, the chill in the air was felt by all of us. We got out our jackets that we had been carrying around for this express purpose for the last three months and put them on.

'Did I mention that it can be really windy here, guys?' I said, actually forgetting if I had remembered to tell them.

'Yeah?' Joseph replied. 'Like how windy?'

'Well, like, you'll need your hat, let's put it that way.' We were used to gale-force winds in Ireland.

'Let's see how these winds compare with those at home.' Niall said, giving me the eye to desist with my warnings in case Joseph baulked. I desisted and zipped up my coat and wheeled the luggage cart out of the baggage claim.

We were met by a rental-car agent who had been subcontracted by a contact we had discovered on the Internet by the name of Erika Schmidtt, a Patagonian of German descent, who guided us in our tour by arranging car hire and booking hotels for our six-night stay. Our rental car turned out to be a sort of truck, a red four-by-four, with four seats and a covered cab in the back to hold all our luggage, along with a yellow plastic petrol container and two spare wheels. We hopped in and followed the signs from the airport. The single-lane road goes in two directions, either down to Punta Arenas or up to Puerto Natales, the gateway to Torres del Paine, our destination. Once again the weather was with us. In between the clouds on the horizon, the foothills of the Andes loomed from the pampas. But it would be many miles and many hours before we would see the famous towers themselves.

On and on we drove. The printed itinerary that we downloaded from one of Erika's emails in uncertain English guided us:

You drive to Puerto Natales (254 km) a cruise ship and ferry terminal for the region. On the way, you stop to enjoy the beauty and charm of the southern Patagonia landscapes. In Puerto Natales you have to tank with gasoline your car, please do not forget. If you like to eat something, go to 'Centro Español', Calle Magallanes 247, Pto. Natales or at Hotel Eberhard (there is here a beautiful view to the bay from the restaurant). After a drive distance of 60 km north you then arrive at Cerro Castillo, which was in the earliest twentieth century a farm of one of the big Sheep-Societies. You drive from here 31 km north. At your right side you will see the Sierra Cazador and Los Baguales and at your left side you will see

Lago Toro. After driving 31 km you will see the sign to NP Torres del Paine. You will have now at your left side the Lago Sarmiento. Please be careful all this way, because it has many curves and is very narrow in some places. Then you entrance the NP Torres del Paine and drive until the Administration of the National Park (if you have time on the way back you should have a look in the museum). From here you will have another 18 km more or less until you arrive at Hostería Grey, where you will stay for the next three nights.

'More or less' being the operative words, Erika was off her calculations by about 100 km. When we finally arrived at the entrance of the National Park of Torres del Paine, it was six in the evening. We had already been driving for four hours. Judging by the map, we still had a long drive ahead of us, three more hours, *mas o menus.*

It is so often said of Torres del Paine that you can experience the four seasons in one day, but so far we were being blessed with wonderful spring-like weather. The notorious wind of the Patagonian spring and summer, which can sometimes reach over 100 km per hour, was more like a strong breeze that day. As we rounded yet another spectacular bend, a sudden view of the Torres, the granite skyscraper-like mountains, stopped us dead in our tracks. We jumped from the car in the wind and twilight above Lago Pehoe. The milky turquoise water rustled in great gentle gusts. It was awesome, and immense: peaceful, majestic and magical. Breathing deeply, we relaxed into unfamiliar beauty. Guanacos gathered and grazed on the grassy slopes in groups while lone guanacos stood as sentries on hilltops watching for the hungry but rarely seen pumas. We stood there in the blustering scene with such a shared sense of excitement, of arrival, that already I felt the trip to Patagonia fulfilling all of my expectations. There was that feeling known to all travellers, when the ground on which you are standing is both real and somehow a position, a point on a map on a wall, so that you are in both places at once. You can see the map of the world and the distant corner that is Patagonia, and at the same moment you feel the thrill running through you and the three words: *I am here.*

Throughout our journey, an unanticipated bonus had been the spotting of a variety of animals that we had never seen before. From the grizzly in Yellowstone to the iguanas and squirrel monkeys of Manuel Antonio now to nandus, guanacos, black-necked swans and condors of the Torres. (We had looked everywhere in Peru and Bolivia for condors, but saw none until we arrived past Puerto Natales and drove closer to the National Park, where we easily saw the giant condors sitting on wooden farm fences.)

We continued for miles across large-stoned, gravelled roads with dust flying everywhere behind us, just a little nervous as to what we would find at the end of a road which was beginning to seem never-ending. Rarely did a sign appear to indicate direction. Just a single stony track in an awesome landscape. Hardly a car or truck passed us. If anything was coming you saw it a long way off as a plume of dust rising from the stones of the road. Occasionally we saw a hiker or two, but little else. It was an eerie kind of journey, full of a bleak kind of startling beauty, all the time imbued with a sense of this being *a faraway place*, an end that had attracted travellers from all over the world – partly just because it was there, it was a furthermost shore. Eventually, after nearly eight hours of driving, we arrived at Hostería Lago Grey which lies at the base of Grey Lake and the Grey Glacier.

'This is it?' Deirdre announced from the back seat. 'This is where we're staying?'

'I'm afraid so, Dee,' said Niall, pulling himself achingly from the car. We all crawled from the dusty red truck and headed toward what looked like the main building, a white wooden single-storey ranch. Red ribbons decorated a few wind-worn trees. The gravel path was edged by long grass. There was no sign of porters or other life from the hotel and we dragged our many bags behind us, ready to collapse. It was about nine in the evening and the kids were starving. We checked in only to discover that dinner was finished. However, the chef agreed to rustle up some pasta for Deirdre and Joseph. Niall had the main course on offer: boiled meat and croquette potatoes with canned carrots, while I had the soup. If you ever go down to that part of the world, go prepared to eat little. Just about everything comes out of a can. Fresh produce doesn't arrive regularly due to the distances that supply trucks have to travel. *Refugios* – hostel-like accommodation – which are sparely stocked, do sell food to campers, but they are tens of miles apart and not exactly signposted. Suffice it to say that you are not there for the food anyway. It's the scenery that sustains you. And that is what we lived on. The Cipro was making my already nauseous stomach even more nauseous. I adhered to the diet prescribed by Roberto and, slowly, the pains began to ease.

The three-star accommodation of Hostería Grey was simple. It reminded me of a camp. We slept in sparsely decorated, cabin-like rooms that were built above ground. The air was free to circulate, presumably keeping the underneath dry during the long stretches of cold, wet weather that can easily arrive in mid-summer. When another guest walked along the wooden planked-way, the entire one-storey building shook and echoed with hiking boots. But the rooms were clean and dry and quite adequate, and the view just beyond the window of the meltwater of the Grey Glacier with floating icebergs and the massif was extraordinary. The electricity closed down at midnight and came back on at sunrise, so Deirdre and I stayed together and Niall and Joseph slept next door. There are only a few hotels inside the National Park and, while they tend to be overpriced, I think it is worth every peso. (When we win the lotto or when one of Niall's novels is made into a movie, we will luxuriate and book the Explora Hotel, one of the fifty hippest hotels in the world, situated on the very edge of Lago Pehoe, where the view alone is worth the hefty price tag.)

Torres del Paine National Park is a lonesome kind of place, extremely remote and without much in the way of tourist amenities. People who come here come for the beauty of the landscape and sense of awe-inspiring wilderness. Perhaps too they come for the solitude. Nearly half a million acres make up the park, which is ideal for hikers in the fine weather, but inhospitable when it turns wet and windy (which it can do at a moment's notice). The park has several treks, the most popular being 'El Circuito', a five- to six-day hike which follows a trail around the Torres and Cuernos del Paine.

On our second morning, we left the hotel after breakfast for a tour of Lago Grey and to voyage out to see the Grey Glacier. Along with twenty other tourists, we boarded the red boat of the Hostería that was large enough not to remind us of our last boating episode a week earlier on Lake Titicaca. With the sun shining strongly, we clipped along the lake. We could already see the glacier on the horizon. Floating islands of abstract blue ice shapes perched on the water, silhouetted against the rising mountains of grey granite and green forest. The Grey Glacier is at the tip of the Southern Patagonian ice cap, the *Campo de Hielo Patagonico Sur*, which together with the Northern Patagonian ice field, constitutes the third largest ice cap in the world after Antarctica and Greenland.

'If that's the Grey Glacier, I'd like to see the blue one!' Joseph quipped as we got nearer. The condensed oxygen gives the glacier an impressive blue colour like giant blue cut-crystal slabs. None of us was anticipating the stunning splendour of the glacier, nor the immense quietude that emanated from its jagged walls of cobalt ice. It was a place unlike any in the world we had seen before. A place so itself, so imbued with a resonance of age and endurance, of timeless beauty, that it simply stopped you in front of it. You put away all of your preconceptions, you lost intellectual response, and just stared. It was one of those rare moments when the passengers merged with the panorama in a direct symbiotic relationship of man and landscape. We were witnesses of wilderness, and felt as if we had to be there, perhaps to attest to God's natural beauty. It was a moment of that often inappropriately used word: awe.

'It's amazing,' Deirdre said, 'isn't it?' She leaned over the edge of the boat and snapped a photo, turning back to me with a look in her face that I hadn't seen in quite a long time. A look you don't easily find in teenagers: wonder.

For Joseph there was a giddy thrill, his eyes wide, hatted head bobbing, a grin telling you that he knew exactly where he was, in front of his first glacier, and it was so *cool!* We had done it, we had brought our children here. I looked at Niall and saw the way he was gazing at the ice and absorbing the scene, gathering it in for future images, storing the experience as he always does, returning to it later. He turned and caught my eye, and we smiled at each other without needing to speak. In a way, I thought, such moments are unshareable with others. No one we will meet later on who has not been here will understand our excitement and wonder standing before this immense blue-white ice wall. But in our family, for us, it will be a thing forever: Remember the day... And that alone is reason and reward for starting out. The four of us huddled together and asked a fellow passenger to take a photo of us with our digital camera. Dressed in the red life jackets of the ship, with hats and gloves, against the ice mountain of blue, we stood for a frozen memory. Then Deirdre turned to me, first to hear the noise.

'What's that?'

The blue-grey stillness was disturbed by a splintering sound.

'What? O my god!'

Following the sound, the passengers moved to one side of the boat and looked across at the glacier that towered over us. The noise grew louder until it became a deafening creaking and roaring as a great chunk of ice cracked and split away and fell crashing sensationally into the lake water. There was a white powdering fall and splash, and for an instant we watched stunned where the ice had vanished, before realising we should hold on. For a large wave soon formed and the swell came and rocked the boat back and over. A part of the glacier was no more, a cautionary note, added to by the captain who told us that the ice had retreated many metres in the last ten years. We stood holding on and the boat slowly returned to stillness. Then there was the deepest silence once more.

For two hours afterwards the boat sailed slowly along the foot of the glacier, dwarfed in size. Wind-carved sculptures rose skyward with fissures and crevices and ravines in a hundred shades of blue. Every imaginable formation was paraded in spectacular contour and colour. The boat stopped and a crew member eased himself gingerly down a ladder, cut some chunks off a floating iceberg and returned with an ice bucket. We clinked our drinks with 10,000-year-old ice.

'And if that doesn't cure you, Chris, nothing will!' said Niall, as we toasted ourselves, arrived at a place of pure wonder, and at the southern most point on our itinerary.

Dear S,

Hola mi hermano! Que pasa? *We made it! We're nearly at the bottom of the world. Had drinks today with 10,000-year-old ice on board a red fishing boat as it skirted the blue Grey Glacier. Cool. Awesome place. You'd love it. Bring the boys down here. Go hiking and camping, only bring plenty of food with you. There isn't a thing to eat! Tomorrow we head back to Punta Arenas and onward to Northern Patagonia.*

Our experience of being in Torres del Paine was nearly everything I hoped it would be. It was exotic and distant and mysterious in its unfamiliarity, quite different from the life we had stepped out of a few months earlier. It was also beautiful and wild, and at times I felt complete in this landscape. I was expanded by it, although isolated at the same time. I was aware that we belonged at that moment to a privileged group. Looking about us in the large-windowed dining room with its magnificent view of the glacier and mountains, I could see that we were in the company of fellow-spirited travellers with whom we shared a common goal – a journey to seek out the world's most remote, beautiful natural landscapes while travelling independently in relative comfort. I call us the comfort-class travellers. Not the first-class, Abercrombie and Kent subscribers, although at times we did dip deep into our pockets to pay the extra few bob for luxury. And not the hostel-sleeping, tent-carrying, budget on a shoestring tourists either. We were the travellers who couldn't afford the Explora Hotel (or felt it was greedy extravagance which is closer to the mark), but who didn't want to camp either. No one at Lago Grey had booked group tours.

I also noticed that, largely, the people we encountered along the way stayed to themselves. I hadn't expected that we would travel in such self-containment. More often than not, it was I who struck up conversation with people. Joseph would too, especially in the hotel's Jacuzzi or swimming pool! I decided that it was because we weren't among novice travellers who feel so excited to be on holiday – somewhere else, in another country – that they have to shout about it. Like Americans on their first trip abroad who catch another American voice and say spontaneously in loud tones, 'Hey, where are you from?' The people with whom we shared meals in hotels, or joined in mini-excursions, rarely spoke to us and likewise us to them. Sometimes it was too impersonal for me. It was as if once in a while we were invisible, which was alternately discomforting and comforting. Discomforting because on occasion I wanted to be the loud American shouting, 'Hey, here we are, The Travelling Breen Williams Family Quartet.' I wanted to share our excitement. But, like Niall and Deirdre, who are naturally more reserved, our fellow travellers kept to themselves and, I imagine, savoured their own experiences for sharing 'back home' with family and friends. We were all just passengers in a landscape, moving on to another destination in a few days. As usual, Deirdre and Joseph were the youngest travellers and in all probability we looked somewhat self-contained. And hadn't it served us well so far? When I thought more about it I realised that I was possibly understanding something about myself. That my desire to communicate is stronger than average, which, given my somewhat solitary nature and social unease is a bit ambiguous. In any event, I wasn't just gliding through this landscape on the way to somewhere else. I was preparing to be touched by new experiences that spoke to me in an as yet unknown language, but whose message would in time find expression. I was more than privileged. I was blessed.

The third day of our stay inside the park we brought a picnic of peanut butter and crackers we had bought in Santiago. We stole a banana, two apples, some cheese and breakfasts rolls from the skimpy breakfast at the hotel and found a cosy spot tucked in out of the wind overlooking a lake and lay in the sun. There was no place else to have lunch except back at Hostería Lago Grey, or at the Explora, which at $200 we naturally turned down. I had one more day left of taking Cipro and was continually getting better. The dreadful concert of noises and gurgles was, I hoped, in its final movement and the pain in the centre of my gut was easing. But the whole experience had left me weak and tired. Still, I found the energy to trek along a trail that wound its way up a grassy, rocky slope which got wilder and windier as we climbed higher and higher, nearly blowing us over. Joseph and Niall stopped halfway and rested, while Deirdre and I continued along until the path disappeared and we crossed the top, our faces peeking through our hooded rain jackets, our hands tucked into the sleeves wishing we had brought gloves. It was sheer exhilaration. We didn't see another soul. I was thinking the whole Patagonian experience would soon be closed away, added to the growing 'zip' files accumulating in my memory. I was reminded of something else too. Something I had read about restoring health to the body and harmony to the soul and was grateful to be in pursuit of both.

~

Chile is nearly as long as North America is wide and it is unlikely that you will find a map of the whole of the country on a single page, which made pointing out our next destination to Deirdre and Joseph a bit tricky.

'And how, exactly, are we going to get there?' asked Deirdre when she saw that it seemed to be surrounded by water and that the red line where a road should be had disappeared.

'Easy,' I answered. 'We fly.'

I knew from my research that Parque Pumalin was inaccessible by direct road from either northern or southern Chile. We would have to fly there once we arrived in Northern Patagonia. We left Punta Arenas and boarded a plane for Puerto Montt. I had read an article about Parque Pumalin in a magazine during my many hours of research for the trip and was intrigued. What would it be like to be inside a privately owned national park whose sole intention was preservation and environmental protection? At the time of my research there was only one company sanctioned to operate inside the park, Alsur Expeditions based in Puerto Varas. After many emails with a woman named Rocco we settled on an itinerary which included a guide for three days who would travel with us and take us trekking. Our accommodation was arranged in Caleta Gonzola, where half a dozen cabanas had been built along the shore of the Renihue Fjord. Niall had several times hinted that it was too much. This *adventure* side trip, as he called it, involved too many logistics. Things could go wrong. We shouldn't press our luck. Hadn't we seen enough in Torres del Paine? I remained insistent. I hadn't done all that work for nothing. I had already agreed to give up on Vietnam as part of the itinerary back in October and had settled instead for China as our Asian leg of the trip, but on this I wasn't compromising. No wayo, Niallo.

After two nights in Puerto Varas on the banks of Lago Llanquihue with the near-perfect cone of the Volcano Osorno rising from the eastern edge of the lake, we headed back to Puerto Montt with our athletic guide, Mauricio, for a short flight to Chaiten. We were joined by two older ladies, Laura and Viola, who were Chilean cousins out on a bit of a jaunt. Mauricio eyed them suspiciously. Viola, the chattier of the two, was wearing a black lamb's wool coat and her walking shoes were heeled. Laura was less stylishly attired and quieter but both assured us they were game for anything and Viola, who spoke excellent English, conversed easily with us as we awaited our plane. Before long, Deirdre understood that either the plane was going to be empty or it was going to be small. Considering it was less than a forty-five minute flight, she worked it out.

'Mum,' she said, 'I can't go on a small plane!' She still hadn't got used to the idea of aeroplane travel. She had a real fear of being up in the air, and occasionally I would give her a combination of *argentum nitricum* and *aconite*, two acute fear remedies. She also carried her own bottle of Rescue Remedy but, mostly, I think, she just needed to vent.

'I'm sorry, darling,' I said trying to calm her, 'but there is no other way to get there.'

'Then, why do we have to go? Dad doesn't want to go. I don't want to go.'

'C'mon Deirdre,' said Joseph in one of his gentle humours, 'it'll be fun. You'll see.'

'Ha,' she replied. 'I don't want to have that kind of fun. What if we die?'

'Now there's a thought,' said Niall. 'What if?' He put his arm around Deirdre and said, 'Don't worry, Dee. I'll land first and catch you.'

The plane finally arrived after being delayed because of cloudy weather and we saw that it was indeed small. In fact, it was the smallest plane I'd ever climbed into. It was a ten-seater, and the back seats were stuffed with our cases. Talk about scared. I sat behind one of the two pilots, the one who turned out to be *in training* and strapped myself in. Crikey, would Deirdre make it? I turned to Niall and whispered, 'What luck, eh? A trainee pilot, bad weather and a twin engine, ten-seater!' He eyed me back as if to say, 'I told you this was a bad idea.' I looked to Mauricio and he nodded reassuringly and the Chilean gentlewomen acted as if there wasn't a thing to trouble them. I later reflected that they had survived Allende and Pinochet and this was just a walk in the park, or a fly in the sky. The plane approached the runway quite quickly and took off. No turning back. I swung around as we lifted upward and saw that Deirdre had her eyes closed, Joseph was looking out the window and Niall was ready to nod off. I sat frozen in my seat with my heart in my mouth as the plane swayed back and forth in the windy rain. The windshield wipers on the plane worked blindly. The trainer pilot kept his eye on the gauges in the front panel and I tried to keep myself from imagining the worst. For the first time, I understood what it meant to be 'out of your body'. I let my imagination run riot and was thinking only in panic proportions. I had more or less abandoned my body to suffer the anxiety alone. Once I realised I didn't have an ounce of control I surrendered and focused on steadying my breathing and listening internally to my pounding heart. Through the blind, grey air we flew, buffeting wildly. The landscape below, when it appeared, was nothing but trees, and the long, thin finger of a cold water fjord. Not a house in sight.

The flight took a long time, although in reality maybe only forty-five minutes. We eventually emerged from a cloud, almost upside down, and turning 180 degrees to approach the runway. A great sigh of relief expanded the plane and I wondered if, once again, I had neglected to think the whole thing through. What if? Had we signed a waiver?

～

Billionaire Douglas Tompkins, former owner of the clothes company Espirit, bought the Renihue Ranch in 1991 with the intention of protecting its 42,000 acres of evergreen temperate rainforest from possible exploitation as was happening in much of the rest of Chile, where logging was decimating the country's natural forests at alarming rates. Tompkins and his wife, Christine, have since added another 750,000 acres, establishing Parque Pumalin as a nature sanctuary, a special designation of the Chilean State, which grants it additional environmental and non-developmental protection. The Conservation Land Trust (a US environmental foundation) which currently administers the park plans to eventually donate the protected lands to Fundacion Pumalin, a Chilean foundation, for the administration and continual development of a unique type of National Park, albeit under private initiative.

Neither the Foundation nor the Park receives any financial assistance from the Chilean government. Being a new form of private environmental philanthropy in Chile, the project met with political opposition, initially from those not understanding how such an initiative would work, but also from those who questioned Tompkins' motives. It seems he had in fact bought an entire section of Chile, stretching from the water to the Argentine border, in effect establishing a private domain in the lower middle half of the country. In the years since Tompkins bought the land and established the park, confidence in his altruistic intentions has grown and the project is advancing locally and nationally and internationally, and is now considered by some to be the world's most important conservationist project.

Small farms with productive activities such as animal husbandry, cheese-making, honey production, eco-tourism, wool handicrafts and organic gardens function as park stations and visitor help centres. The main idea being fostered is that conservation and a productive contribution to the local economy can work hand in hand. The guardians of the Conservation Trust are aware of the need to include neighbours in its conservation lands and aim to create a shared feeling of the need to protect wild lands and their biodiversity. No less a primary objective is to provide a place for Chileans and international visitors to experience pristine nature, to have a heightened understanding of the magic and beauty of the natural world, thereby becoming, it is hoped, more active in their daily lives in valuing and protecting nature. Douglas Tompkins and the partners of the Conservation Trust are hopeful that Parque

Pumalin can set an example for other private gestures, not just at a large scale, but at any level. Nature and wild lands philanthropy has been responsible for thousands of projects all over the world, protecting and securing naturelands, animal and plant life, forest, prairies, deserts, and wherever natural habitats are endangered.

Originally our three-day visit to Parque Pumalin was to include a guided hike each day, but with the delay of the plane and our late arrival we ended up having dinner instead. From the airport, it was another hour and a half to Caleta Gonzola in an old mini-van with holes that flooded us with grey dust from the gravelled road beneath. We had arrived in a temperate rainforest. Mist lay on the tree tops and the grey and green landscape was familiar to us. Mauricio, our Chilean guide, was elf-like. Not so much because of his smallish stature but because of the twinkle in his eye and his constant good humour. His dark hair was cropped short and he wore an earring in his ear. His skin was brown, probably like his Mapuche ancestors. He was swift and agile like a puma and spoke English well and was interested in literature and music. We had much to chat about. He was equally at ease talking with Joseph and Deirdre as he was with his Chilean compatriots whose charge he took seriously, inwardly wondering how he was going to get these lovelies out trekking.

First he settled us in to our wonderfully romantic, wooden-shingled cabins, half obscured by green growing things and ringed by rivulets of mountain water. Grey and brown woven blankets lined the wooden beds. Curtains framed timber windows, and the bathroom was tiled with slate and green ceramics. It was subtle and elegant in its simplicity and startling when you consider how difficult their construction must have been. We were literally in the middle of nowhere you might say, on the edge of a fjord. The only access to the organic farm, from where most of the food came, was across the fjord by boat or private plane.

As soon as we arrived it began to rain. Again for us recognisable scenery. Joseph felt right at home. The constant rain must have touched in him a personal chord and he felt comforted by its familiarity. He made himself cosy and ran back and forth from our cabin to the main cabin where he quickly made friends with Jerry from LA, who was on vacation from his teaching job in an inner-city school. Joseph was reading *Catcher in the Rye* and Jerry and he talked about it. Unless you wanted to walk in the rain before dinner there wasn't anything else to do but hang out in the main cabin and warm yourself by the open fire, chatting with strangers. Another young couple, also from LA and on their honeymoon, arrived after supper and he, like Jerry, was also an English teacher but at a private school. It was a setting for a one-act play. Three English teachers from three different walks of life find themselves together in the temperate rainforests of Northern Patagonia with no entertainment but *Catcher in the Rye,* a game of Scrabble and an eleven-year-old. This one had a happy ending. The *craic*, as they say in Ireland, was only mighty and Joseph chatted to his heart's content. Jerry wore a woollen hat pulled down nearly to his eyes. He was tallish and wiry and looked like Mike Nesbith, the former guitarist with The Monkees. He had the same quizzical but game-for-anything gaze and had arrived in Parque Pumalin as if the wind had blown him like a seed. He wasn't sure where he was off to next, or when the next transport would take him to his next location. The newlyweds, Jeff and Diane were reading Steinbeck's *Of Mice and Men* to each other. I can only imagine what fun they were going to have when they got to their cabin that night, especially as Jeff was well over six feet tall and Niall had already hit his head on the cabin timbers. The atmosphere in Caleta Gonzola was distinctly different from that of Torres del Paine. In both places we experienced a unique sense of place, but perhaps because of the rain and the singularity of the landscape, the atmosphere at Parque Pumalin was one of intimacy. The food was simple but delicious with freshly baked bread and organic honey accompanying every meal. There was a sense from everyone there of *caring*, of being a small part of something bigger than any of us, of being truly fortunate to be in that magnificent natural wonderland, deep, deep in a forest with no sound anywhere but the rain falling and the hissing of the logs in the fire.

We slept well in the shelter of the wooden cabins even though we were a bit cold. By morning the rain had eased but the waters of the fjord looked grey and choppy. We watched a small boat battle the swells and swing into the shore.

'If that's our boat, there's no way I'm going with you,' Joseph said. He gingerly made his way over the large stones on the shore and felt the water.

'I thought so,' he said, 'it's freezing. If the boat sinks, we'll die from hypothermia. I'm not going!'

Niall looked to me and said, 'All right Joseph, you and I will stay here and the girls will go.'

'I want to go,' said Deirdre.

'Okay we'll go then. You'll be all right?' I asked Niall.

He nodded and I knew from his quick response that he hadn't wanted to go in the first place. It meant that we had room for Jerry and we offered him Niall's spot, which he gladly accepted. Laura, Viola and Mauricio were the other passengers. The six of us climbed on board the tiny, ten-foot aluminum boat. There was only room for the four females inside the cabin plus the 'captain'. Mauricio and Jerry stood outside grasping whatever they could. It was then that Mauricio said he too was a bit weary of ocean-going voyages and for that reason rarely went in a boat. The Chilean cousins were undaunted. Deirdre and I assumed the captain wouldn't be risking his life, so we felt assured the trip ahead was navigable.

Once we reached open water the swells got larger and their white caps threatened the boat's head-on steering, making the captain zigzag across the fjord. Jerry and Mauricio were being assaulted in the open back by sea spray, Jerry smiling the whole time, while Mauricio looked slightly concerned. He spoke rapidly in Chilean Spanish to the captain who simply nodded his head.

'He says the forecast isn't good. We stay only one hour at the organic farm.'

Deirdre and I were getting well practised at these hair-raising adventures by now but it wasn't getting any easier for my body, which seemed to have a mind of its own. No matter how many times I told myself I wasn't destined to die of hypothermia crossing a Chilean fjord if I hadn't died crossing Lake Titicaca with a drunken Bolivian in a fedora, it didn't work. I was petrified and held Deirdre's hand. I found that by not looking at the swells I was less frightened, but when the boat careened down with a thud that forced us off our seats, it didn't help. Visions of George Clooney in *The Perfect Storm* rose before me.

When we arrived forty-five minutes later, the mist was steadily falling. We were met by farm workers in two vans and brought to the main building where the honey was made and where the offices of the park's administration were housed. We had passed Tompkins' house apparently, but couldn't make it out through the descending fog. He had a private landing strip for a small plane. We were surrounded by trees in thick groves that rose like small mountains. It reminded me of Ireland with rain falling like a thin steady veil across a green landscape, only this landscape held trees instead of green fields, and there were no houses about, and no roads for a way out.

'Please, do not worry,' Mauricio told Deirdre. 'We will stay here overnight if the weather does not improve.' While we were on the tour of the beekeeping and honey operations he stayed behind. Suffice it to say that the business, run by local workers who lived in comfortable dormitory-type accommodation, was first class. Nearly every material used for the production of the organic honey was recycled. The timber for the honeycomb trays was made from fallen trees of the park. The wax was cleaned and recycled. A cluster of wooden, shingled houses that surrounded the main building housed the manager, his wife, the head gardener and the pilot. They had their own satellite for Internet hook-up and communication and their own generators for electricity. As a model of co-operative farming it was exemplary. We were hurried through the warehouse and workshops back to the head office and ushered back to the boat. It was wet and wild. The captain couldn't gauge the roughness of the sea until we reached the open water. Life jackets on, we squeezed into the boat. With teeth chattering from a mixture of cold and fear, I sat stiffly and alert. What could the life jackets do for us if we capsized? We'd freeze to death first. Joseph had been right. To my utter amazement, Viola and Laura were not anxious. Jerry was philosophical. It was Mauricio and I who were playing the possibilities out in our minds. After fifteen minutes we hit the open water and within seconds the captain said we must turn back. It was too rough. Like lambs to the slaughter we sat silently and returned to the farm where we were told the manager of the park would soon arrive from Puerto Montt on his twin jet to tell us what to do. Meanwhile, it was a hopeless situation in terms of accommodation for the night. There was no room for six of us. When the manager of the park arrived he breezed in like a knight on a white horse. Black wavy hair, highlighted with designer grey specks. Pressed blue jeans and a white knit sweater. Tanned and charming, to my great surprise he kissed Deirdre and shook hands with the rest of us.

'There is no problem. The sea is rough, yes, but the boat is strong and with two motor engines you are perfectly safe. But,' he smiled, 'I think it is best for you to return in two groups. Yes? All right?' He was a man for whom 'no', in any language, was not part of his vocabulary. Jerry and the Chileans were to go first. The captain would return in an hour and half and take Mauricio, myself and a very calm Deirdre back for the second trip.

'I'd fly you in the plane, you see, but the fog is too much. No, no, the boat is very safe.' And with that the first three said goodbye and disappeared.

'Is there anything you want us to say if we make it and you don't?' I asked Jerry, trying to fortify myself.

'Yes,' he said. 'Tell them I died laughing!'

That night back at the Caleta Gonzola Café we had a story to tell Niall and Joseph and we bought a bottle of wine and shared it with our new friends. As we had survived, the telling of it was both funny and fascinating. Deirdre and I and Mauricio had been taken by the manager to his private house while we were waiting for our brave boatman. We had cups of herbal tea and pastries. God only knows how the delicacies got there. I expect that his job as manager of the entire nature preserve commanded a rather healthy salary. His home, finely crafted from native trees, was a wooden sanctuary in the middle of the rainforest. Top-of-the-range appliances, designer furniture and earthen-tiled counters. It was like arriving in a five-star hotel on a desert island. This was no wellie-clad, mud-speckled Chilean lumberjack. On the contrary, he was a rather charismatic, well-groomed man in the prime of his life, overseeing nearly a million acres of protected rainforest. Big job, big responsi-bility. Lots of trees, lots of rain. It felt like we had walked into another world when we came through the door of his home, in out of the rain and away from the swelling sea. An oasis of protection and exclusivity. I was hoping that our captain would have to stay in Caleta Gonzola and we would have to stay the night with our charming host, but it was not to be. He brought us back to the boat in his jeep after showing us the organic garden and glasshouse, and kissed us goodbye. I imagine he was as interested in us and we were in him. It's not everyday two beautiful damsels in distress walk into your life, in out of the rain, in need of a cup of tea and a blazing fire, in the middle of a rainforest.

~

Christmas was around the corner. We had been in Chile since the second week of December and had been travelling for a month in South America, staying no more than three consecutive nights in one place. Every moment was as rich as the one before, even the bad ones. The children were holding up well and I think Joseph surprised himself. But Deirdre's ability to adapt was the greatest surprise to us. She eased herself in and out of trouble spots like a prize jockey in a steeplechase – the catamaran in Bolivia and the stomach disturbance, the shaky flight to Chaiten, the wild boat journey to the honey farm. Her recovery time was brief. As long as Joseph had plenty of opportunity to express himself, he too was all right. Yet, with the calendar moving quickly toward 25 December, it was difficult for both of them. They missed getting ready for Christmas in Ireland.

On 22 December we hired a driver and a van from Puerto Varas to take us to Los Lagos in the lake district of the X region of Chile where Ian and Maggy Staples were expecting us for the holidays on their farm, Fundo Chacaipulli. It was another of my Internet finds. Originally we had hoped to spend Christmas in North America with my brothers in Seattle but our Oneworld tickets didn't permit return travel to a continent once you had left. Ian and Maggy were from England. Similar to our initial move from New York to Ireland, they had left England for Chile when they decided to sail to Patagonia, and spent nearly five years in between living and sailing in the boat. Once they landed in Valdivia they decided to put down roots, so they pulled up anchor, sold the boat, and bought a 400-acre farm with cattle and horses. Maggy was a horse woman from way back so it seemed a logical progression once the farm was on its feet to offer Chilean-style farm holidays to guests from abroad. They were in their second year of operations when we contacted them from Kiltumper. Ian wrote in an email:

Dear Christine and Niall,

Your letter arrived this morning but we were rushing off to Valdivia to pick up lots of trees that we are planting at the moment but now a proper reply. We went to your web page. Very interesting. In fact a very attractive web page. We will now hunt down Four Letters of Love. We love 'love stories'. Firstly Joseph will be surprised by Chile. Tell them they don't bury people alive anymore. It is a very civilised and friendly country. We think that we are in Europe, except they speak Spanish – very quickly! You will love the farm. We have had quite a lot of children to stay and families tend to stay longer than they expected. Our very first family guests came for four days and stayed for eleven. The farm is incredibly beautiful and I think you will enjoy meeting the folks who work on the farm. Do Joseph and Deirdre ride? I suspect that they will enjoy the riding here and at the end of your stay feel very confident on horseback. We have a very good guy here, called Antonio, and he and Maggy seem to have the knack of making young people feel relaxed riding. Our horses are pretty sensible and used as working horses all the time. There are also two very friendly Labrador semi-puppies called Jet and Mackay that the children will love. My suggestion is you enjoy Christmas with us. Last year we had a full house and had a great time. We will also roast a lamb outside over charcoal. The weather at Christmas is usually warm to very hot so we put up a Christmas tree but basically live outside. I shall probably be in the south just before Christmas helping pilot a yacht south but be back before Christmas. I hope all of this is helpful and we look forward to helping you have a really memorable stay with us at Fundo Chacaipulli. From the very green and currently Indian summer south.

Ian and Maggy

Maggy greeted us when our van pulled up the gravelled drive of Fundo Chacaipulli in front of a reddish, chocolate-coloured shingled farmhouse softened with shrubs and flowering plants. We kept forgetting that it was their summertime.

'Welcome, Niall and Chrissie and Deirdre and Joseph,' she said dropping a handful of weeds that she had picked from the flowerbed and shaking our hands. I guessed Maggy was in her mid- to late fifties. She wore her riding jodhpurs and riding boots under a long shirt. Her eyes were blue, and greying blond hair framed her face at her shoulders. She was a beauty. She spoke slowly and, as we were soon to find out, peppered her sentences with Spanish.

'*Bueno, bueno*,' she said, and turning, called into the kitchen, 'Alicia? Alicia? The Williams *estan aqui*. Oh there you are James,' she continued, smiling and turning around again when a man in his thirties came from inside. 'Come meet Niall and Chrissie and Deirdre and Joseph.'

'This is James, a friend of our son's from England. He'll be staying with us for Christmas too.'

She led the way to our lodge, a large cabin built from logs, a hundred yards from the main house. She talked as she walked. 'As soon as you're settled we'll get a Christmas tree for your house.'

In the way of these things you suspend your thinking and go with the flow. We thanked our driver, emptied his van of our dozen bags, and deposited them inside the lodge which surpassed our expectations. It was bigger than we expected with wide glass windows that overlooked the steep valley below. The rooms were warmly decorated in blues and whites with a mixture of terracotta and wood and stone. Maggy was under the impression, and not mistakenly, that we had been expecting our rooms to look a bit Christmassy so the first order of business was to get the tree. We hardly had time to look around before we set out down the drive in a line behind Maggy and James. She neglected to explain that it was across a few fields, through some barbed wire and through the high grass to a grove of very tall pine trees. We stood in the dark centre of the grove, sidestepping cow plops and puddles and looked at each other in amazement. It had started to rain. Before we had time to question her, Maggy said, 'Here, James, cut down this branch and this will do for the Havers' house.'

'Right Maggy,' James said in his cheery British accent as if it was the simplest and most logical thing he had ever heard. So the four of us followed suit and looked above us for a proper branch-cum-Christmas tree.

'You see, Ian wouldn't let us cut down one of his trees but these will do nicely.' We hadn't been in Fundo Chacaipulli an hour and we were wet with rain. Our hands were sticky with sap and our feet drenched by the time we trudged back to the houses bearing the Christmas tree-branches. In a way it reminded me of early Christmases in Kiltumper when Niall and I had gone up the hill to cut a spruce and carry it home. But here we were in the rain in Chile and a little unsure of triumphing over the burden of expectation Christmas can sometimes bring. I imagine it is the same for all parents at Christmas – the desire is always there to make it the best one ever, to create the perfect memory for the children, a kind of fantasy fulfilment. All this then was running through my head as we carried the wet branches back to the cabins in the rain. We left one at the first house, where two units had been recently built for guests, another at the main house and the last one back at our own.

'James will bring you a bucket for the tree and we can start decorating as soon as you're ready.' Maggy said as she went through the open door of her house.

One of the many activities that Ian and Maggy advertised on their website was an art studio because Maggy was also an artist, although the demands of the farm had left her no time for painting. The art studio was somewhere upstairs, I think. We never saw it, probably because it wasn't finished. Deirdre and I had been looking forward to working with Maggy in the studio. I had had half an idea that I might prepare some sketches from photographs in the quiet of Christmas. We let it slide and went with the flow that carried us along. Maggy invited us back to the main house and suggested we could make some ornaments for the trees.

'We've been so busy I haven't had time to get ready,' she said, disappearing through the open door past the large figure of Don Israel, a man in his sixties who was shucking peas under the roof of the porch and looking like a Chilean Buddha with a straw hat. Half a dozen boots and hats of every description greeted us. It was true.

Looking around us we saw no evidence that Christmas Eve was two days away. I could see the kids were disappointed.

Fortunately the comfort and wonderful space of our lodge allayed our disillusionment somewhat. Large, plate-glass windows stretched almost the whole length of the cottage. There was a horse grazing just feet from our window. Both children had their own rooms and they set about unloading straightaway. The nesting instinct took over for me as well and I began unpacking everything we had.

'It's great, isn't it?' Niall said. I smiled back.

'Yes, it looks pretty good.'

'It's better than I was expecting.'

'Yeah, me too.'

After some hair-raising experiences in South America we were due for some rest and relaxation and were looking forward to sleeping in the same bed for ten nights. We hadn't been more than three nights in any one place since we'd left Costa Rica at the end of November. Only one thing was missing. Where was Santa Claus?

A knock came at the door; it opened and the silver-haired Ian arrived.

'I see Maggy's got you your tree. Good. Good. How are you? Niall isn't it?' He shook our hands like a west Clare farmer, sturdy and firm. 'And this is Deirdre and Joseph and you must be Chrissie.'

'Yes, hello, Ian?' we replied, presuming it was he, and smiled back. I noted that they called me Chrissie sometimes as a result of reading the first of our books about our life in Ireland, *O Come Ye Back*. It was kind of endearing. I could see straightaway that it was his charisma that carried him through life. It probably got him into a bit of trouble too. But here was a very engaging, charming Englishman. Ian was about fifty-five, I guessed; to the manner born, as it were. Life in Chile obviously agreed with him. He wore wellies and jeans. His brown eyes were bright and round and rather youthful.

'You've been on a great adventure so far, haven't you, Joseph?' He smiled at the thought of it. 'And Deirdre, we'll have to get you set up for horse riding in the morning. Here, Niall, let me show you how to light the stove.' He dropped the logs he had been holding all the while at the stove and lit it for us.

'There should be plenty of logs outside your lodge every morning. And Alicia will make sure you have all your breakfast things.'

I was the one who had done most of the corresponding with Ian by email. So I felt in some ways I was meeting a friend. We shared some wonderful emails back and forth.

'Thanks, Ian,' I said, 'it's so lovely to be here. And we're very pleased with the lodge. Thank you very much.'

'You're going to have a brilliant holiday here. Just make this your home away from home. See you at dinner and we can talk all about it. It's just us tonight. The Havers arrive tomorrow and Nancy and Wally, the Americans, arrive on Christmas Eve.' Before he bounded out of the lodge I asked, 'Ian? Any packages arrive for us?'

'I don't think so. But I'll check with Maggy.' And off he went in a flash. Deirdre shot me a look of despair. She said, 'Mum! Christmas is in two days! It's not fair. I thought there'd be some packages for us by now. We won't have anything.' Deirdre was more than disappointed. Her friends Kate and Sheila had promised to send her Christmas boxes. We had ordered books for the kids from Amazon way back in October. My sister Deirdre had posted us some presents. Marie in Kilrush had said she was sending us a big box to remind us of Christmas in Ireland, and so far nothing had arrived. There are times when there is nothing you can do about your children's disappointment, never mind your own.

'I'll ask Ian what the deal is with the post. Maybe something will come tomorrow,' I said in a feeble effort to be positive. So far, though, it seemed that the Christmas spirit in Chile was not a match to what we were used to at home in Ireland. We had expected to find something in Puerto Varas for the children but it was slim pickings really. We had decided to wait until we reached Valdivia, the nearest city to Fundo Chacaipulli, where we were hoping to go on Christmas Eve for some Santa shopping. It was Joseph's first year without the magic of Santa Claus and we didn't want it to be too much of a letdown.

We hadn't had room to bring presents with us but I had given thought to the tree already and had bought some ornaments in Santiago as a surprise.

'Look what I found.' I appeared from our bedroom with an armful of ribbon and wooden Santas and candy canes. Niall hooked up the Sony speakers to my laptop and the *Christmas Greatest Hits* from our collection of CDs blared through the room while we clambered up and down the stairs and around the branch to decorate our tree, singing, 'I saw three ships come sailing in, come sailing in, come sailing in. I saw three ships come sailing in on Christmas Day in the morning.' I pulled out the Santa's hat that we had been carrying since September and put it on Deirdre's head.

'There you go, sweetheart, Santa's little helper.'

They were handling their disappointment well. I was proud of them. I come from a long tradition of Christmas celebration and, for good or bad, I have transferred it to them. Every year my mother had a blue tree, as we called it. She decorated it in blue lights and large blue balls and silver tinsel. The tradition of decorating the tree has become even stronger with my mother's six children. Niall and I have a collection of ornaments that started when we married. Most of them have the year written on them from when they were first acquired. Trying to duplicate that in Chile was never my desire, but going some way towards it was a priority. However, I was busy in my mind figuring out how to soften the blow that might be around the corner. It was obvious that Ian and Maggy were not really that much 'into' Christmas. While we had anticipated Christmas pudding and/or mince pies on the table for dessert, I decided the best we could hope for was some sherry trifle. The only positive thing I could see on the horizon was that for once Deirdre wasn't going to be left off the menu. Four of the seven other guests were vegetarians!

We arrived for dinner our first night and Ian handed around Pisco sours and Cokes. We sat in comfortable sofas in a wood-panelled room while the dogs cosied themselves around Joseph and we toasted each other. James had joined us and told us all about Sydney where he had lived for a year and we learned more about Maggy and Ian's own five-year sailing trip. We were among kindred spirits and felt warmly welcomed. I had the sense that something was preoccupying Maggy, but I was never to find out. I guessed it was probably something to do with the fine balance that needed to be struck between inviting strangers into your home as paying guests and treating them like friends. While it was definitely Ian who talked the talk, it was possibly Maggy who was left with the rest.

The Havers, an English family on a three-year job appointment in St Lucia, arrived the next day and while Joseph had been looking forward to spending time with three boys around his own age, it didn't quite work out as we had hoped. They tolerated each other, but found they had little in common. The Havers had come for a horse-riding holiday and had expected a bit of a riding school with proper hats and boots and crops. What they found was something similar to what I had found with the art studio. It wasn't there, but what was there was next best thing. Four hundred acres of land to trek across and, before lunch, Ian had saddled most of us up (except Niall who refused, saying he rode only imaginary horses). We followed Maggy and Antonio, the Chilean gaucho, down the grass track and across the meadow. Summer flowers and tall grass waved across flat fields before the trek dipped steeply down into gravel and bare earth. Joseph wanted off. Even I was frightened. Ian was walking beside the youngest of the Havers.

'Don't worry, horses have four legs. If one stumbles there are three others left.'

'Oh, that's comforting, Ian.'

During our first trek, the youngest Haver did have a fall from his horse after it bucked him off and Joseph decided that he wouldn't go out again. Deirdre on the other hand was in love with her horse, a chestnut brown gelding named Sephy, and was thrilled to be asked to go out again in the afternoon with Maggy and Antonio. Joseph reverted, as he usually does when things are not going according to his expectations, to his books and a table where he could draw. I had hoped he would kick the ball around with the other boys, but he was happier in his own space. The calm small horses that Ian had written to us about didn't exactly materialise, but we made do with what was before us. I was familiar by now with Joseph's rhythms and knew that once he got it off his chest he would adapt. For myself, I was just happy to be stationary for a time in comfortable surroundings where the food was home-cooked and the company engaging. Things were not quite as Ian had advertised, but his charm and Maggy's gentleness more than made up for it.

Ian managed to hire a car for us which enabled Niall and me to drive the two hours into Valdivia on Christmas Eve. A modest old city built along the mouth of the river where old grey-bearded sea lions sang an out-of-tune refrain to the fisherman, Valdivia, like Puerto Varas and Puerto Montt, was devoid of Christmas decorations or a Christmas spirit anywhere close to what I was familiar with in Ireland and America. Alongside the river there was a small market where fish and vegetables and blocks of seaweed were for sale. Deirdre, on finding out that no mince pies were on the menu, insisted that I return with all the ingredients for making them. Maggy too had given us instructions to buy fish and vegetables for dinner. Again in the way of these things you can either object or feel pleased that you are being treated as one of the family. She also asked us to pick up something small for the second cook as a Christmas present. Entrusted with what seemed to me as important tasks I went about the market surveying everything carefully. We had even brought a cooler with us to store the fish. Vegetables and fruit and fish were incredibly inexpensive and we bought two bags of everything. Of course I had to keep reminding myself that, although this was the end of December, it was summertime in Chile. I think I was still expecting a dusting of snow to fall by midnight.

We bought Deirdre, and the second cook, lovely hand-crocheted bags with embroidered flowers. We filled Deirdre's with some Chilean undergarments bought at the department store. Niall spotted some fashionable tops and we found a stylish belt for Deirdre. We had already bought her a leather bag in La Paz and silk pyjamas and a necklace in Santiago. Joseph was more difficult to buy for because he never really wanted anything. Deirdre and I had bought him a teddy bear in the market in Pisac in Peru, made from alpaca, and, although he was a bit crushed from being hidden in the bottom of Deirdre's bag for three weeks, he looked like he'd strike just the right chord with Joseph on Christmas morning. Niall insisted that we buy Joseph a toy and we scoured the streets of Valdivia in search of one, ending up with a stuffed replica of Hagrid from Harry Potter. Fortified with a few CDs and more art supplies and Christmas candies, we headed back to Fundo Chacaipulli for Christmas Eve.

Wally and Nancy, two Americans from the DC area, had arrived by the time we got back and turned out to be two wonderful companions with whom to spend the Christmas holidays. They taught martial arts and, as it turned out, they were both good singers, so they too were also lined up for the Christmas concert that Deirdre and Joseph had been sporadically working towards. The nicest thing about Nancy was that she reminded me of my sister. She had that kind of spirit that aligns itself with the greater universe. One of the first things she said to us was that she could tell by how well we were all getting along that we too were star seeds of Orion!

'It's in the matrix of your bones,' she chirped. We smiled back, Joseph with wide eyes and a giggle which he suppressed

Okay, she was probably a bit too much outside the mainstream, but she was genuine and her New Age approach to life was refreshing. You might have described her as a ditzy blond but when you heard her credentials you understood she was more than a free spirit. She had a black belt and had been to China and trained with a T'ai Chi master. She used Reiki healing in her practice. Her husband Wally, formerly a military man, seemed to be as much in awe of Nancy as we were. Both were in their second marriages. Nancy kept us laughing with the outrageous things she would sometimes tell us, but her energy vibrations were harmonic with our own and we enjoyed every moment we spent with both of them. Lucky for us, Ian had arranged that they would join us on an overnight river-rafting expedition that would see us back in time for New Year's Eve. I think we were looking forward to further conversation with Nancy more than we were to the river rafting.

Ian had forecast that weather would be brilliant for Christmas, saying if it was anything like the previous year we would be in shorts and T-shirts. But as it was, when we awoke on Christmas morning in Chile, the weather had turned rainy and cold and was not unlike Christmas in Ireland. In an odd way, it made us feel better. For a few moments Niall and I lay in the bed in the log cabin wondering how we were going to do. This was to be one of the most testing moments of the whole trip. When you plan a year away you think first of all the wonderful places you will be outside of your own life and its familiar places. But familiarity and family tradition are the very things that make Christmas. So many people when we had told them about the trip asked: 'So where will you be for Christmas?' Well here we were, in a cabin in the middle of Chile.

'Merry Christmas,' Niall whispered to me.

'Merry Christmas.'

'Cup of tea?'

'Yes, please.'

I lay there in the quiet while he slipped into the kitchen and made the tea, lighting the fire as silently as possible. Setting the scene. With the dozen Christmas touches I had added to our living room and the mince pies that Deirdre and I had managed to whip up the night before, I thought we were pretty well set for Christmas morning. On the couch we had set out the children's presents, trying to make them look a good-sized collection. The organic honey from Parque Pumalin was ready to grace our toast as we opened our presents. Niall brought me the tea.

'All asleep?'

'All asleep.'

'It's Christmas morning,' I said. 'It's hard to believe.'

'I know.' Niall sensed my anxiety. 'It'll be all right.'

'I hope so.'

'The kids know. They know we're away, and that it can't be like home. And we've made a great effort, Chris, we have. Come on.'

I carried the tea to the living room and took a moment to take in the scene: the decorated branch of our Christmas tree, hung with painted eggshells and ribbon and the few decorations I had bought in Santiago, the gifts wrapped in unfamiliar wrapping, the horse standing at the plate-glass window and the broad view of the Chilean valley outside. Niall put on the Christmas CD and the children stirred and came out to us. The moment they saw the little stack of presents, their eyes widened and they smiled the smile of children at Christmastime everywhere. I think I realised right then how great my kids really were, that they had been preparing themselves to have nothing at all, and were truly surprised to see the things spread on the couch.

'Merry Christmas!'

Hugs and half-tears and a family teetering between laughing out loud and breaking down crying. That was how it was.

A package had arrived from my father in Florida with some cash and a CD of Dylan Thomas's 'A Child's Christmas in Wales', and half a dozen Cadbury's chocolate bars had arrived in a package from Deirdre's schoolfriend, Sheila. Apart from that, there were only the few things we had managed to get while shopping in Chile. Deirdre, of course, was delighted with her Bolivian leather bag (almost as much as Niall was to have it finally out of the bottom of his suitcase and now looking for a home in hers!) The box of books from Amazon failed to make it, so we were a bit short on gifts for Joseph. But Joseph being Joseph, he didn't seem to mind. He is a child who never expects gifts, who gets as much joy from some new pencils as he would from something more elaborate or expensive. He looked at his presents and smiled and hugged us in gratitude, although all the time my own heart was aching a bit for him, thinking this is his first Christmas without the magic of Santa and how the real world must seem a bit grim to young hearts. Right there and then I secretly vowed to have the best Christmas ever next year in Kiltumper.

I never enquired of Ian why he was a bit of a humbug about Christmas, but I could see from the absence of cards and presents that five years living on a boat had had an effect. Ian was probably of the opinion that no day was more special than the next. However, upon hearing that Joseph was expecting a turkey, Ian had, and fair play to him, gone out and found a 12 lb hen. I never knew what was previously on the menu, but Alicia, the wonderful Chilean cook, always with a nod and a smile, had made a delicious nut loaf for the vegetarians. No plan was ever quite cast in stone in Fundo Chacipulli, and so despite Niall's best efforts to find out exactly when Christmas dinner would be, Ian and Maggy would only turn to each other and say 'when do you think?' and leave it that. In mid-afternoon, so, we headed up to the main house, and there met the Havers and Wally and Nancy and sat around the big fire with a kind of unspoken hunger and hope. Ian and Maggy were as relaxed as ever, and chatted away offering drinks to everyone. There was no apparent sense of schedule or plan, the opposite of the kind of thing Niall was used to in his own Christmases, where the day was marshalled through Mass and presents and visits and dinner and so on. Here we were sitting around on Christmas afternoon in a strangely unreal scene, and in the pauses between conversations I couldn't stop myself thinking of what family members and friends in other corners of the world would be doing, and how very different their Christmases would be. In a way too, I suppose, I was thinking of our own Christmas back in Kiltumper, and seeing us back there as well, as though we could be in both worlds at once. And in that way I think I found a way to appreciate each one more. I watched the children carefully, and again marvelled at how well they were handling things.

Part of the attraction of Christmas in Chile with Ian and Maggy had been the musical evening that Ian had been arranging. I guessed he equally talked up Deirdre and Joseph as accomplished young Irish musicians to the Chileans as he had talked up the band he had organised for the evening to us. He insisted that the Chilean musicians were so good last year that he helped them record a CD. That evening after dinner, five young black-haired Chileans in their twenties arrived, dressed in yellow cotton Oxford-style shirts and black pants. They had guitars, wooden flutes, a mandolin and a keyboard. Ian was master of ceremony and introduced Deirdre and Joseph to the band, who seemed a bit reluctant to make their acquaintance. But one of the musicians took a great interest in Joseph and his fiddle and asked him to play a tune. Another of the musicians, a handsome young man named Alonso, seemed to be taking a good few sideways glances at Deirdre who had agreed to play later in the evening. We had bought wooden panpipes and bell shakers in Peru and brought them out. Maggy handed around castanets and hollowed gourds to us as we all settled ourselves on the sofas, chairs and floor. The farm workers and their families and the kitchen staff joined us at the edges of the room, leaning against doorways, and the room became alive with music and tapping feet and the beats of our percussions.

We could have been in an Irish country house, it was such a familiar warming environment of hospitality. The atmosphere, designed by Ian and Maggy, radiated a synchronised harmony. It was slowly dawning on me that here was Santa Claus in his ruffled tucked-in shirt and blue jeans presenting us with gifts of goodwill and good cheer. And Mrs Claus nestled in among her staff, sang in Chilean Spanish the words to 'The Black Lady'. On and on the tunes continued. The band was excellent, whether playing traditional Chilean pieces or even singing lively versions of Elvis songs or Creedance Clearwater Revival. In this wonderful mix of cultures and peoples, Wally took out his guitar and played a sad American Civil War ballad. Nancy sang 'Killing me Softly'. Juan, Antonio's brother who was married to Alicia, appeared fully dressed in traditional costume, and a woman named Margarita came out of the kitchen in bolero and black hat with her heels clacking and her arms upturned. The traditional dance, the Cueca, complete with much gesturing of a bandana and fiercely passionate Latin looks, was played out with Juan who looked a bit nervous.

Finally, Deirdre took out her silver flute and began to play Bach with grace and elegance, a kind of cool beauty that stunned and silenced the Chilean boys. As I watched her, following the Bach with a haunting Irish air, I thought of how you cannot know when such moments will occur on a journey like this. You cannot know what will happen and that suddenly there before you, thousands of miles from home, your children will flower right in front of you. I didn't even know then of all the wonderful moments that would follow in our days in Fundo Chaciapulli: of days spent horse riding in Chilean meadows; of Deirdre becoming quite a natural rider under Maggy's encouragement; of the overnight river-rafting trip with Nancy and Wally clinging onto Joseph into the back of the raft as we plunged into a 'hole' in the river after a class IV rapid; of the hilarious football match Ian organised between the 'staff' and the guests in the cow field where the Chileans got to show off their far superior skills and Ian himself, the patron, would spin on a through ball and land spectacularly in a cow pat; of the New Year's Eve barbecue and the return of the Chilean band when Alonso would slip into the kitchen with Maggy in an attempt to learn the words of Elvis's 'Love Me Tender' to sing to Deirdre. All of this was still ahead. But we both knew right then that this was indeed a special time, that here was a warmth of companionship and caring, a gathering on a Christmas night that would form a very special memory for all of us. It was for moments like this that we had thrown caution to the wind and uprooted ourselves for nearly a year to travel and see a bit of the world.

Well after midnight, with the music reaching its end, encouraged by Maggy and offered a private warm-up session in the back bedroom, Joseph finally brought his fiddle into the centre of the room. He took up his stance and the audience watched and waited. Out came the first shaky notes of the fiddle tune 'Home Ruler' that he had learned from Seán MacNamara, of the Liverpool Céilí Band the previous summer at the Willie Clancy School in Miltown Malbay. After a few notes, he found his rhythm. And soon there he was, in the centre of a farmhouse in Chile, deep into Christmas night, playing 'The Cameronian', 'The Rights of Man', reels and jigs from the west of Ireland. The feet were tapping and the eyes of all were smiling, a happy, merry Christmas.

New Zealand

Four months of travelling, heading to our ninth country, checking five and sometimes six bags, carrying on another seven in hand luggage between the fiddle, camera bag, two laptops, Deirdre and Joseph's backpacks as well as my own leather satchel with the essential oils that our Tiberon friends had given us in California. In all that time not a single thing had gone astray. At the Santiago check-in desk at Lan Chile we watched as the lively baggage clerk tagged all six of our bags. Deirdre had carefully labelled everything. The conveyor belt stopped and started worryingly but eventually relinquished our bags into its dark mouth.

'Feeling better?' I asked Niall, rather impishly, knowing what he would say.

'Yes, much,' he responded. 'I can relax now that the bags are gone.' He looked at me in that quiet way of his. It was easy for me not to get too excited about these transfers as Niall orchestrated most of it. He also bore the responsibility of the bum bag which carried our bulky tickets for the nine months, and our money, passports, licences, and a copy of our marriage certificate should I need to declare myself as married to an Irish citizen. (You never know when you might want to be someone else, as in *not* American, or when it might be beneficial for Niall and the kids to be *attached* to an American.)

'Sorry,' I said, 'if I was making fun. You are doing a terrific job and I really do appreciate it. But don't worry so much about it. We'll get there.'

The 'transfers' as he called them, were the only dreaded parts of the journey. Packing all our gear, stuffing our growing stuff into our bags that seemed to shrink after each arrived-at destination, and loading ourselves back again like a small army into a mini-van: it was a major accomplishment. Transporting us from airport to hotel to airport tested Niall's reserve each time, each time taking a little bit more out of him. It never got easier. In fact, it was getting downright tiresome. But he soldiered on, a weary yet noble captain.

We had tried several times to unload stuff and kept sending boxes by Fed Ex home to Ireland, but with the multiple climates that we planned to encounter over nine months, we seemed to need everything we had. Deirdre, admittedly a shopaholic and proud of it, wanted to buy one of everything we saw. But to give her her due, if it wasn't for her we probably wouldn't have bought many of the treasures we will be thankful for in years to come. The handwoven, butterfly blanket from the Pisac market, the gaucho hat in Santiago, the carved, wooden Dutch-like clog stirrups from our horse-riding escapades in Los Lagos, the panpipes in Cusco and the gold Inca charm in La Paz. The list was precious and growing and it *all* had to be sent home.

'Well, there you go now, all the bags have gone peacefully forward. Soon to be digested by the machine and spurted out on the other side,' I said grinning.

'We can only hope,' Niall replied. 'Let's go. Another continent awaits.' He rechecked his bum bag, making sure the tickets and passports and boarding cards were all there. Plus, the phone, his wallet, telephone numbers and a pen. I picked up my laptop bag and led the way.

Getting out of Chile was harder than getting in. We waited in a long queue that saw an entire Chilean family squeeze in ahead of us, late for a plane, involving long goodbyes from their granny. We had plenty of time as Niall insisted that we always leave extra. What's another hour? Better there than late, he said. The Chilean officials examined each passport holder leaving the country long and hard, especially Chilean passengers. There is still a slight air of secrecy around. As we headed with our carry-ons to the X-ray security checkpoint, the floor started vibrating. I looked into the duty-free shop and the streamers advertising items were waving like flags in a strong breeze. I imagined it was a large plane taking off nearby. The clerks about us were clearly unperturbed. As we sat down beside a sporty-looking Australian lady from Melbourne in a white tennis polo shirt, she remarked,

'Did you feel it? The tremor?'

'Really?' Joseph asked in amazement. 'Was that an earthquake?'

'Yes, it was. Not such a bad one however. Or they would have turned off the lights.'

Much to my surprise Joseph declared, 'Cool. My first earthquake!'

And there I was thinking he'd be jumping up and down trying to stay off the ground – just when I thought I was getting to know him inside and out. I was glad we were at the airport because we had seen what an earthquake can do when we were in Fundo Chacaipulli the previous week, where years earlier one had caused the land to shift thirty to forty feet, resulting in what is known as a rift valley. We quietly waited for the boarding announcement. Joseph meanwhile struck up a conversation with the lady from Melbourne, who was a teacher. She was separated from her Chilean husband and had been living in Chile for the past twenty years. I wondered why she hadn't gone back to Australia. 'Yes,' she consented, 'I *am* lonesome for my family in Melbourne, but this is my home. My children are here.' I knew what she meant, lonesome for New York but living in Ireland…

Fourteen hours later at half four in the morning, 8 January 2003, we arrived in Auckland after a surprisingly easy flight (helped by the most unhomeopathic of aids, a 10-mg sleeping tablet, yielding five hours of uninterrupted dozing). We had missed the 7th of January completely. Forever gone. Felt a bit weird. We left Santiago close to midnight on the 6th and arrived on the 8th, crossing the international date line after about ten hours of flying across the Pacific. The kids loved the idea. I think from now on I can say that I feel a day younger than I look, or I look a day younger than I am, or something like that. We were so pleased with ourselves having survived the fourteen-hour flight that we took no notice at first that our bags were slow to come out. Airport dogs were everywhere, trained at sniffing for banned food items and plant materials, which the Kiwis are exceedingly vigilant at keeping out. They checked over more than once the bagels and muffins that Deirdre had bought from New York Bagel in Santiago (where inside the front door is a letter from Bill Clinton who seemingly also enjoyed their bagels when he was in Santiago a few years earlier). Five in the morning, bagel in hand, Deirdre watched as the bags eventually appeared. One, two, three, four, five bags... *Where was the sixth and final bag?* Our best bag, the Karimor we bought in London, was missing.

It's become a thing in our family that if something is going to happen, it's going to happen to me. I have that kind of luck. We all know it. Don't ask me to pick a queue to stand in, for it's sure to be the longest. *I* got Altitude sickness, *I* got Bolivian Belly, and now this: Lost Luggage. (At least I had skipped a few letters in the alphabet.) I like to think that rather than being jinxed, I have subconsciously contracted with my maker that I will take on the pitfalls of travelling so that my children and husband won't have to. It was after all mostly my idea to take this trip in the first place and it was up to me to pay the piper if payback were due. Bleary-eyed, I gave the lost-baggage attendant the details and we emerged to a prearranged driver who, miraculously, was still waiting for us. It was nearly six in the morning. Niall had arranged with his publishers in New Zealand, Macmillan, to help us plan the first few days. A very friendly New Zealander named Vanessa had arranged for the transfer and booked us into a hotel across the city of Auckland with a most magnificent view of the Sky Tower and the harbour. Because it was still so close to Christmas, the tower was lit up in blues and reds and could be seen from miles away, like a space-age building in a *Star Trek* film.

We drove from the airport under threatening grey skies. Rain was falling. We were tired and I was mulling over all that was in my bag, which, not to put too fine a point on it, was everything. Now I wished I had half my stuff still in Niall's bag. I had only the clothes I was wearing.

All that day in Auckland it rained – enough, the news channel said, over a twenty-four hour period for a whole month. The tail end of a cyclone in the Pacific was sweeping across the North Island of New Zealand. It was an unwelcome greeting for us. We had left behind unerringly blue skies and ninety-degree weather in Santiago. But yet, someone was happy. Was that the English language, although Kiwi style, that Joseph was hearing?

'Good on ya, full on, eh?'

By the time we reached the hotel, the watery morning had brightened somewhat and we decided to risk our reserves and stay awake until nightfall. The jet-lag part of travelling is best met head on. Let that ol' pituitary gland see the light of day and reset the clock. We headed into the city after breakfast. It was only half seven in the morning. The day seemed to drag on endlessly and we walked in a daze for hours, without raincoats, checking the clock, and wishing for nightfall. Joseph and I managed a trip up to the Sky Tower, the tallest building in New Zealand and the whole southern hemisphere for that matter, and he seemed to come alive for awhile. Sections of the floor are made of glass. To walk across them nearly 400 metres above the traffic was rather terrifying. Talk about vertigo. Joseph jumped up and down on the glass displaying his bravery. Unfortunately, the rain and grey skies veiled any sense of that wonderful Auckland harbour below with its sailboats and yachts and islands in the gulf that was preparing for the trials for the Americas Cup. After lunch, we hopped on a bus tour of the city, partly to pass the time and partly to see what sights piqued our interest enough to trigger a second look. It was still raining. We disembarked too early for Parnell Village, the upscale boutique and speciality shopping area of Auckland, and found ourselves scurrying along rain-heavy Parnell Street like coatless waifs in need of a good ol' cup of tea. The rain had made us not only wet but cold and, after a dip into a few shops, we hailed a taxi and sailed back to the hotel across the Auckland Harbour Bridge. So much for the city. Nothing had really inspired us for a second visit, and the rain had once again confirmed how important weather was in affecting the pros and cons of a destination. Our first impression of New Zealand wasn't as impressive as the photographs or postcards of Auckland that showed it as a city of sparkling sunlight on the harbour, with thousands of glistening white sails, where iridescent water laps against the dock and yachts bob gently. More boats per capita than any city in the world. Even the Sky Tower, silver and glinting, looks like a giant sail mast towering above the city. But so far the City of Sails failed to enthuse us.

~

New Zealand is like Ireland in many ways, a smallish country, inhabited by around four million, green and friendly. Rugby. Rain. In great contrast to Dublin, however, a bustling, lively city, we found in Auckland a laid-back Northern California-like mindset. Here was casualness taken to the extreme. One couldn't help but notice how sportily the Aucklanders took the weather we were encountering. Shorts and T-shirts and sandal-footed they walked about carefree. Dubliners would be grumbling in their winter coats. A surprising number of New Zealanders walk around barefoot, even in Auckland in the rain. There were very few suits, yet every sort of short pants you could imagine. The immediate feel was of a city that was at ease with itself, not trying to be anything other than it was. Or was it something else? Was it complacency, a kind of what-the-hell-does-it-matter attitude? New Zealand is the most isolated country in the world. Joseph was discussing this with Stephen and Jane Burn, the owners of the Island Guesthouse that we were renting for a week and to where we moved just two days after arriving in Auckland.

'Yeah,' Joseph said, 'people think that New Zealand and Australia are right next to each other. But it's actually the same distance as Dublin to Moscow.' Out came the maps and the ruler and they measured. Joseph, naturally, was right. Stephen laughed,

'Good on ya, Joseph!'

The Island Guesthouse is nestled in a forest of tea trees and New Zealand vegetation at the bottom of a plum-strewn sloping garden and was typical of what the Kiwis call a bach, a beach house or holiday house with a simple box-like construction of wood and treated corrugated-iron siding. Blue agapanthus was in bloom everywhere, like wildflowers. Stephen said they had become a nuisance. The sound of the unseen sea filtered through the leaves to the wooden deck of the bach.

Whether it was the Auckland rainwalk or a feeling of letting down our reserves once we had left the South American continent, within a day of settling in at Stephen and Jane's, sore throats, colds and flu symptoms invaded us like we were defenceless prey. We were completely vulnerable. And the mozzies were eating Deirdre alive. For the first four days of our stay on Waiheke Island – a beautiful island in the Hauraki Gulf, a forty-five-minute ferry ride from Auckland – we succumbed to our bodies' processes of healing. Niall stayed in bed one full day dozing, sipping tea and Collidial silver, and taking Echinacea, Vitamin C, aspirin and ImmnoMax tablets. He felt like a hammer had hit him in all his joints. I gave him *Euporeum Perforatum*, a homeopathic remedy, and by morning he was much improved. South America had taken a bigger chunk out of us than we had realised. It was as if we knew it was safe now to let our bodies catch up with us. First they had to let go of some unnecessary baggage. Quickly surrendering to the relaxed, easy pace of summer in Waiheke, letting our tiredness and jet lag drain away, we didn't want to move. It was as comfortable a place to convalesce as we could have hoped for and our hosts became immediate friends. I had found The Island Guesthouse on the Internet and corresponded with Stephen off and on for half a year. (It was another one of those times where we were really looking forward to meeting the person behind the email and another one of those times where we weren't disappointed.) Stephen and Jane suggested we stay a few extra days. (One couple the previous year, on a similar adventure to ours, liked it so much they stayed three months, Jane told us.) It was tempting for us to consider the same. Here was where our scheduled itinerary could become a millstone. 'Couldn't we at least stay an extra week in New Zealand?' I asked Niall.

Next to Bolivia, New Zealand had been high on my list of places to visit in the world. (I was sure to have better luck in the land of the long white cloud.) We were sitting on the deck of Stephen and Jane's house overlooking the sea and the sailboats, sipping some of their freshly brewed Island coffee and talking about the South Pacific.

Jane said, 'Oh, you've got to go to Rarotonga. It's so-ooo beautiful!'

Deirdre looked at me. 'Roara-what?' She laughs at herself now, for compared with Joseph who is a geographic whiz kid, she sometimes hasn't a clue where on the globe somewhere is. Mind you, she got an A in geography in her junior certificate examination last summer, but she puts that down to hard work rather than global awareness.

'Where is that?' she asked, unmoved by Joseph's snickering. Her blueberry-coloured eyes widening at the thought of more sun and sand.

'It's the capital of the Cook Islands,' Jane, one of those gorgeous, blond-haired, tanned Kiwis, replied smiling. Jane had been a model in her twenties and at thirty-five still exuded a healthy sporty look that I envied. She wore a sarong or jeans most days with one of her own Island Coffee T-shirts that she designed. For along with being a coffee roaster she was also an artist. And the icing on the cake was that she was straightforward and friendly. I could see that we would have been friends if our lives had turned out geographically amenable. New Zealanders talk about having been to the South Pacific Islands like Europeans talk about having visited Paris or London or Venice. Kiwis have been to Fiji, the Cook Islands, Tahiti – locations in the South Pacific that New Yorkers dream of, ending up in the Caribbean while Dubliners end up in Spain or the Canaries.

We got out the map and looked west of New Zealand into the mighty Pacific.

'There.' Stephen pointed out to Deirdre, his head, with its sand-, sun- and salt-bleached hair looking like he just stepped away from a photo shoot for *Surfer Magazine*, bent over the table. A collector of maps, he was on the ready for any 'Where in the World?' question we might ask. I could see that Niall was not taking the bait. Having an itinerary was a kind of safety net. He had survived South America and I could tell he was secretly shoring up for China. Joseph had asked a number of times if we really had to go to China. Even I was feeling shy of it. Deirdre was the only one still keen.

'We *have* to go to China. We've been planning it all year. What will Jeffrey think if we give up? I'm going anyway!' she said.

Niall and I took a walk down in the early evening to one of the dozens of coves of Waiheke. Long shadows lay like puddles of cool, green air. I was in one of my 'I could live here forever' humours, a frame of mind that descends over me like a good glass of merlot and colours my thinking. It happened in Bainbridge Island in Puget Sound off the coast of Seattle a few summers ago. It happened near Amagansett. It happened in Mendocino in Northern California. It nearly happened in Canon Beach in Oregon and it happened in Belvedere on the edge of Tiberon across the San Francisco Bay. Now it was happening again on Waiheke. Instead of moving, couldn't we stay at least a week longer? And what about Rarotonga, hey? Good on ya. We've got heaps of time. Full on!

I took a seashell and drew a large square in the sand with lines across and down until I had sixteen smaller squares, each representing sixteen weeks, four more months of travelling, which we would still have at the end of January. According to the itinerary, at the start of February we were due in Sydney. The sand calendar went something like this: five clam shells for five squares/weeks in Australia, two razor shells for Bali, three large grey pebbles for China, four leaves for France, two bottle tops for the two free weeks that had previously been earmarked for Vietnam, and two empty squares, which I quickly filled with a piece of seaweed, representing the extra week in New Zealand and a sea sponge for a week in the Cook Islands. Eighteen weeks. Two too many.

'I think thirteen days is too long to stay in Perth, Niall,' I said. 'And we could shorten Bali by a few days as we are still unsure about travelling there anyway. And,' I continued excitedly, moving my tokens around on the sand like a child with a game board, 'we could go back to our original plan of two weeks in China and only three or four days in Hong Kong. What do you think?'

Niall looked at me, I could see the tokens adding up in his eyes like symbols on a slot machine. He was dizzy with my calculations and permutations.

'Yes, it might be do-able,' he said nodding his head and fingering the seashells.

'See, by my calculations, by spending less time in western Australia, Bali and China, we gain another two weeks. We could still go to Central Europe, perhaps, in exchange for the two weeks we had earmarked for Vietnam.'

He grabbed my hand.

'C'mon,' he said. 'The kids will be wondering where we are.' But I could see he was ruminating and, as I looked back, a seagull had landed and was tiptoeing across my sand-board. It was looking good. Deirdre would be delighted. I went directly on line to see what New Zealand Airlines had to offer. I was happier that Niall had agreed in theory about an extra week in New Zealand, but was still needling him to consider moving to Waiheke, if not forever, for a year anyway.

We were back in the groove and, although stationary, looking ahead to continued travels. I went ahead and booked the South Island after Jane and Stephen said we could stay another few days. The following week would see us flying from Rotarua, the centre of the North Island, to Nelson on the South Island, then driving down the west coast alongside the Southern Alps, ending up in Queenstown. We could decide later where in New Zealand we would stay for the extra week. Rarotonga in the Cook Islands would have to be booked soon if we were going to do it. Not in its favour, however, was the news that evening that another storm in the Pacific, Cyclone Anne, had just hit Fiji with winds of 185 miles per hour. Two weeks instead of one in New Zealand would be icing on the cake for me. Kiwiland is, after all, an island in the South Pacific, isn't it? I would ask Joseph and he would later respond, 'No, Mum, it's several islands in the South Pacific!'

It occurred to me that it was the first time we had deviated from the planned itinerary, and it felt good. Brave and bold. Making plans for the South Island was accomplished in a just a few emails and the itinerary came together with the help of Terry, the owner of boutique lodging in Queenstown called Pear Tree Cottage. We'd make up the rest of the month as we went along. The relaxed atmosphere of the Kiwis was having a good effect on us. Even Niall felt completely relaxed and settled into a period of steady writing. Every morning on Waiheke he wrote. He was in good form. For a writer to stray too far from the work requires a tremendous effort to get it rolling again, a bit like restarting a steam engine. We left him alone and hoped that he was chugging forward once the inevitable retracing of his steps had made clear his route. When we heard him murmuring the words as he was writing, we knew all was well. He was navigating the rapids.

We awoke in the guesthouse, which was surrounded by trees. Only the white or blue sky above us told us whether the sun was shining. Through a veil of ti tree branches, New Zealand tree ferns and banana trees, I could just about make out the ocean. I wished the view wasn't masked by the bush, but Stephen said you couldn't cut anything down, it had to fall down first. A path wound its way through the bush past our door down to a pebbled beach. It was secluded and rarely visited. The bach itself was small yet perfect. Jane had decorated it in browns and blacks and chrome inside its totally white interior. Creative floral arrangements decorated every room. On the long black table where we had our meals stood a high vase with wide green flax leaves that looped back into the vase with tall purple flowers in the centre. Very minimalistic. Very chic. Plainly *not* cottage-y, which was a relief to Joseph and Deirdre who both agreed that's how they wanted *their* houses when they grew up. Our accommodation looked like the pictures you see of New Zealand in house and garden magazines. We felt so peaceful and relaxed and seemed to settle into the pace quickly. Niall and Joseph swam nearly every day. Deirdre joined them when she wasn't sunbathing. But even when we weren't swimming it felt like we were sort of 'beached' on Waiheke like some large ocean animal resting ashore in the sunshine.

Waiheke was originally home to Aucklanders who were not well-off. They moved to the island because it was cheaper. It was not a desirable address then, but now it is thriving. Wineries have sprouted all over the island and host a wine and jazz festival every February. Artists have also made their homes here, making the island one of the most chic addresses in the whole of the North Island. Between tours of the wineries' testing rooms and hiking the dozens of walking trails, I thought I had found a paradise. Everywhere we went on the island we could see the sea.

Meanwhile, we were still awaiting the arrival of my bag that had gone walkabout. Turns out it went to Sydney and was picked up for another Williams, probably by a tour company operator, and sent directly to a hotel where another Williams was disappointed, I imagine. The good people in Sydney returned the bag to Auckland and my suitcase was located after about a week that had seen me wearing the same clothes day in and day out. I hadn't bought anything new except some underwear, one red sleeveless top and a pair of black Capri trousers. I don't have the sort of body for which I can easily buy off the rack and I hum and haw over the rare purchases I do make. My mother was fond of calling me a ragamuffin and, try as I might, I always seem to be out of step with the fashion, not to mention being a stone overweight. My daughter, on the other hand, takes good care of herself and has developed a style and sense of fashion that I envy. She has a slim figure, looks well in anything, and loves shopping – qualities that my mother passed on to her, I think. It was a joke between us that it was *my* bag and not hers that went missing because she would have delighted in having to buy a whole new wardrobe. But for me it was a different story. And, another year was going by before my eyes when those ten pounds I had promised myself I would lose were quickly turning into fifteen, which prevented me from buying clothes because inevitably they fit in some places and didn't fit in others. Trying on ill-fitting clothes only depressed me. The Bolivian Belly Bug had left me ten pounds lighter, but thanks to Maggy and Ian's hospitality in Fundo Chacuipulli, I had successfully regained every ounce. Deirdre took it as a message from the cosmos that here was my opportunity to discard my rags and buy anew. Could I do it? She was only dying to help me. The gauntlet was thrown down, but when I didn't pick it up it vanished. My bag was returned with all my old favourites and worn-in clothes and I had missed the bus, completely. I couldn't let go of my stuff. I was too attached to my things and to the clothes that camouflaged me. I wasn't ready to break from my safety net of the idea I had of myself – my props – even though I fully intend to. Even though I knew there was a freer self below the surface and I could sense her seeping up through my pores, whispering words to me as I wrote. My mother said to me before she died that I should try to do one thing instead of several. Would I learn that the strength I needed to complete the tasks I had set for myself was of superwoman proportion? And when did perfecting my figure before I turned fifty get on the agenda anyway? I still had a year to go before I would return to Ireland to de-size. Give yourself a break, girlfriend. Because if you don't, don't expect anyone else to.

~

We stayed about ten days at the Island Guesthouse and agreed to come back for another few days after our tour of the South Island. Stephen and Jane wanted us to come back and held some of our luggage for us. They said they'd keep the coffee hot until our return. We took the ferry to Auckland, rented a Honda CRV from Avis and headed to Rotarua which Joseph was desperate to see. He wanted to understand more about the Maoris and to visit the sulfur mud baths there. However, it turned out to be a bit of a disappointment. Under sixteens weren't allowed in the mud baths or the hot sulphur baths. We contented ourselves with a family indoor spa pool for four in the famous Polynesian Spa. Nothing can compare with the geothermal activity of Yellowstone that we had already seen. But ours is a democracy in the Breen Williams family and there were two things Joseph really wanted to do: go to Rotorua and go to Uluru. (I think he has sympathy with the Maoris and the Aboriginal people because of the injustice done to them and so in order that he could make up his own mind about the current state of affairs of the indigenous people of these two great islands we were happy to grant him his wish.)

We visited the Interpretive Centre where we were taken on a tour by a very proud Maori guide and shown traditional crafts and the meeting house with the large wooden carved entrance and an original long wooden war boat. We were a few minutes late and missed the traditional welcome of nose-rubbing, about which I think Joseph was secretly delighted. It's a very interesting time in New Zealand at present, with the Maoris demanding that the government return most of the land to them, declaring that the original fathers were tricked into the treaty by the British. Time will tell how the Kiwis handle this, but much like what has been happening in Australia, where land is being returned to the Aboriginals, the English translations of Maori names are being changed back to the original pronunciation. Whakarewaerewa is Ta-fouck-erru-a-rua, confusing a lot of the older New Zealanders. Finn and Jane and Tom began to teach Joseph how to sing the national anthem in Maori, a thing young Kiwis learn now in school in an attempt to reconcile the two cultures, and which some older Kiwis find threatening. We stayed two nights in Rotorua. Rather than driving and ferrying across to the South Island we bought tickets on Air New Zealand and boarded a plane painted with a scene from *The Lord of the Rings*.

Our first two nights on the South Island were spent at a lovely B&B in Nelson, a creative seaside haven of painters, potters, jewellers, knitters, and ceramic artists. We could have easily stayed a week. We didn't make it out to the Abel Tasman Park, a stretch of golden sand that takes a few days to hike between the tides. But as Niall was probably tiring of reminding me, 'we can't do and see everything.' The people we met were friendly, and we noted many non-Kiwis who had moved here for the climate and atmosphere. It struck me as that kind of place, a bit like south-west Cork in Ireland – not that people moved to Ireland for the weather, but the fishing, food and art is great and the scenery is superb.

Deirdre had a bit of an epiphany after visiting the Museum of Wearable Art in Nelson, a funky, avant-garde museum and probably the only one of its kind in the world, filled with the most creative use of objects-turned-clothes, like feather dresses, tin-cup bras, cellophane pants. Those were just the basics. Dresses made around a tea-party theme. Dresses that moved on wheels. Bras made from every imaginable thing – from fish fins to parrot heads. I watched her look at everything in the same way I would look at flowers in a garden. She was delighted and sensed a place inside her that resonated. This was later reinforced after a stop in a boutique in Nelson selling a creative range of stylish handbags and jewellery.

'Mum,' she said as we stood inside the tiny shop eyeing a silver neck choker that dropped at the neck with a paua shell, 'I know what I want to do when I finish school.'

'What's that?' I said, anticipating her answer.

'I want to do design. I want to *be* a designer.'

I had known for some time that she had a penchant for putting things together and that she enjoyed it. She just has a knack for it. Every since she was a toddler and could use a scissors she had been making cards and paper things. She has a keen sense of what goes well together, whether it's clothes, food, furniture, or accessories. She has that sixth sense.

'Well done, sweetheart. More power to the woman who knows what she wants.' I could see she was pleased with herself and I was pleased for her. I always regretted that art was not something that was fostered in my childhood and I was thrilled that it was now an option for Deirdre. Guiding her through this time by my, sometimes obtrusive, hand was part of our entire experience that year. Watching her unfolding during her fifteenth year and being alert to her blossoming talents, to her strong and weak points, was one of the highlights of the trip for me. That time will never come again. We both knew it. It was like a secret we shared that needed no discussion. I felt we'd both be ready when she returned to Ireland to spend the next two years shepherding her gifts towards college. I couldn't help but be reminded of Tom-Tom, Jane and Stephen's two-year-old who days before was jumping on the white couch, naked and headfirst, and shouting *à la* Buzz Lightyear, 'to imfimity and b'yongd!'

~

You can't talk, write, or think about New Zealand now without referring to *The Lord of the Rings*. As Niall observed one day, 'I think *The Lord of the Rings* was only waiting for a New Zealander to turn it into a film.' We were driving down the southern part of the South Island. Like they said about the actor who played Forrest Gump, 'Tom Hanks *is* Forrest Gump', well, New Zealand *is* Middle

Earth. Lonely Planet's latest poll says New Zealand is the number one holiday destination. It's easy to see why. It has everything. Landscape ranging from mountains and lakes to islands and oceans. From vineyards and rolling hills with rounded crests to volcanic peaks. Beneath it all is the Maori culture whose roots reveal a time before Europeans where the virginal beauty of 'the island of the long white cloud' was uncontaminated by explorers and invaders for 500 years. The air is infused with a mist-like wistfulness especially when the summer light stitches golden rays across the land. It's a photographer's playground. We ourselves had shot about ten rolls of film in New Zealand alone. We put on the soundtrack of *The Lord of the Rings* and drove.

In fact, everything about New Zealand seduced us. We hit it during a good stretch of weather and to me it seemed like it was Over the Rainbow. From around the pointed topped hills rising suddenly from a meadow I expected to see Frodo or else the Munchkins. The South Island turned out to be as beautiful as anything we had seen so far on the trip. It even rivalled Patagonia in places, with Mt Cook rising 3,500 metres into a blue sky. We visited one of the glaciers there and walked along the river bed to where the melting ice met the grey, stoney bed. It was disappearing by 100 metres a year. Like the water in parts of southern Chile the colour of the rivers near the Southern Alps was an astonishing milky blue-green.

We arrived in Queenstown after a few days driving down the west coast of the South Island, stopping at Westport and Punakaiki with its famous Pancake Rocks looking like hundreds of flat, grey pancakes piled in towers toward the sky and its mile-long beach with fiercely rolling, crashing waves and white foam. The sea wasn't forgiving there. The waves rolling in were powerful. We counted twelve rows of breakers. The roar from the ocean reverberated against the stone mountains and was deafening. It nearly sucked out all your energy to contend with it – talk about breathtaking.

Dear D,

Hello from the South Island of New Zealand. Just wonderful now. Kids are great. Joseph too wants to live here. Got a gold Lord of the Rings *ring the other day in Nelson, where it turns out Peter*

Jackson, the director, first spotted it in a jeweller's. We saw the original. A good bit of the film was made here. It's everything I imagined it would be. It's like Napa Valley, Tuscany, Montana, Donegal rolled into one. Cool, hey? Tell Daniel we went to the place where bungy jumping first started. Tell Larry that Joseph and I went on a wine tour of Gibbston Valley Winery. He really liked their Blanc de Pinot Noir! Tell Julia that Deirdre and I went horse riding for two hours on a 450-acre deer farm. Will you consider moving here with me? Sell the business and buy a winery!
Love, C

We arrived to Pear Tree Cottage in Queenstown in the early evening just as the light crept across the land, casting pinkish violet hues. The surrounding hills and mountains reminded me of Sun Valley in Idaho. In our accommodation we had gone from one extreme to another. Here was a wooden cottage covered in roses and flowers of every description. Petunias hanging out of a rusted old bathtub. White geraniums in baskets. An old bicycle stood artily against a tree. If you can picture the kind of arrangement that the old woman who lived in a shoe must have had, then this is it. I mean this in the best possible way. Instead of children spilling from every lacehole and busted seam there were flowers. Joseph declared he had had the best sleep in the best bed so far on the trip for the four nights we stayed at Pear Tree. We were told that the actor, Sam Neill, had a house across the valley high up on the Coronet Mountains. Inside the house was like a museum for every kind of household item, past and present, arranged in themes. In the twin-bedded room Deirdre and Joseph slept in, a music stand stood with sheet music open. A few old electric guitars rested against the scores and old sheet music wallpapered walls. In the bathroom with its copper flush tank was an old gas mask at the ready. I imagine guests have fun trying to find something they don't have. Every imaginable object had its place: from hot-water bottles to pin cushions, from old irons to bedpans, from a bicycle pump to an old-fashioned coffee grinder. It was something they prided themselves on.

We agreed that when we return again to New Zealand we will head directly down to Queenstown, after a brief stop at Waiheke and the

Northern Beaches, and explore Milford and Doubtful Sound. Five days wasn't nearly enough. Queenstown is sometimes called the adventure capital of the world and it was easy to see why. Every kind of adventure sport is available, some I've never heard of. There was Zorp, where you roll downhill in a giant ball and luge-mobiles zipping at breakneck speed around hairpin corners. There were jet-boat rides on the Shotover River that whizz past outcropping cliffs to within inches of your body. New Zealanders have a thirst for adventure sport that is second to none and goes with their devil-may-care attitude. But what attracted us was none of these. It was the incredible beauty of the landscape. Fewer than one million people call the South Island their home and it's a well-kept secret. Walking out by the guesthouse in the falling evening, with the green hills turning golden, Niall said: 'It's easy to imagine people arrive here and never leave.'

I took his hand.

~

Deirdre said to me one day after we had arrived back in Waiheke, 'You know I haven't talked to anyone my age for months!' She was right. When I considered what she had said I realised that she had not met a single person her own age since we had left California. Joseph also turned to me one day and said, 'I wouldn't mind going home now. I want to go to school.' The children wanted the habit of their lives back. They wanted friends to talk to, routines that shaped their days for them. All this with the sun shining for endless days. In the end, we had opted for two extra weeks in New Zealand. Rarotonga had been eclipsed due to hot, sticky humid weather and cyclones, not to mention exorbitant airfare. After a few days, we rented another house near Palm Beach in Waiheke because Stephen and Jane had visitors already booked in. We found ourselves there for ten more days in an eco-friendly house of wood and cotton. The sun was still shining, the ocean a few hundred yards away from the house. A sloping cliff, like a green cutout against a blue canvas of sky painted with unhurried puffs of cloud, slipped into the sea. Boats reflecting the sun floated by like white birds in the distance. Cicadas sang in the ti trees and agapanthus blossoms coloured the paths like blue confetti thrown by well-wishers at a wedding march. Peaches dropped from a tree at the top of the driveway.

As I walked along the beach one evening I watched the twilight touch the blue liquid colour of the sea in a thousand places, stippling it with black diamonds. Infant-white sails tossed and tipped above the horizon line. My bare feet skimmed across the velvet sand. Amber, black and gold patterned ripples like scallop shells shimmered beneath the thin film of outgoing tide. I was lost in a moment that I didn't want to end. Sometimes a moment is so perfect you think to yourself 'I could die happy this very instant'. Thankfully, the good Lord had other plans for me...

Niall and I were both able to find peaceful time for writing, and sat each morning facing the ocean which we could see from the windowed walls of our rented paradise. I had finally settled into the fact that I was writing a book after all – about our travels together in the world during a year of our lives. It was more than a mouthful. It was a three-course dinner. There were our travels, the world, and our lives. My laptop told me I had accumulated over a hundred pages. It both thrilled and terrified me. The path of my future might be veering before my very eyes. Suddenly I was saying something. And even if no one else was listening, *I was listening*. I could see myself say things – words appeared from beneath my fingers on the computerised page in front of me. *Voilà*! From a blank, white space communication materialised. I found I enjoyed the simple act of making words come together in sentences. A bit like gardening, lining up the perennials along the path that leads down to the weeping pear tree. First comes the small white and grey cerastium, maybe some purple veronica, followed by Pacific Giant delphiniums. Finding just the right word was like planting an anchusa if you were lucky enough to find it in the garden centre. At times, the writing process for me *is* a bit like gardening with words. Other times I feel like I am painting with words. The sheer organisation of my thoughts has the power to comfort and inspire me and something from deep within me communicates. Talk about being with yourself in the moment. Here I was: me giving and me receiving. Deirdre and Joseph leaned over my shoulders now and again and read patches. 'Hey, that's good, Mum. That sounds a bit like Bill Bryson,' said Joseph in amazement. 'Yeah, I can't wait to read it,

Mum,' Deirdre added. Niall said, 'Send it to Marianne when we get to Australia.' Marianne is a great friend and Niall's wonderful agent. That was good enough for me.

~

Contending with sunshine day after day isn't as easy as you think. At times, even in this paradise, we were getting a bit blasé. I thought about our lives in Ireland where we were conditioned to a kind of survival against the elements that could sometimes make a journey to the village for a carton of milk an event, whether it was racing to the car through the rain, stopping for Downes' cows to squeeze past on their way to the field, chatting with Mary Breen, or giving Mrs McMahon a lift to the village. When a blue day comes our way, it is like a gift for work well done. A reward. It takes some getting used to, this sun shining nearly every day. What was the reward for? Living? Now there's an interesting idea.

Deirdre and Joseph had to find things to do; they could sit on the beach for only so long. The Waihekians had gone back to school. Joseph had read *To Kill a Mockingbird* and *Catcher in the Rye*, which is more than you can ask of any eleven-year-old and was now into his fourth or fifth Bill Bryson travel book. Niall sat down with him on an irregular basis to dip into his sixth-class maths book and his Irish book, but as parents we didn't expect them to do homework really. The experience of the world trip was enough. If he ended up being behind in maths or Irish when he started secondary school, we knew he wouldn't be long catching up. When he wasn't reading, Joseph drew at a small desk in his bedroom from where he could see the Kiwi bush rising in a green mishmash of palm trees and ti trees with its tropical scents of underbrush like the scent of Costa Rica. Deirdre practised her flute a bit and, as she had no real studies to attend to with her classmates in Kilmihil free from academics for a year, we let her learn other things. She now made lunch almost every day for us and tidied up the dishes. She was also writing in a journal from which she prepared a few articles for an Irish teen magazine called *Face Up*. Deirdre was also crocheting a skirt of creamy-coloured sheep's wool that she had bought in Nelson. Her determination was admirable. I was watching her moving closer and closer to choosing a path for her future. She could do nearly anything she put her mind *and* her hand to.

We left the kids one night playing with two black kittens that had come with the rental, and their mother, and headed over to Stephen and Jane's. They were up, as usual for them in the summer, roasting coffee late into the night in the tiny shed attached to their house with its two red and chrome Turkish roasting machines. We sat on hessian sacks and helped them label bags for the farmers' market in the morning – the smell of freshly roasted coffee our fifth companion.

'What made you decide to get into the coffee-roasting business?' Niall asked Jane.

'I was looking for something else to do after I stopped teaching when the boys came along. I'm a bit of a 'foodie' and love coffee and I looked around us on Waiheke and saw there was an opening for freshly roasted coffee. Eventually the business really took off and Stephen was able to leave his job in Auckland.'

'Cool!' I said. (I had seriously got into the habit of saying 'cool' to everything in New Zealand and it was beginning to annoy me.) I sensed a soul mate in Jane and already felt the loss of our seedling relationship which would probably never see the light of a full summer.

'And what about your painting, Jane?'

'I know, I keep saying that I will get back to painting. But I know that it's always there for me. I have half a dozen unfinished paintings around the house just waiting for me.' In his surfer shorts and white T-shirt, Stephen funnelled some organic coffee beans into a brown bag. I penned in the date on the back and attached the adhesive label.

Sometimes Stephen was quiet and other times he 'rabbitted' on, as he said himself (I supposed he was, in homeopathic terms, 'doing a proving' of the remedy coffee and was under its powerful influence) and he was in one his pensive moods at the moment.

'Yes, I know what you mean,' I said. 'I keep meaning to get back to painting myself but so far I've only managed a few sketches.'

'You will,' Jane said.

'Hang on, Christine,' Stephen said stepping aside from the roaster into which he had poured another half bag of fresh beans, 'I thought you were a homeopath.'

'Well, yes…'

'And she's also a self-taught artist and a gardener and writer and was studying Italian last year for her graduate course in Bologna in homeopathy.' Niall interrupted. 'Chris can do many things.'

'Yeah,' I mused, 'Jack of all trades and master of none.'

'That's not true,' replied Niall. 'We were all healthy for the last six months thanks to you.'

'A lot of good it did *me* in Bolivia!' I reminded him.

'But that's usually how it is,' said Jane. 'If the family stays healthy it's the mother who gets sick.'

'No, you're right,' I said. 'It's worked out pretty well on that front.'

'And if we can get through China without a hitch, then I'll think you're a miracle worker too!' We all laughed and went back to talking about the coffee business. I told Jane that Deirdre wanted to set up a coffee-roasting business when we got back home and call it the Cowshed Cabin Café.

'Oh, what a great idea,' Jane said.

'It might just pay for all her shopping expeditions!' Niall chuckled.

'Yes. And we'll come over and help you set it up,' said Jane.

'Cool,' Niall said and I smiled – it sounded funny coming out his mouth. Stephen looked at all three of us and broke into one of his characteristic laughs, a laugh that sounded like a guffaw if ever there was one.

We left the roasters roasting and returned to Palm Beach. We were leaving New Zealand in a few days for Australia and I had many things to think about. The Cowshed Cabin Café was only a pipedream but getting back to painting and finishing my book were not. Returning to homeopathy was a whole other ball game. Gardening would always be there for me in the same way that painting would always be there for Jane, and sometimes I thought that it was what I truly wanted to do. Just garden. Nothing else. One thing I was sure of: I wouldn't rush into anything. As they say, time takes time and first things first. I just had to decide who was on first.

On our last night in New Zealand we had fish and chips on the white beach in Oneroa, the chief town on Waiheke. It's Kiwiana: fish and chips on the beach. Reminded me of a chipper in Sandymount. Same paper wrapping. Jane said she remembered many dinners like that throughout her childhood. We spread out our towels and shared the chips: tomato sauce dotting the paper with designs made by our hungry children's dabbing. The sun was setting, the water was warm. We played Frisbee with the kids and swam with the waves. Then the eight of us walked along the beach and back again. Six-year-old Finn stopped to dig a hole with Joseph. Tom-Tom dragged a piece of seaweed like a souvenir from battle. I had to bring myself back into the moment. We were leaving the next morning. As a parting present, Stephen gave Niall a pair of jandles (thongs or flip-flops) and a rather groovy-looking blue Mambo shirt with surfer dudes. We had joked with Niall that he ought do like the natives and let his toes out of his sneakers for a bit of fresh air. Jane gave me a pair of paua shell earrings. It was a sad leave-taking and, as they waved goodbye from the dock, Jane was crying and I felt miserable.

'Mum, Jane is crying,' Joseph said a bit surprised. 'Hey guys, those are real tears *not* because we didn't pay our bill but because we're leaving!'

~

It was easy for me to imagine a life here in my future. And if it weren't so far from London and New York, it wouldn't be a hard decision. Perhaps I am being characteristically naïve, because if it wasn't halfway around the world, it would change everything and it likely wouldn't be what it was, a laid-back, easy-going country, out on its own and self-contained. When it came right down to it, would I really want to live in New Zealand? Because of the isolation, there is a high incidence of suicide among teenagers. (Ireland comes in a close second.) But unlike Ireland, where the landscape is also beautiful, New Zealand has sunshine – plenty of sunshine – and perhaps that is what I find so appealing. The answer was something I could see myself thinking about for a good time to come. Niall was always telling me in these situations that I had to remember that I was *on holiday*. That life isn't the same when you're living the *business* of your life rather than the *holiday* of your life. But from where I was looking, life in New Zealand sure looked the same. I had told Stephen and Jane that when they decided to take their gap year I would come to manage their guesthouse and coffee business. No worries. I'd bring my paints and sunscreen. I'd learn how to surf and fish. I'd cut my hair real short and swim every day in the summer. I'd walk down the street looking the ragamuffin that I am at heart and feel right at home in New Zealand.

Australia

It felt like we were going home even though we still had three and half months to go after we left New Zealand. It unsettled me. I had anticipated that I would love New Zealand, and when it was time to leave I felt like I was leaving behind a suddenly unburied part of myself, a newly surfaced shell that the tide had laid bare against the sand. Do I dare to pick it up? I felt freedom in New Zealand. Besides the beach and sun of summer, the walks along the white sand, the seashells, the fantasy landscape, there was calmness and a feeling of relaxation that came easily to me. I was feeling lonesome for a way of life in New Zealand that I hadn't encountered before. I was feeling lonesome for a part of myself.

The idea of heading towards home once we had reached the furthest point around the globe had thrown me into a tailspin for another reason: I was in a bit of a conundrum about continuing with my postgraduate studies in homeopathy. There was a course in Boston in April that I had booked myself on prior to the idea of our trip. Attending it would mean leaving the family behind in Paris for ten days and rejoining them later in the south of France. Interrupting the trip would have its own consequences, but I was troubled over the larger implications. I was reminded of a conversation I once had with a *New Yorker* cartoonist who told me that he eventually had to give up drawing for *The New Yorker* because he could see the world only through a cartoonist's eyes. Everything became a *New Yorker* cover or cartoon. He couldn't stop himself. He had to go cold turkey to see reality. (He turned to writing and illustrating children's books.) I felt a bit like the cartoonist. For the past ten years I had been increasingly looking at the world through homeopathic lenses, interpreting everything though the language of homeopathy. But, having stepped away from it to some degree during the trip, I felt I was being invited to look anew at its value in my life. I had made a lot of deliberate choices but it occurred to me that some of them had been more headstrong than heartfelt. Confronting me was an opportunity to question my role in homeopathy and homeo-pathy's role in my life. As Van Morrison sings, 'if my heart could do my thinking and my head begin to feel, then I would know what is truly real.' My head said one thing and my heart was saying another.

Ten years ago I began to study homeopathy in a world as the adoptive mother of two young children in a rural, quite isolated environment. I also watched two of my brothers wrestle with a chronic disease. A disease that carried with it, at that time, life-threatening consequences and also called into question emotional and spiritual wellbeing. My mother was also very ill and was treated by medical doctors in a scenario which fixed one health problem only for another one to emerge. (She had the appallingly bad luck to be misdiagnosed with bone cancer when in fact she had osteoporosis deterioration. Her osteoporosis had been brought on prematurely because of a treatment with excessive doses of cortisone in a misjudged effort to alleviate the pain of fibromyalgia, a condition not well understood twenty years ago. My mother was sixty-seven when she eventually did die from cancer.) Meanwhile my brothers take the recommended conventional drugs for their illnesses and are *living* with their diseases. Homeopathy has played no role in their lives. Helping them was the main reason I went into homeopathy. Since, I have ceased waving the banner and recognise that health care is a personal choice involving many factors. For me and Niall and the children, homeopathy has been our first port of call during any illness and has given us more choices in the administration of our own health care. Our choice not to take vaccinations was one of these.

But my current dilemma concerned my role as a homeopathic practitioner in the lives of others. Homeopathy is like learning a new language where new words are added every day. In order to speak it fluently you have to keep learning it. Learning it was no bother to me in terms of study-time and concentration. But in order to be a fluent speaker I needed to go great distances to learn it and spend a fair amount of money to get there. Not to mention needing to buy the homeopathic software necessary to facilitate finding remedies, and needing to acquire a stock of remedies for prescriptions. Unfortunately for me at times, I have to go the whole hog, the whole nine yards. Anything else goes against my grain and I suffer from it. Call it delusions of grandeur or delusions of neglected duty. It's who I am. However, the present situation was also a question of timing. Was I in the right place at the right time? It seemed that I was always swimming upstream against the tide without a paddle. Is this how I wanted to spend the next thirty years of my life? Don't get me wrong, I love homeopathy and I love assisting people in finding solutions for themselves. But perhaps for too long I have been *mother's little helper* and somewhere along the way I forgot to stop and take stock of my own wellbeing. Perhaps it was time for me to get back to writing and painting, pursuits that I had put aside to take up homeopathy. Perhaps I could continue to look at the world through homeopathic tinted lenses while exploring the other creative visions within me. Either way I would have to make a decision soon.

~

We were glad, in more ways than one as it would turn out, that we had delayed our trip to Australia and beyond. When we finally arrived, two weeks later than scheduled, it was raining. The clouds provided cool weather much to our relief. Two weeks earlier the temperatures had been in the high thirties. Niall's younger brother Paul and his wife and kids used to live in Sydney and he recommended that we stay in the Quay West Apartments in the Rocks district. Taking his advice we booked a two-bedroom apartment. It was a bit on the pricey side, but Sydney apartments on the Internet were in short supply so once again we splurged. Our rooms were on the thirteenth floor and looked straight out onto the bustling steely blue waters of Sydney Harbour with a lively view of the Opera House and the grey-black Harbour Bridge.

The twilight views of the harbour in the fading light of summertime were stunning. Some evenings I shouted with delight, and even leaped into the air, much to the amusement of Deirdre, as another cruise ship pulled into the harbour. Possibly the biggest thing on water I've ever seen. Looked like a skyscraper turned on its side, floating white and covered in fairy lights. I was reminded of the Brio train set that I kept adding to each Christmas for Joseph. One year I got him a boat which looked disproportionately larger than the trains. We played with it on a blue plastic harbour on the kitchen floor, turning the boat and sliding it across the top of the plastic, pulling into docks waiting with trains. The giant cruise ships that appeared in the Sydney night looked like oversized playthings, gliding like a toy guided by some mysterious hand over the night water, sometimes nearly touching the bottom of the Harbour Bridge. There was a robust aliveness in the harbour. In any moment it could be a place of splintered rainbow blocks of colour with flashing movement from the large yellow and green ferry boats and lemon-yellow water taxis and white sailboats, red kayaks, black and white tug boats, Captain Cook harbour cruise ships. It was still for only a few hours after midnight when the surface of the water was motionless like a polished mirror in the dark. Some nights, I found myself getting up just to see if a cruise ship had pulled in past midnight. About four in the morning was the only time the harbour went to sleep. Without its harbour, Sydney is just another city. It is the harbour that defines it and its location in the Pacific has become strategic on the world stage. Sydney has come of age, considered by many to be one of the best cities in the world, and after a few days there I was already beginning to agree.

We sat at the table in our dining-cum-living room, eating Chinese food and watching the activity at the Opera House. Tourists and Sydneysiders mingling around the architectural wonder that it is. It ranks up there as one of the most recognisable structures in the world alongside the Eiffel Tower and the Taj Mahal. Described as open seashells or the sliced quarters of an orange, it's a thing of pure imagination. We watched the Opera House catch the sun in half a dozen places like little fractured spotlights. Its white pebbled-coloured jaws opened to welcome travellers who had journeyed along the immense waterway. It confirmed for Deirdre that she wanted to live in a city when she finished school and Joseph was naturally struck by the architecture all around him.

'Do you know the Opera House is built on reclaimed land?' he said.

For me and Niall we quietly looked forward to the time in the future when city life would become part of our living. So, for the moment, we let Sydney become our *designated* city, our city of culture. Ever since our San Francisco experience had been rather eclipsed by a bad start, we had been looking forward to 'living in a city'. Our visits to so many less populated places now laid the way for this, city experience Aussie style. What we wanted was to wake in the heart of a city, to walk out and wander, to drop into bookshops, to pause for coffees, slip in to galleries, meander among the crowds and feel part of the cosmopolis, the very opposite of life back home in west Clare. So now that is just what we did, strolling along the harbour beneath the big blue Australian skies, taking time, feeling the pulse of Sydney.

~

What we felt in Sydney was a kind of freedom similar to New Zealand. It was more than just freedom from winter. Maybe it was life in the Southern Hemisphere. In the mornings we would watch the traffic cross the Harbour Bridge and see the commuter trains below our window. Next we'd slip down to the Rocks for a coffee and take a stroll along the quay, stopping to watch the boats. Our view of the world had expanded to include so much more than any of us had previously understood. I was reminded once again of that *New Yorker* cartoon where New York City is at the heart of the world, larger and more significant than anywhere. It was the other parts we were now seeing and living in.

In Australia, it's clear to see they can get on perfectly well without waiting for their cue from the US or Britain. In fact, many prefer to get along without any connections with the world's superpowers.

And yet, it does feel to some extent that, while the apron strings tying them to Britain are greatly loosened, American culture has become quite prevalent. In Sydney we were able to see four of the Oscar-nominated best movies of 2003 and, on everyone's lips, naturally, was the star of *The Hours* – Nicole Kidman – Sydney girl made good.

We were invited to tea at the Tea Rooms in the Queen Victoria Building, a smaller version of Harrods, by two young women in the publicity and sales department of Macmillan, Niall's publishers. It was a bit of relief to meet up with them because we were feeling a little adrift in the city. Joseph was excited finally to meet an Australian because, besides the hotel staff, we hadn't met any. Like New York, all the taxi drivers were non-nationals. We had drivers from Bosnia and Ghana and Greece and Iran, but no Australians.

I told Annie, the publicist at Macmillan, that I had started to write about our trip.

'Oh,' she said, 'I'd like to read about a family like yours and how you did it.'

'Really?' I said. 'Why?' Here was a young single woman in her late twenties and her comments surprised me.

'It'd be very interesting I think,' she said. 'Like, what did you argue about? What are you like as a family travelling together? When did you feel love?'

'Yes, well it has certainly been interesting,' I replied. 'Sometimes I wish that we were the kind of family that could travel with just a backpack each, and sleep in one room. But it turns out we aren't, not by a long shot.'

Deirdre laughed.

'But that's good,' she said 'to find out what kind of family you are.'

'I'm sure you are right,' I replied.

'Niall,' said Kathy, the other publicist and true Australian, 'we were sorry that you couldn't come to the Perth Festival this year.' Niall had been invited by the publishers, but the timing was wrong for us and he had to decline.

'I'm sorry too,' Niall said. 'It was just too difficult to get there with the kind of itinerary we had, we would have had to leave New Zealand too soon, skip over Sydney, double back, just...' He shook his head as if it were now a familiar puzzle, but one that was never quite completely solved.

'What's Perth like?' Joseph immediately asked, jumping in with both feet and eager to speak with a real Australian.

'It's nice,' replied Kathy, her blond hair and cheerful features conveying a robust kind of energy that I associate with Australians. She engaged with Joseph generously.

'Some people love it. It has a unique kind of atmosphere, I think. But some people think after Sydney it's a bit bland.'

Hmmm. Joseph was mulling this over. He had wanted us to go to Perth but it had moved off the playing board when we voted to stay in New Zealand longer. Again, another time.

'I'd still like to go there. It's the most isolated city in the world. It's exactly the opposite of Sydney. The sun sets over the ocean instead of the land. Cockatoos are black there, and it is apparently a really good place to live. It's not spectacular but dry and sunny whereas Sydney can be wet and cloudy. And Bill Bryson says it's the kind of weather that can get a postman whistling.' I could see there wasn't much she could tell Joseph about Perth. She turned smiling to Niall and said, 'Yes, you must come to Perth another time. You know, your books are doing well there too. Are you writing a new one?'

Niall laughed and made one of those Frenchman-like poofs with his lips, his arms flying up in the air.

'Yes. I've been working on a book since before we left. I had thought there was... *maybe*... a hundred pages or so to go back in September, and that it would be long done by Christmas. I thought by now I'd be writing travel articles or stories or something. Then I cut a hundred pages in San Francisco and thought it was awful.'

'Oh.'

There was an awkward hush for a moment. I could see the two women weren't sure how to take this information, so I assured them it was fine.

'Don't worry, he is back on track,' I said.

'Yes, I think I recovered the book somewhat in New Zealand.'

'Is it difficult to write while you're travelling? It must be.'

'Yes. It is sometimes. Because places are so… so real and vivid and it makes it more difficult because you don't have the consistency of landscape you have sitting at the table in Kiltumper. It makes it harder for me to find that doorway.'

Again there was a pause. The children were sitting there listening to their father talk about his work in a way they hadn't perhaps before. This was the first conversation with anyone in the book business since we left.

'When do you hope to have it finished?' Kathy asked.

'It's so hard to say really. What's funny is that in saying "when" I'm saying "where" too. Will I finish it in Bali, in China? It's so strange, also because the book is pretty rooted in two locations, in the west of Ireland and New York. So part of me is always elsewhere.'

Deirdre smiled at this. Sure, Dad, she was thinking, that explains everything.

'I'm hoping to finish it in France,' he said. 'When we have a month to be still and to settle.'

I sensed that Joseph could have stayed talking with them about Sydney and Australia all day. And I too wanted a deeper connection but said only that I hoped we'd meet again. They wished Niall luck on his book and me on mine, they promised to send books to Ireland for us, and wished us all luck on the rest of our journey. We could feel their genuineness and generosity, and also something of how wonderful our year of travels had looked in their eyes. We left them and walked out into the Sydney sunlight, feeling the warmth of having shared a fragment of our lives, that sense there is of optimism when you encounter the unexpected kindness of others on a long and wandering journey.

~

A few days after our arrival in Australia, peace rallies were held across the world. Sydney was no exception. A quarter of a million marched up George's Street and crammed into Hyde Park. It was the biggest demonstration of its kind in the history of the country. Across the globe, 16 February saw largely peaceful protests and placards of 'No War' waving to television cameras. A million marched in New York and Rome. From small towns to cities. One of the most talked about placards in Sydney carried the words: 'Some small village in Texas has lost their idiot'. Other placards showed pictures of Prime Minister Howard being led around by Bush like a dog on a lead. Sydneysiders were especially outraged at their prime minister. At the time it seemed that the people of the world were sending messages to their governments that would be hard to ignore. Time would tell.

Meanwhile Deirdre was gearing up to go with Niall to a Bob Dylan concert and Niall was on cloud nine that I had got them tickets. Joseph and I stayed in the hotel room, me watching the harbour and my son drawing. As it happened, the concert itself was quite an event, but not for the reasons anticipated. The opening act was a young American singer/songwriter, Ani diFranco, whose intense songs were much like Bob Dylan's of forty years earlier. There was an angry edge to her performance, Niall said, which reached its climax in her final number. 'This,' she announced, 'is going to be a long poem.' At the same moment, the shadowy figure of Dylan emerged to listen at a doorway at the back of the stage. The poem began with a bitter attack on American foreign policy. Her words were very anti-American and, when the poetess/singer said, 'Mr Bush you make me ashamed to be American,' the forty-something-year-old man sitting next to Deirdre could take no more.

'Bullshit!' he shouted loudly. He was also American.

The woman on stage continued without pause.

Again the man shouted, 'Bullshit, bullshit!'

Deirdre, needless to say, was very uncomfortable, especially when other American voices in the huge crowd joined in booing the performer and heckling while the poet herself didn't miss a beat and continued with her poem. It wasn't long before the Australians got in on the act. One clear voice shouted across at the American beside Deirdre, 'Shut up! In this country we have free speech.' From then on, there was a three-way battle: American voices, the antiwar Australian voices, and the lone voice of the artist on stage, who was now struggling to finish her piece as the crowd erupted. Probably because the Dylan concert was on only a day after the peace rally, emotions were intensified. It was a flashback moment to antiwar protests in Dylan's own era and demonstrated how powerfully feelings about the possibility of war in Iraq were running. For Deirdre, of course, it was shocking to have first-hand experience of how mild-looking, middle-aged people could be so passionate. It seemed to encapsulate a moment of history and was the thing that they spoke most about when they returned – that, and the fact that Dylan himself spoke not a word in reference to his opening act through his own performance, but ended the evening by playing 'Blowing in the Wind', his encore and only statement.

~

No visit to Sydney is complete without a trip to the Opera House and better to be in it than just outside. We were lucky to get tickets to Offenbach's classic operetta, *Orpheus in the Underworld* in a new Australian version, *Orpheus in the Down-Underworld,* and it was sure to be much less contentious and very enjoyable. First, Deirdre insisted that we get our hair cut and styled and off we went to a rather chic salon where a Frenchman razor cut Deirdre's long hair in a perfect line and then spent two hours curling and pinning her hair into brown, glistening squiggles. She was delighted at all this attention and I was pleased to see the staff making such a fuss. We had bought her a lovely dress in Santiago for Christmas, and a linen wrap. She was the only one of us who was appropriately dressed for a night at the opera. An 1850s social satire was definitely on target after the Dylan concert. Non-stop gags, fire-works and a distinctly Australian slant with local topicality and Aussie vernacular thrown in provided us with three hours of raw inventiveness produced by first-time director and former punk rocker, Ignatius Jones. In this version Orpheus was gay and Eurydice his wife found hell to be a much more attractive place than earth. Hell was a turn-of-the-century Parisian café full of fine-looking things, especially men. When Orpheus himself gets to hell, he too finds that they simply wear the best clothes down under. We found it to be superbly produced and stage-managed. It was an exciting evening of theatrics and fun and, while probably not for the opera elite, it certainly drew a big crowd who seemed uniformly to declare it well worth it. The talent on stage and behind stage impressed us considerably. Niall commented at the time that it was refreshing to see because he felt that there was a confidence and inventiveness and boldness. 'That,' he said, 'is for me the mark of being pure Australian.'

~

In all, we stayed in Sydney nearly three weeks and took one day trip out to the Blue Mountains in a tour bus filled with sixty-year-olds and a bus conductor who didn't stop talking. His name was John, and he wore the traditional bus conductor's gear with Aussie-style hat and string fastener, white shirt, blue shorts and long white knee socks. He looked like an overgrown kid. We learnt more about his wife and brother-in-law than we care to remember. It was a nightmare and we regretted every moment of it. Maybe it was just because the weather was bad and the spectacular views that were promised were misty and grey, but I'd take the mountains of the Northeastern United States any day over these. We did learn some interesting details about fire and forest regeneration from our loquacious driver, but breathed a great sigh of relief when we returned back to our apartment.

'Don't ever take me on one of those things again!' Joseph roared when we were safely out of earshot. We all agreed. There is enough to see in Sydney itself without having to venture out to the Blue Mountains. A couple of visits to the beaches to see the golden sand and the surfers and the dozens of small children in their tiny cloth bathing caps in organised swim groups was plenty. Manly, Balmoral, Palm Beach in the rain. Bondi, Bronte, Coogee. We visited all of them and were impressed by the yellow sand and the fact that the harbour was now so clean that the sharks had returned. Needless to say, we ventured into the sea only at Manly Beach but couldn't make out much past the first line of breakers. Niall, who had loved swimming so much in New Zealand, tried his best, and gave us all some comic moments as he got tossed time and again in currents stronger than any he had known, coming up covered with seaweed and sand with a wild, dazed look on his face as the next wave rode up just behind him. These beaches were a surfer's paradise and from the shore we watched in awe as dozens of figures caught waves, crouching and curling – almost like members of a beach religion, briefly on a wave of faith – and occasionally crashing into the white tumbling waters. We had fish and chips on the beach at Manly and watched as the sun faded and the evening arose as if emerging from the sea. We walked back though the seaside town and soaked in the twilight as the Manly ferry carried us back through the harbour, passing the giant cruise liners on their way out to the open ocean onward to Hong Kong. I couldn't wait.

~

In Sydney we had pleasantly discovered another city, much like Seattle, that we would feel pleased to live in. We took a bus tour of the city. Went up the Sydney Tower. Walked along the harbour and listened to street musicians along the quays. Besides the movies, the theatre and opera, we visited museums and galleries. We walked back and forth through the Rocks market on the weekends and went to Paddington Street Market. We ate Chinese food at the Harbour and watched the moon rise. We met an Australian designer by the name of Alistair Trung and bought some of his fashions, talking with him for over an hour about his style. He combined Asian and Australian with a French twist, as far as I could discern. He used no buttons or zips for fasteners, instead relying on ties and strings. His fabrics were soft and natural like silks and hessian and cotton with mostly muted colours. His trademark seemed to be a rather layered look which flattered Deirdre's tall slim figure and left me looking rather lumpy. But it was exciting to be in his showroom and he was generous with his information and furthered Deirdre along in her budding ambitions as a designer.

'Give me a call when you graduate,' he said. 'You can come work for me.'

'Don't be surprised,' I answered, smiling at Deirdre, who was calculating the years and the miles.

'Okay,' she replied. 'Thanks.'

Before we knew it we were packing up again. This time to leave Sydney. Just a month to China. Joseph gathered up the hundred drawings he had made during our visit – the city skyline against the water, buildings full of colour and windows. Deirdre packed up the new things she had bought at the markets, including a pair of suede boots, and stuffed them into her shrinking suitcase. We sent home Joseph's viola and more clothes and bits and pieces that we'd been collecting for our scrapbook. We'd be in Melbourne for St Patrick's Day, but before that, we were on target for visits to the Great Barrier Reef and Uluru, destinations expressly asked for by Joseph.

~

We found a deal on the Internet for a week's stay on Hamilton Island and flew there in the beginning of March, sad to leave Sydney behind. In Australia one must fly everywhere and luckily our Oneworld tickets allotted us five internal flights. We decided to visit the Great Barrier Reef from Hamilton. You hear the words Great Barrier Reef so often in connection with Australia and you assume it is one of those places you must visit if you go Down Under. In my ignorance I thought it was more of a place that you arrive to than an actual area. I had never looked on a map to see exactly where it was and was therefore surprised and embarrassed when Joseph told me the Great Barrier Reef was the size of Japan. It is in fact a combination of many types of reef stretching along 2,300 km of coastline. Hamilton Island is one of those holiday resorts that can be managed on a budget. It is much less up-market than Hayman Island, but both are part of the Whit Sunday Islands, the famous islands of white sandy beaches surrounded by blue Pacific water. Our trip was turning into a year of holidays as our young friend Tommy Kilkenny had suspected and this was no exception. This was more like a holiday within a holiday. We arrived by plane and were met by the hotel's mini-bus which dropped the guests off at different accommodation units. Ours was a fifteen-storey building with one bedroom, two sofas in the living room and a kitchen and bathroom. A large balcony overlooked the ocean from our rooms. Once again we were on the thirteenth floor. (I wondered if it had any significance, but it was only a passing thought.) The resort boasted a large gym, tennis courts, a pitch-and-putt course, and free water sports. Six or seven pools with Jacuzzis and hot-tubs stretched between the beach and the hotel. A variety of eateries inside the compound catered for holiday-makers not wanting to cook and a number of restaurants and shops were available down by the marina. There are no cars on the island, but golf carts were available to rent if you didn't feel like walking.

It was as close to a South Pacific feeling as we were going to get, having forsaken a visit to the Cook Islands back in February. Palm trees, coconuts, balmy breezes, colourful small rainbow birds and ocean everywhere we could see. In the mornings a line of white cockatoos with lemon-yellow crowns flew onto the railings of our balcony. Their squawk may be loud and brazen, but the birds are a spectacle to watch. Their round black eyes are watching you. The whiteness of their feathers suggests what heaven might look like. I suspect for Australians, however, they are as much a nuisance as magpies are in Ireland, as we found out later in the week when an army of them broke through the double screen doors of the balcony to ransack the apartment. Every crystal of sugar, every flake of cereal, every grain of rice was scattered on the table and counters and floor. A gluttonous and messy feast was had by the beautiful cockatoos that resulted in cockatoo droppings galore. They weren't so cute after that and we kept the windows closed and the air conditioning on. They continued to watch us, waiting for an opening.

Joseph and Niall went pool hopping most days and Deirdre worked on her tan, read and convinced me to join her in the gym nearly every afternoon. I tried my hand at a few watercolours and saw to my dismay that I was much in need of practice. But mostly we relaxed by the pool and looked out at the ocean. With no museums or sights of cultural interest to visit, I was able to enjoy the sheer relaxation of having nothing to do. Niall was still beavering away on his book and spent some part of every day writing when he wasn't in great demand by Joseph, his swimming companion. It never ceased to amaze me how much a water sprite he was, my merchild. And it never ceased to delight me how wonderful a father Niall was to our children. Many times it had occurred to me on this trip that Niall was like a silent partner. I mean that in the best possible way. He hardly ever imposed his needs on us like we did on him. He was our guardian angel. Entirely unselfish. I knew it was probably burdensome for him to be responsible for the tickets and passport and finances but ours is what good marriages are made of. We have a good partnership. I had done the researching and planning for the trip and I was writing about it, keeping the spirit alive. Niall was our journey's chief executor on the road. If there were decisions to be made as to *where to next*, then I got to work on the Internet. Niall took it from there. We didn't have any time *alone* together as a couple but from the outset we had wanted to do this thing as a family. We lived 24/7 with our kids. Our time alone together would come again.

~

Sometimes I forget where I am. I am sitting and typing on the lap-top and I pause, look around me and say, where am I? Sometimes it takes a few seconds to remember. I wake up in the night and am not sure where I am sleeping. It's not frightening, but oddly comforting. You can be somewhere else so easily yet still be where you are inside yourself. Like a journey within and without. My gratitude never wanes.

~

We had come this far to see the Great Barrier Reef and so booked four round-trip tickets to Reef World a floating station in the Pacific, a two-hour boat ride from Hamilton Island. A full day's adventure, including snorkelling, or scuba diving, luncheon and a glass-bottomed boat ride in the reef. The seasickness was free and, as we found out, par for the course. Two kinds of seasickness tablets were on offer as soon we pulled away from the marina: a homeopathic version which I was pleased to take, based on ginger, and a standard over-the-counter medicine which Niall and Deirdre tried. Joseph took the ginger too but complained straightaway that it hurt his chest. But we all survived, barely. The swells reached three metres on the way out before we came into the shelter of the reef where suddenly the water turned a cerulean blue tinged with green.

'They don't call it aquamarine for nothing,' Joseph said.

We arrived at the station, which consisted of a large floating platform with a centre building that housed the dressing rooms. A large area around the circumference of the station was roped off with buoys here and there demarcating the safe snorkelling section. It was entirely bizarre to be on this floating platform in what felt like the middle of the Pacific Ocean, not a speck of land in sight. I was waiting for sharks and whales to appear and swallow us up. But I assured myself it was too shallow. Lifeguards scouted all corners and life jackets were available for beginners. An underwater viewing room provided us with a constant moving picture of the hundreds of fish swimming by and of Wally, the male Maori Wrasse, the second largest fish in the Great Barrier Reef, whose territory he kindly let us share. Once in the water, we could pet him as he swam alongside us. Getting outfitted with all the snorkelling gear and manouevring ourselves to the edge was an event in itself. Joseph wasn't sure he wanted to go in at all and at first just dangled his feet in the warm water. Niall wasn't exactly that keen to begin with either and stayed with Joseph until he felt confident. Deirdre and I jumped in with both feet first as it were and quickly found that the water was like our own body temperatures and that we floated with ease. We soon got used to the snorkel and managed a few dives without taking in water in the process. It was a remarkable experience. Hours passed in moments. The sheer beauty of the reef floor with blues and purples and pink anemones, yellow and blue trunkfishes, wrasses, and angel-, butterfly-, box-, lion-, rainbow- and parrot-fishes provided a feast of colour that was extraordinary and not easy to explain with just words. Joseph found his way into the water when he felt safe and Niall and I took turns staying close to the station with him. Snorkelling in the Great Barrier Reef was a life-affirming experience for all of us, a nearly pure body experience. Swimming, feeling the water on your skin, the sun on your back as you skim the blue surface with your eyes like portals to another world where the human mind is unnecessary. Pure visual joy and sensual delight that needs no mental interpreting. Sensations that of their own power can trigger dopamines in the brain releasing a sense of wellbeing. If looking at the photos of us, taken by the staff's photographer, are anything to go by, you can see total enjoyment on our snorkelled faces and know that on some level we all received some kind of natural healing that afternoon in the Great Barrier Reef. In one moment, all four of us in the warm water, the myriad coloured fish flowing around us, I caught the wet smiles of all our faces, and thought *yes, yes, for this we came.*

~

The only downside of our trip to Hamilton Island was the threat of the *Irukandji* – the stinger as he is known by in Australia – the jellyfish with a sometimes fatal sting. We quickly surmised that there were so many swimming pools because you couldn't safely swim in the ocean. Signs posted on the edge of the beach said:

When the ocean is warm and specific wind, tide and weather conditions occur, the Whit Sunday Islands experience an increased presence of the Irukandji *jellyfish, a small, transparent jellyfish found in deep water. If stung, symptoms include severe pain, muscle constriction and breathing difficulties which require immediate medical attention. The preferred alternative is to swim in the range of pools on the island instead.*

There had been a few deaths the previous February because of the jellyfish and most people, ourselves included, were quite fearful to swim. The Barrier Reef was safe for swimming because the conditions there are not ideal for the jellyfish. But it was startlingly odd how dangerous it was to go swimming in Australia. With the sharks in the harbour and jellyfish in the sea, one gets the feeling of danger on the doorstep of Australia's shores. That said, the old Breen spirit within me that has braved a few near life-threatening experiences was determined not to leave Australia without one dip into her waters, dangerous or not. Within eyesight of Deirdre I headed towards the sea. It was horribly warm and brownish at the tidemark. I waded out slowly until I was chest deep and dunked myself. Not a stinger in sight. With two fists raised above my head like Rocky Balboa I punched the air and jumped up like an elder mermaid, screaming with fear and delight, and, as quick as lightening, plunged out of the water to Deirdre, like a bolt from the sea.

'You're mad, Mum,' Deirdre laughed and screamed at me at once. 'You really are!'

'I know, but I just had to do it.'

'How was it?' she asked with a look that seemed to say *will I have a go*?

'Scary, really, honey, but thrilling. Do you want to go in? I'll go in with you if you want,' I said, hoping she would not.

She hesitated.

'Not to worry, I did it for both of us.' She smiled and I couldn't tell if she thought I was crazy or wonderful or both.

～

Back on Qantas a week later, we flew to Uluru, for the red centre of Australia. We had one passenger who was beside himself with excitement. Ever since he had done a project for school on Australia the year before, he was eager to be there. When asked why he wanted to go, he said, 'I dunno. It seems like a magical place. It's like there's so many different worlds to it – like the desert, the rainforest, the barrier reef, you know. And I want to see all the different cities that I wrote about and to see the differences in the parts of Australia. To see it for myself.' Australia had never been on my top ten places to visit around the world. But for Joseph it was number one. Bruce Chatwin writes in *The Songlines*, 'America's young. Young, innocent and cruel. But this country's old. Old rock. That's the difference. Old weary and wise. Absorbent too. No matter what you pour on it, it all gets sucked away.' We were about to see first hand what he was talking about. When we disembarked from the plane we had to walk along the tarmac to the arrivals hall. It was hot, very hot. As we approached the doors I noticed that people were swatting at flies that seemed to land out of nowhere on faces. One lady had a netted thingamajig around her face. Was she for real? Must be American. Sure enough, she was. But I have to say at this point, she was ahead of the rest of us. Because within moments of arriving at our hotel we all followed suit and we bought four face nets to cover ourselves. The flies were atrocious. What is it with Australia and creatures? At any given moment, there could be twenty flies feasting on you.

When you get out to the centre of Australia to visit Uluru there is really only one place to stay, Ayers Rock Resort, which comprises five hotels from a five-star to a camp ground as well as the exclusive Longitude 131°, which is accessed by climbing over a sand dune on a path of red earth with a direct view of the rock. We booked two rooms at Sails in the Desert and were escorted by the resort bus to the hotel. I felt a bit like an old camel being herded across the desert, but was pleased enough with our accommodation. We managed to duck the flies and find our adjoining rooms. When we had to change our itinerary back in New Zealand, we had reduced our days in Uluru to three, which was unfortunate, because once we arrived I felt I could have stayed longer. We had a lot to organise and headed straight to the front desk, only to be told that the Sounds of Silence dinner in the desert was booked for both nights. Would we like the barbecue instead? Disappointed, we signed on for the Aussie barbie the next night, which started with a visit to Kata Tjuta, formally known as The Olgas, sunset viewing, and ended with a stargazing talk after the barbecue. It was the next best thing.

'You'll love barbecued kangaroo,' the pert blond behind the desk chirped.

'Yes,' said Niall, 'I'm sure. Not sure, though, about my daughter who is a vegetarian.'

'Oh,' said the young lady. 'I'll send word on to the chef to make some veggie burgers as well.'

As we had come this far primarily for Joseph's sake we asked him what he wanted to do next.

'Go to Uluru, now!' he said.

A few other guests were of the same opinion and within half an hour of arriving we boarded the Uluru Express to visit the cultural centre and catch the sunset at Ayers Rock. The Australians we encountered were friendly and laid-back yet very energetic and our driver was no exception. She dropped us at the centre and said she'd collect us at the car park at the base of Uluru in plenty of time to reach the viewing station for the sunset. But the two American ladies on the bus with us were talking over their strategy of climbing the next day. They had come to 'do' the rock.

'You know, Leo did the rock last year. He said it was awesome.'

The speaker was a woman in her late forties, rather plump in the lower half of her body, and she wore bright white sneakers and khaki trousers with a flamingo pink T-shirt. Her travelling companion hailed from North Carolina and had long painted fingernails.

'Yeah, but you know Richard? He said he wouldn't climb it because the Aborigines didn't want him to. But he was just using that as an excuse. He doesn't like rock climbing.'

It was for times like these that I was glad my partner could put on a thick Dublin accent when he wanted to. I pretended not to understand American and got off the bus first. Niall came behind, shaking his head.

'Friends of yours, honey?'

The local Aboriginal people of this area are known as the Anangu, *the people*, the Pitjantjatjara and Yankunytjatjara, the traditional owners of Uluru. As they say themselves,

Ancestral beings emerged from this void and journeyed widely, creating all living species and the features of the desert landscape we see today. Uluru and Kata Tjuta provide physical evidence of feats performed during the creation period. Anangu are the direct descendants of these beings and are responsible for the protection and appropriate management of these ancestral lands. The details of the activities and travels of the ancestral beings have been taught ever since, in story, song, dance and ceremony. The knowledge of how to take care of the land, animals, plants and people has been passed down from generation to generation in the form of the Tjukurpa, Anangu Law. Uluru and Kata Tjuta and the land are part of a timeless representation of the past, the present and future and of the relationship of all beings to one another.

This religious ideology is the essence of the 'The Dreamtime' and the basis of Aboriginal life. The 'creation ancestors' created the landscape. Places where they have been thought to emerge from are sacred. Uluru is one such place. It is the wish of the Anangu that visitors not climb the rock because of its sacred place in their culture. It was the traditional route taken by ancestral Mala men on their arrival at Uluru and of great spiritual significance. Among other things, they ask visitors not to take photographs of the

Aboriginal people or of any important spiritual sites without written permission from the Board of Management. This is strictly enforced by the guides, although the decision on whether or not to climb is left up to individuals. Considering the Aborigines possess probably the longest cultural history of any society on this planet, 40,000 years old, we didn't hesitate in respecting their wishes and bought a badge that said: 'I didn't climb Ayers Rock.' Very topical, and very topical too was the flow back to Uluru of its scattered sacred pieces. Tourists have been known to take away bits of Uluru, a taboo of sometimes immense dimensions. Inside the Cultural Centre there is a book in which are kept the letters and testimonials of people who have returned their bit of the rock, all with apologies to the Anangu. There is more than one record of people having been healed upon returning their souvenirs and of others who had suffered illnesses until they had relinquished their part of the rock.

Also inside the centre were short film documentaries showing traditional crafts and food gathering and hunting methods of the Aborigines of the surrounding landscape. But most interesting of all to me were the paintings. The paintings depict the stories of creation. Because of its subject matter, Aboriginal art conveys an entire culture and its beliefs rather than the thoughts of just one artist as most of the paintings illustrate the 'Dreamings'. The 'Dreamings' is a concept that is hard to get your head around at first. It has nothing to do with sleeping. Each dreamtime story relates to a particular landscape. As one landscape connects with another, these stories form a 'track'. These tracks are called songlines and crisscross the Australian continent. Some paintings portray maps showing physical features, campsites, animal tracks mostly executed by the use of dots, a distinctive aspect of Aboriginal art which has it origins in blobs of paint that come from the pulp of ground-down plant material. As you fly in over Uluru, the landscape below looks like one of the Aboriginal paintings. It wasn't hard to believe that these artists possess a knowledge of the landscape similar to what you could call a bird's eye view or that they must have some great out-of-body experiences because the colours, the contours, the shapes are the very landscape of Australian desert itself. I think one of the most exciting aspects of the paintings is that non-aborigines will never know their full spiritual significance and if you buy one you buy on faith as it were. Faith is implicit in the paintings, faith in the past, present and future of creation. The true meaning cannot be revealed because the paintings themselves contain sacred symbols and elements that belong only to the Aborigines. Because the stories of Uluru are synonymous with the culture, they belong solely to the Anangu and may not be used or reproduced in any form without written permission of senior Anangu custodians.

We learned all this before heading out on the beautiful Liru (meaning snake) Walk, to the base of Uluru where our escort met us and transferred us promptly to the sunset viewing platform with a hundred or so other tourists. The vast population of flies vanishes as soon as the sun goes down. One by one, people took off their ridiculous-looking face nets and took out their cameras.

'Take one photo every five minutes or so and you will be amazed when you get them developed. The naked eye can not appreciate the colour changes that will appear in your photographs.' That's what the guide explained to us and we did as he suggested. The colours of the sunset are reflected in the rock from orange to blazing red to purple-grey to brown as the sun sinks into the horizon. The shadow cast by the setting sun inches up to the monolith and eventually envelops it like a blanket. It's like a performance. And we, a captive audience.

'Ready for the sunrise walk around Uluru?' our guide asked us as we hopped back in the bus for the return journey to the resort.

'What time is that again?' Niall asked.

'Bus picks you up at the hotel at half five in the morning. Sunrise is just before six.'

'Aagh!' In unison, Deirdre and Joseph groaned.

'C'mon guys, it'll be grand. But how will we ever get the mother up?'

'Hmmm, yes, that'll be a feat,' I replied.

The Anangu ask you not to walk up Ayers Rock but they do encourage you to walk around it. We retired early in preparation for the next day's activities. The full base walk, nearly 10 km, would take us about three to four hours with a rest for lunch. Joseph and Deirdre were eventually game for it. Getting up was not easy. But we were there standing in the dark waiting for the bus with ten other guests. We had our woven water-bottle carriers from Peru that Deirdre had remembered to bring and our face fly-nets. We had been encouraged to dress in lightweight long trousers and long sleeves and even so shivered in the morning cold. When we arrived at the base in darkness and met our guide, she quickly ushered us to the path and explained that the sun would be up soon. We would see it light up the rock. As we went further, she stopped occasionally to tell stories from the Tjukurpa – the laws of creation. All of the extraordinary features of the rock are explained in story. Places where huge spears were stuck with such force that holes were made in the rock. A dark line across the surface of the rock was left by an angry mother racing after the offender. Loose rocks at the base lie in the aftermath of a violent event. A woman's laugh is carved in the rock in the shape of her mouth. Such is the wealth of legends and beliefs that the hours passed easily. The sun was slowly climbing and the tremendous heat that reached thirty-six degrees centigrade in the afternoon was only warming up. The ubiquitous flies, however, were up at the crack of dawn. No rest for the wicked, as they say. They were on us at first light, in full force, like bees to the honey hive. I watched Deirdre struggle and eventually succeed in drinking from her water bottle without lifting her face net in case one fly slipped in.

Niall and Joseph tagged along at the end of the line, while Deirdre and I walked up front. We didn't see any snakes or lizards or honey ants during our walk. No birds. No kangaroos. We were there during late summer and most of the flowers had faded. But all around us was the sound of the wind and the sound of the earth itself; the colours of the rock and the sand and the spinifex. It was an unexpected surprise because I hadn't anticipated how much at home I would feel in the centre of the Australian continent. Maybe it was the sheer expansiveness of the flat plain, like standing on the edge of the ocean. Here was an oceanic desert of red sand and green dots of plants and shrubs. Listening to everything was a meditation. It felt like a place where peace flowed as easily as breathing, as easily as the sun rising and setting and that to be there soaking up the atmosphere, dry and hot as it was, was an incomparable experience. In great contrast to the high expectations I had had of The Island of the Sun on Lake Titicaca, I had none here and was greatly surprised. Joseph, on the other hand, did have expectations of the rock. He was hoping for it to be smooth, so he could touch it, or rub it like quartz or marble. He thought it would be redder and that the sand around it would also be red. (It is in fact a kind of mulchy brown.) But nonetheless I watched the rock work its magic on him as the sun came up. He was truly fascinated by it, and by all the stories that linked its various parts. He liked the heat because it was dry heat, not thick and humid like Costa Rica had been, and walked on kilometre after kilometre without complaint. Deirdre liked it less, because it was physically discomforting not only on account of the flies but also because, after many bottles of water, she realised there were no places to pee at a sacred rock, and it was too hot for her. She found it really affected her enjoyment of being there.

And much as I realised on the trip that my daughter may prefer cities and the energy of the consumer markets of this earth, I know too that she'll never be without some perfect moments of real beauty, like a smile tucked into her back pocket. Niall and I have helped to give her that. And that will always stay with me.

The sun rose into an immaculately blue sky. We shot some unforgettable scenery of nearly abstract compositions with our assortment of cameras. By mid-afternoon we were at Kata Tjuta for another walk. This time the tour organisers insisted that we bring two litres of water a piece. They couldn't stress enough the importance of drinking water. A litre an hour is recommended for long walks in the heat of the red centre.

'Mum, that's fine, but where are we going to pee?'

Some say that The Olgas, the thirty-six rock domes with their deep valleys and gorges, are even more spectacular than Ayers Rock. Niall and Joseph didn't care as much for them. Deirdre and I joined a walking group, but after about an hour along the Valley of the Winds walk, we turned back. It was too hot and we were tired from the morning's adventure around Uluru. After toasting the sunset with plastic glasses of champagne and potato crisps, we boarded the bus for our Australian-style barbecue somewhere in the middle of the desert in the dark. The landscape had transformed from red to black. It was easy, Niall said, to imagine Australia now as an ancestral place. It seemed to come alive in an altogether different way in the darkness – the awareness of creatures and ancestral beings moving in the primordial darkness. No light pollution. The sky was speckled with stars.

The barbecue itself was less than wonderful. Dubious-looking desert salad for Deirdre, and perhaps even more dubious kangaroo for us. I was reminded of when we visited friends in Norway for the winter holidays and went further north, up to reindeer country, and on the menu for New Year's Eve was reindeer. The kids asked, how we could eat it. It was like eating a teddy bear, wasn't it? Here too, we couldn't quite eat a kangaroo no matter how tasty it was supposed to be. Our tall, thin, chatty Australian guide who was bustling with energy, strode around and pointed out high in the night sky the Southern Cross and how, as far as we Northern Hemisphere people were concerned, Orion was upside down. The nightscape was stunning. In the vast quiet of the Australian desert, imagination was free to roam. I watched Niall staring up into the stars, and Joseph wandering about with the excitement children can feel in complete freedom. Deirdre too was clearly taken by it, the sheer simplicity of the place, the rock in the red desert, and the sense of how minute we all were there in the great starry darkness.

On the journey back to the hotel the guide treated us to a remarkable half hour of didgeridoo playing. Like the Aboriginal paintings, the music of the didgeridoo tells a story, this one of a kangaroo crossing the Australian highway back into the desert. And although it might seem a page out of the Australian Tourist Board's manual, much as Irish musicians playing for American tourists, sometimes even clichés can escape and become real, and this was pure magic, the skill of the player and the respect he brought to the music enthralling. And so after walking about the rock, and seeing the sunrise and the sunset, and the barbecue and kangaroo and the didgeridoo, we were able to leave Uluru in the morning completely sold, hook, line and sinker, for a return visit to Australia's red hot centre.

~

Our final stop in Australia was Melbourne. We arrived just in time for St Patrick's Day and expected some excitement with so many Irish in Australia, but there was no evidence of anything green or Irish or lucky. Although the Irish president Mary McAleese was also in Melbourne, we didn't see or hear news of her. One hundred models dressed as brides were on the steps of the parliament house for L'Oréal Fashion Festival. We missed those too. We watched CNN from our apartment in Melbourne and didn't do much else. Didn't feel like doing anything. We were all citied out after Sydney and three of the four of us agreed that we preferred Sydney. Joseph preferred Melbourne, calling it a livable city. I said to him, 'I think you are right about that Joseph. Melbourne was voted top among the world's most livable cities.' How he understands these things, I don't know but livable or not, I didn't have the energy to explore. I was garnering my energy for Indonesia and China. We did walk up to the Queen Victoria market which rivals the Pike Street market in Seattle and bought organics and listened to a band playing on the corner. We heard the sound before we saw them and immediately recognised the music from South America. Peru or Bolivia? We were not sure. But the pull was instant, the sound from the mountains tugged at us and we stood momentarily lost in a music that touches your soul if you have ever been in those high green spaces. The band turned out to be from Bolivia and it was surreal to see them on a street corner in Melbourne. Long, black, shiny hair falling to their shoulders. Black woollen ponchos. Wooden pan-pipes and flutes, strumming on instruments that created a sound reminiscent of a dozen rivers flowing down the Andes. I imagined spirit-like mist rising from crashing waterfalls and drifting across the Pacific to where we stood, lifting our faces to catch it.

～

I watched another full moon rise in a different place in the world. 18 March. For the past seven months I had seen seven full moons rise. Eating pizza pie on the beach in Amagansett, from the corner of Delancy and Bryant over the Bay Bridge in San Francisco, on Manuel Antonio Beach on the Central Pacific of Costa Rica, over the lake in Puerto Varas in Chile in December, having dinner with Niall at Vino Vino in Waiheke Island in the Hauraki Gulf in New

Zealand, and from a Chinese restaurant in The Rocks district overlooking Sydney Harbour. Watching for the full moon is something I do. I once heard a line in a movie where a character in a desert recites a line from a famous author: 'you will probably never see the full moon rise more than nine times in your life.' Maybe those weren't the exact words and maybe I have got the numbers wrong, but ever since I've made a point of watching the full moon. (It occurs to me now I probably would have had much better luck on the Island of Moon rather than the Island of the Sun in Lake Titicaca back in December.) Most importantly, however, I connect the moon with my mother. She died of cancer on 19 March 1991. And, in the year that she died, there were two extra moons, two blue moons.

When the moon rises, I think of her.

~

We had arrived in Melbourne five nights earlier and in the space of that time the world had nearly spun out of control. We were on the other side from where we had started and the children knew it was a long way home. News of the US and British governments' conflict with Saddam Hussein had been one of the threads of the tapestry of our trip from the start – from our first discussions with Leonard, my sister's father-in-law, in Amagansett back in September, to the first antiwar demonstration Deirdre and I watched in Seattle in the beginning of October, to the Navy war planes in manouevres over San Diego Bay, to the worldwide demonstrations in February. From our hotel room we listened as President Bush broadcast his final ultimatum to Saddam Hussein and sons. We listened on Sky News Australia as the opposition leader hotly denounced John Howard, the Australian prime minister, saying it was a black day for Australia when the government pronounced it was joining the coalition. BBC World Service announced that another English MP had resigned from Tony Blair's cabinet. President Chirac refused to consider any resolution whose ultimatum threatened violence. The European Union was falling apart. The UN was falling apart. News arrived via telephone from my brother Sean in Seattle that French fries had been renamed freedom fries.

Happy St Patrick's Day – how are ya?

Joseph wanted me to keep my voice down.

'Can't you sound more Irish and less American?' he pleaded. I sorely regretted that I had been too lazy to apply for an Irish passport because now my little blue American passport seemed like a red flag to a herd of bulls. I hadn't been able to talk with any other Americans but suspected I felt similarly to many who didn't feel just one way about the impending war. Anti-Americanism was free floating in the air and I felt that every time I opened my mouth neon balloons ensued. I took shelter in keeping quiet but keeping abreast of daily events. I had wanted the UN to support the United States and Britain and Australia in its enforcement of Resolution 1441 and had argued for the justice of the cause in the end of the day. Niall argued for the basic premise that America was in fact not under present threat from Iraq. We were all confused and Deirdre and Joseph followed our discussions with apprehension. Two days before we were due to leave the Australian continent for the most foreign leg of our trip, war in the Persian Gulf was a certainty.

Was it safe to be travelling to Bali now? We heard tales of people cancelling their trips, business and pleasure. It had been less than six months since the Bali bombings in Kuta. These are the times that make you wonder what the hell you are doing. We had discovered that we were not intrepid travellers.

While the threat of war in Iraq loomed heavily, there was another more imminent menace at our doorstep which threatened the remainder of our trip. I happened to spot a short article in *The Age,* the Melbourne newspaper, on 16 March. It reported a mystery virus in Asia. Who knew by the end of the week that it would be headline news across the globe? By the next day it was front-page news in *The New York Times*. I emailed our contacts in Beijing and in LA because I was naturally alarmed. By Saturday, a few days after the article appeared, news that the virus had claimed lives emerged. Its origins were unidentified and its cure unknown. Time to start worrying? It was being called the 'jet disease' because it was spreading by airline travellers. The WHO issued a global health warning. Now the disease had a name: Severe Acute Respiratory Syndrome. By Monday the virus was still resistant to antibiotics.

Our scheduled trip to Hong Kong and mainland China, less than two weeks away, was in jeopardy. Jeffrey, our China tour organiser, emailed back that his friends in Reuters in Beijing were not concerned and that in his opinion our trip was on course. Ah Chun, our escort in Beijing, sent wonderfully expressive emails, encouraging us to keep on schedule and that we would not be in danger. Her brother was a doctor. Jeffrey said to go to Bali, relax, and decide in ten days.

Meanwhile, CNN broadcast the countdown: Forty-eight hours. Forty-two hours. Thirty hours.

Nearly eight months into our trip, I started wondering if it was time to go home.

Bali

'How much time is it now?' Deirdre turned to me to say.

'I'm not sure, honey. We've been on the plane about two and half hours. It's another four hours, I think.'

She was shaking her head.

'That's not what I meant. How much time before the war?'

Her question blindsided me. A fashion magazine was opened on her lap. Her headphones were on and she was half watching *Everybody Loves Raymond* on the television monitor above us. She hates to fly at the best of times. My heart broke open to include her.

'This time tomorrow, I think,' I replied holding her gaze steady in my own. 'We should be safely in the hotel by then. Don't worry, Deirdre,' I added touching her arm gently. 'I'm sure we are perfectly safe right now, and we will be safe in Bali.' I said this to reassure her when, in my own mind, I wasn't so sure.

She looked away and it was impossible for me to decipher what she was thinking. I had been reading in the Melbourne paper when she spoke to me of a man who had closed his restaurant in Baghdad, sold his luxury car, and headed with his family to Jordan where he said he would watch the war on CNN. It was 19 March. With one eye on the news headlines for the start of the war and both ears alert to any passenger excessively coughing or sneezing (signs of SARS we had been told to watch out for), we flew to Denpasar. Six hours after boarding, we touched down on the island of Bali in Indonesia, the world's fourth most populous country and the fastest-growing Muslim country in the world. We didn't know what we would find, and we were all more than just a bit nervous.

Flying over the ocean between Australia and Bali gave me passing relief, however. From my window I looked across the world to where the horizon line was a heavenly haze of smudged blue like a chalk pastel in aquamarine. The ocean blended seamlessly into the sky. Havens of golden sand arose here and there, isolated in their own splendour. I rested in that energy of pure beauty, allowing myself to be replenished. I thought about my responsibility to let the children see for themselves that the world itself is a beautiful place, despite the conflicts of its people. As we approached Bali, dozens of white smoke columns were spiralling into the sky. We stepped into the hot air, which was perfumed by the burning piles of harvested rice stalks. We were warmly greeted by Ari of Bali-Tourist.com who had booked us into the Natura Resort and Spa in Ubud for four days.

'Welcome to Bali. Thank you for coming to visit,' he said, vigorously shaking our hands and introducing himself to the children as well. We piled into the van and headed off, yet again, from an airport to a hotel.

The narrow streets of Denpasar were crowded with men and women in sarongs and sandals on motorbikes. Beeping horns filled the air as vans passed motorbikes and motorbikes passed vans in a continuous parade of slow-moving traffic, punctuated by toots and beep-beeps and coloured cloth ribboning in the wind. A small motorbike buzzed against us, weighed down with a child on a woman's lap, and a second woman with pyramid of fruit balanced on her head like a circus act. Others seemed to carry entire families. Giant white statues of Balinese deities rose from roundabouts. As we skirted the city of Denpasar on our way to Ubud, the cultural capital of Bali, it was not what I was expecting. The roads were teeming with life; Balinese people engaged in the daily ritual of their lives. People washing in roadside drains; thin men, barely clad, carrying machetes; people heading to temples in sandals and neatly ironed sarongs. Small groups of men sat in the shade, some stroking cockerels. Woven cages on the roadside housed poultry in rows like cloches over prized lettuce plants. We passed a Banyan tree where fifty or more women and children were gathering. Like colourful, shiny sweet wrappers and gold foil gently swirling in the breeze, they sat in groups with their fruit offerings around the base of the tree. Colourful litter edged the road.

I hadn't researched Bali. It wasn't one of the top destinations for me on this trip but we thought it would be a good introduction to Asia, and was easily accessible on our Oneworld Alliance tickets. Qantas in and Cathay Pacific out. A kind of hiatus between Australia and China. Now that I think about it, I shake my head at my ignorance. Had I presumed from too many magazine photos that it would be designer exotic everywhere I looked? It was of course anything but. Our hotel had a small reception area under a bamboo and reed roof. No walls and one desk. We stood in the heat while Niall passed his credit card to the escort who swished it through a machine that appeared from nowhere, while the assembled staff stood around smiling and bowing and waiting. If this was the reception area, what the blazes would our rooms look like? At this point there was no sign of anything you might call a hotel. Just a reception area in thick trees. Small marble steps led down to a planked teak walkway that was covered by another bamboo and reed roof. Hindu statues with flowers appeared in tiny alcoves. It was beginning to look more promising. On either side of the walkway, jungle leaves and flowers enclosed us in a tunnel of green, and led eventually to a wonderful villa, as each of the rooms were. In its centre was a six-foot square four-poster bed with a high canopy of thick muslin. The floor was marble and long windows overlooked the river valley. Discreet bowls of flowers were displayed on tables. Down a set of windy stairs beneath our rooms was a day bed large enough for a family of six and our own plunge pool. Exotic and luxurious and heavenly. And so silent. At first it appeared that we were the only guests.

The hotel's villas are set into the landscape, and merged with it in more ways than one, as we would find out when Deirdre tucked herself into bed to write in her journal only to discover that her legs were covered in ants. An army had made a nest in the underneath part of her mattress. The hotel staff quickly came and changed all the linen and the mattress and Joseph's bed too. Throughout our stay, ants and tiny spiders found their way from the reef thatched roof to the floor and chairs. It was only a minor nuisance until one night when I crawled into bed, enclosed in muslin, and looked up at a giant spider above my head. He was up in the canopy. Black on white. I scrambled out and my ears starting ringing as they do when I see spiders. Niall came to the rescue with a broom and a member of staff and managed to dislodge him, whereabouts unknown. Eventually convinced that I'd be safe, I tucked the muslin under the mattress and around the pillows and slept motionless until morning.

The hotel had advertised satellite television and, as soon as we arrived, we attempted to tune into BBC or CNN, but found only TV5, a French-based channel, local Indonesian stations, and two Japanese channels. The countdown was still on for war with Iraq, yet we could only guess at what was happening. We felt very cut off, and yet were disinclined to enquire in case we appeared pro-war, or anti-Islam, or red, white and blue Bushies. We also determined to let the staff know at every opportunity that we were Irish, well mostly. Not British. Not Australian. Not American, exactly. We had yet to experience the nature of the Balinese, a truly gentle people who were as saddened by the bombings in October as the Australians and the rest of the world. But during our first few days, we stepped softly and spoke quietly yet with thick Irish brogues when in earshot of the staff.

The end of March in Bali is the end of the low season. Between that and the fact that the tourist industry was only beginning to recover after the bombing, we found the hotel hushed. The Balinese staff greeted us in the Hindu custom of honouring the human being with praying hands at the chest and a slight bow every time we appeared from our rooms. They moved quietly like whispers around us. We felt peaceful and oddly encapsulated. We sat for our meals in a very large, open restaurant eating *Nasi Goreng*, an Indonesian speciality of fried rice and vegetables and chicken, while overlooking the river and valley. Dozens of dragonflies shaded the hot air. A gala of leaves painted the green landscape. In a marble urn on a pedestal, white frangipani and red hibiscus flowers floated. One of the staff sat on the floor and played the gamelan instrument of long rows of bamboo reed, which is played at gatherings to entertain the gods and the guests, inspiring a sense of wellbeing.

~

Our first morning on the way to breakfast we came upon a young man sitting cross-legged on a mat under a thatched roof supported by four teak timber posts. He was drawing on an egg. Spread before him were three rows of painted eggs. Chicken eggs, duck eggs and an ostrich egg. In his hand was an unpainted egg suspended on a thin stick, in his other hand a pencil which he used to trace a butterfly resting on a hibiscus flower. It was like coming upon a poem. He was a young Balinese painter named Komang Mertayasa. The owners of the hotel had given him the space, which enhanced not only the cultural quality for the visitor, but gave employment to a young painter. I showed him my meagre sketch book and he invited me to 'colour' the egg the next day, explaining the various steps. It took him two days to complete an egg painting and he sold it for 60,000 rupees (about $7), a price which we didn't attempt to bargain down when we bought four the next day. I sat with him on the mat under the thatched roof and tried my hand at colouring. I was so inspired by the calm and sacred atmosphere of the hotel in Ubud that I bought a rice-paper journal, made a few sketches during our stay and wrote some lines of a poem on the day the war began.

> *Dream of No War*
> Dragonflies hover
> Still silent green spaces
> Meditating peace
> Ubud 20.03.03

~

Before we had left Melbourne, we had spoken with my cousin PJ in New York and told him of our worries about travelling to Bali and also about the mysterious virus that was emerging from China and

Hong Kong of which we could get little information. As luck would have it, he knew someone who had a business in Ubud and, not only that, the businessman was due to arrive in Bali from Hong Kong on 27 March! A contact. It sounded good. There was no Internet as promised in the hotel so we went into the bustling, crowded, hot market streets of Ubud after breakfast one morning and located an Internet café to discover that an email had arrived from Ardani, the head of guest relations of the factory owned by PJ's acquaintance. Her email was an invitation to lunch which we quickly accepted by telephone.

'Hello Ardani?'

'Yes, yes, this is Ardani,' said the Balinese voice on the other end.

'This is Niall Williams…'

'Oh, yes, yes, very pleased you phoned. Please come to lunch today to the factory. Can you come now?'

'Well, yes, I think we can. You tell me how to get there and we will come,' Niall replied looking at us with his head nodding and his eyes widened to say, *okay guys?*

We nodded excitedly back.

'That is good. We see you in an hour.'

We found a driver, ubiquitous in Ubud, and headed out to the factory through rice-field paddies. Our drive took us along narrow, windy roads bordered by temples and sloping, terraced fields. The statues at the openings of the temples were all clothed in black and white, and gold and white. Stone figures guard entries to temple, hotels, and homes. The black-and-white checked cloths around the statues' waists symbolise the balance between good and evil. In a bend in the road a man stood naked soaping himself in the river; a boy was peeing in the long grass as his schoolmates continued, past him; a child was being washed in the water gully; two boys washed a motorbike from the same water. In the fields, rows of men and women under deep-pointed, round straw hats with bent backs harvested the rice. Men, ankle deep in mud, planted or weeded the rice paddies at a different stage of cultivation. (Three crops of rice are cultivated and harvested in one year.) Ducks paddled every-where and pecked for their lunch. Out in the fields, shrines to Dewi

Sri, the rice goddess, rose above the flat green acres where elevated wooden platforms with scanty roofs stand for shelter and rest for the farmers. Long, coloured ribbon-like cloths spiral into the sky, and scarecrows guard the fields. To the Balinese, every living thing contains a spirit – when they pick a flower as an offering to the gods, they first say a prayer to the flower. The simple journey to the factory was a treat in itself and the marvellous island of Bali unfolded gently before us.

I had forgotten to enquire of my cousin what business the factory housed or how big it was. Were we going to encounter slave labour? We quickly learned upon arrival that it was a factory for the manufacture and production of high-quality jewellery and silver cutlery and accessories for the table. The factory was owned by Cynthia and John Hardy, jewellery designers from New York. Their products were for export only and sold in Neiman Marcus and Saks Fifth Avenue and they employed 600 people. It could have been an embarrassing situation admitting our ignorance but neither Ardani nor Lloyd, an American and the Product Manager who lunched with us, seemed to notice or to mind. I think Lloyd was happy for some outsider American-style conversation. Before lunch, Ardani, a Balinese woman in her forties, took us on a tour of the factory where the jewellery was made. Rooms opening into more rooms of assembly-line like tables where groups of young men and women, dressed in company-issued uniforms, worked quietly at wooden tables. All eyes were on Deirdre everywhere we walked. Here was a Western girl of their age. What was she wearing? How long was her hair? Look how tall she is! Gentle smiles crossed their faces as we passed. I was wondering how Joseph was coping with it all, our socially conscious child. Would he approve of the workers' conditions? When at lunch he learned that all 600 employees were fed from the company's own organic garden as part of their work environment and that they lunched in the open garden-like atmosphere outside the buildings, he was relieved. The Balinese staff here at the Hardys' factory were well paid by local standards and enjoyed good working conditions in modest but pleasant air-conditioned surroundings. In fact, the whole factory set-up was like a small village or compound structured on the Balinese way of living in shared quarters of extended families. We lunched with

Lloyd on plates and silverware and glasses from the product range. Exquisitely designed and elegant were the keywords, combining the renowned skills of the Balinese silversmiths with John Hardy's creative designs. After lunch, we stopped at the showroom and were invited to buy items. Even at lowered prices, the jewellery was a bit beyond our budget, but we bought Deirdre a silver bracelet for her upcoming birthday, a hairpin for me and a silver Christmas ball for our ornament collection.

Ardani told us that John had cancelled his upcoming trip and we guessed ourselves that it was either the war in Iraq or the virus coming out of Hong Kong that was responsible for his decision. We were disappointed and wondered if this was the first sign that trouble lay ahead for us too? But, she added, if for any reason we needed her help we should not hesitate to make further contact. On our departure she gave us each a silver hatpin with one of John's designs as a parting gift. We left comforted and inspired by the visit on two accounts: we had made a connection and had seen first hand an American factory operating productively and successfully without the exploitation that one often associates with products made in Asia. It put 'Made in Bali' in a new light.

We stayed for four nights in quiet luxury amid the antique-like quality of Balinese courtesy of the Natura Resort. Deirdre and I had our bodies perfumed and oiled and polished with turmeric by two young Balinese spa attendants who then stood silently by as we prepared for our petal bath in a marble tub. The warm bath water was covered in a layer of red flowers which we parted with our hands. I had to admire Deirdre, who wasn't used to walking around naked in front of me, never mind strangers. We were equally quiet but absolutely charmed by the experience. The cascading water of the river Petanu below us made soothing noises while we soaked and looked out over the valley through the open walls. Sheer heaven.

Although we sorely felt the lack of Internet service and the lack of English-language news, we did not want to disturb the kind of spell that swathed us there like soft silk. Instead Niall was able to translate the French channel to me which, given the French stance led by Chirac, was lacking in definitive news to say the least but rather involved a number of intellectuals applauding France's position of denouncing the war. News of the 'mystery' pneumonia was equally scanty. Already hungry for information when we left the hotel for the north of Bali, it was without the slightest assurance that we would be any the wiser regarding the war and SARS once we arrived. I had arranged, again through the Internet, to rent a villa on the top of the island for a week, to see the Bali beyond. A man named Blue picked us up at the hotel and piled our luggage into his old van. Would we be returning in a week for our scheduled departure from Denpasar on Cathay Pacific to fly to Hong Kong? I had no idea.

~

Imagine a villa in Bali on the water. Imagine the warm Indian Ocean lapping on black volcanic sand a mere twenty-five metres from your door. The cotton sheets are scented like sandalwood on the four-poster bed of hand-carved mahogany. Thick, creamy-coloured muslin drapes fall to the cool, tiled floor. The ceiling is highly pitched, made from bamboo and reed. Exotic. Just outside your window there is a view beyond the kidney shaped pool where a dozen palm trees lead the way like grey elephant legs walking across the clipped grass to a calm ocean where dolphins swim and early-morning fishing boats glide like water spiders across the liquid-blue iron sea. It is the Bali you've glimpsed at in the pages of travel magazines, even dreamed of on a January evening in the cold northern hemisphere as you dozed before the fire waiting for spring. You rest in that image, that moment, that silence of beauty.

Yet, into that idyll, a noise suddenly breaks the magic charm. The long, slim shadows of the palm trees harbour the rapid-tongued calls of Balinese men who are making a wild uproar of clipped shrill sounds, cheering beneath open-sided plastic tents. On the other side of the lawn of palm trees, vinyl sheets of blue and brown hang from nylon cords strung between them, sheltering a makeshift earthen arena. Imagine that even closer to your door than the sea, these Balinese men are sitting on their haunches clucking like hens. They are entranced while two cocks fight to the death. A feast of gambling and blood. Imagine this is within inches of the walls of that villa in Bali of which you've dreamed. A man pees into the ocean from the edge of the garden. A cock crows and the crowd lets off a cheer that leaves an eerie silence in its wake.

Blue, our chatty Balinese driver, drove us to the northern coast of the island, to the villa we had rented. We felt like the only *foreigners* for miles. It was a strange atmosphere to find ourselves in with war in the Persian Gulf only four days old. Reality is much more than an image. The photo in the magazine is taken out of context. The image on the Internet screen is only a picture. The Bali on our doorstep was a cockfight on a hot afternoon. And, as would soon be slyly revealed to us during our visit, we would be subjected to three more afternoons of cockfighting. People around us were not mindful of the war. It had virtually no impact on their lives. The atmosphere was made even more bizarre because of the four days we had just spent in Ubud in the contemplative setting of Natura Resort where tranquillity and peace floated like clouds in the blue air. Now only a wall divided us from where men were selling machetes to the gathering crowd. It was not the sort of balance I was looking for.

An American in Bali had explained to us, 'You need help in Bali. You can't get anything done without it. I now have a cook and a maid and a driver. It's expected.' And we found the same thing when we arrived at the villa in the North. Blue had seemed to circumnavigate the centre of Bali in ever-widening circles until we reached the north. Because of the cockfighting that was hatching next door, he must have been told by the manager of the small villa to drive us twice around the block as it were. We arrived seven hours later, just after the cockfighting had ceased, unknown to us, and the crowd dispersed. Normally it is a two-hour drive. We had enjoyed a tour of the mountains and rice fields and villages along the way and it was worthwhile but the length of time it had taken in the hot van was not what we had prepared for. Once at the villa, we were introduced to a cook, a gardener, and a housekeeper who were all attached to the house, as well as a security person. It wasn't a big house. A kitchen opened onto a covered veranda with two bed-rooms on either side and a third bedroom upstairs with a balcony. No living room or sitting room except for the veranda which was admittedly quite pleasant and had a magnificent view of the ocean, but there was no place to sit except around the dining table there.

The villa's personnel came and went rather freely, speaking to each other in Indonesian. We moved like chess pieces around them from the moment we arrived wondering where to position ourselves for privacy. We could only surmise that it was the custom and that the Balinese took no notice of the lack of privacy or personal space. The owner, a Greek chap who lived in Hawaii, turned a good profit based on Western rental prices by paying Indonesian wages. Both were happy. Although the staff's job was to make us feel comfortable, we felt extremely uncomfortable. We had been looking forward to cooking for ourselves and didn't want a cook. We didn't want a maid to make our beds and sweep if it meant she had to hang around waiting for a crumb to drop in order to satisfy her job requirements. The young cook spoke very little English and the housekeeper less. We were too full of rice and Indonesian spices already and the children especially wanted some plain simple meals, like boiled potatoes and carrots. We asked her to find some bread and milk and butter and she said these were available only in Singajara, half an hour away. We had no transport and she only had a motorbike. It was not looking good for us.

The first morning, the day of the first cockfight, I was lying in a hammock reading, soaking up the few hours before retiring indoors for the duration of the poultry war. I was distracted from my book when a small Balinese man casually walked past me. He seemed to come out of nowhere and walked straight to one of the palm trees on the lawn. He climbed straight up it, his machete dangling at his backside. He cut branches forty feet up, let them fall to the ground, scrambled back down, collected his branches, smiled, and walked back from wherever he had come. I was too surprised to say anything. Between these abrupt visitations of villagers on business of one sort or another and the villa's staff, Deirdre especially resented the lack of privacy and felt uncomfortable sitting in her bikini at the pool's edge with villagers peering from the nearby shore's edge. She covered herself and tried to read. We felt like we were fish in a fishbowl. People were peering from behind palm trees. Others were edging closer from their group on the lawn waiting for the cockfight to begin. It wasn't that we didn't feel safe, just distinctly out of harmony.

'Away from the hustle and bustle,' is how our driver Blue had described it. He left out the part about the land beside the villa becoming the village's cockfighting arena overnight. The mayor had been approached and the owner of the vacant lot had been asked to rescind his permission for its use but to no avail. It was explained to us in humble tones and with great regret that the event would last just five hours. We had luckily missed the affair on Sunday, but two or three more were scheduled for the coming week. We didn't know quite what to expect and imagined we might manage. How bad could it be? We didn't have to watch. However, when it commenced it was impossible to ignore the sound, which at thirty-second intervals, clearly spoke of bloodletting. Cock crows and crowd roars silenced everything else, like the sound of a door closed against the noisy crowd, when the victorious cock strutted, as I imagine he must have, across the earthen square. Revelling, jubilant villagers flanked the arena and the betting began again.

It was a beautiful location and the picture of the house itself from the Internet was accurate. The sporting arena had appeared overnight and the owner wasn't to blame. I recognised that for some travellers the cockfighting would only be adding spice to an indigenous experience. Here was a slice of the real Bali. We started to walk along the small beach, but turned back when a dead cockerel, legs up, dead as a doornail, lay in our path. We shook our heads. Joseph was distraught. It wasn't getting any better. The signs were everywhere for us. There was more cockfighting to come and we knew we didn't want to wait around. With war in Iraq and the mystery pneumonia in Asia, we needed our wits about us in order to embark thoughtfully on the last weeks of our journey. We didn't want this to be our last experience of Bali before heading to Hong Kong and mainland China.

Aries was clearly ruling and Mars, the God of war, was governing the zodiac.

~

Before twenty-four hours had elapsed in the villa on the water, Murphy's Law, which states, 'Anything that can go wrong will go wrong,' was in full force. After the cockfight, Niall had nearly electrocuted himself when he plugged in one of our laptops. Neither of us had considered that the Indonesian houses in rural places were not properly earthed. *How stupid were we?* When he went to move the laptop, holding it with both hands, he *became* the earth. His hands were stuck to it. He couldn't free himself and was shaking violently, pain shooting up his arm. Eventually he managed to throw off the computer much like detaching a rapid dog that had gripped his arm. He fell to the marble floor, the laptop landing with a thud. Deirdre and I ran to him but he was saying he was all right, clutching his right arm and hand, and rocking back and forth. His life flashed before us. I was afraid to look at his hand in case it was as black as the sand of the beach. The lame gardener appeared from the lawn where he was sweeping imaginary leaves and tried to help him up, practically toppling to the floor. This holiday villa was quickly becoming the scene of a black comedy. It was over in a flash but its aftershock lingered. What would we have done if he had collapsed from electric shock?

Altogether we stayed only three nights. We were confirmed in our decision the next morning when we awoke at seven o'clock to the sound of a chainsaw. Apparently, one of the neighbours had decided to cut down and slice up some palm trees. The chainsawing lasted until one o'clock. We were clearly being blasted out. Between the echoes of the last breath of dead cockerels and the incessant roar of the chainsaw, we couldn't find the peace and quiet we had come for. We couldn't write safely. We could eat only extremely spicy Indonesian dishes. We couldn't summon the energy to combat the elements before us. We experienced a non-tourist Bali, away from the resorts and the Bali-style, architecturally designed villas that have become famous around the world. We saw an island in the archipelago country of Indonesia, where English is as foreign as we were. Where unemployment is high. Where things like earthed electricity are not standard. Where refrigeration and sliced bread are luxuries. Where privacy is not a custom. Where six months earlier a bomb had killed over 200 people. It's difficult to explain the situation we found ourselves in without also admitting to a certain uncomfortable-ness with the way of life as we experienced it in twenty-four short hours. Worst of all was the difficulty in accessing information about what was going on in the world. Our rented villa was an extension of the village and thus we were part of the community. But more than a week is needed to acclimatise yourself. We may have been in the right place so to speak but we were clearly there at the wrong time. I was reminded about what the woman at Macmillan Australia had said to me when she learned that I was writing a book about our year off. She said that she'd be very interested to read about what we were learning about ourselves. Like, what *kind* of family are you? It was becoming certain that we were not intrepid, devil-may-care travellers.

I am being too hard on us because the truth is we could have stuck it out and found our niche and constructed our comfort zone as we had done in similar situations in South America. After all we had learned to adapt ourselves to many situations so far. We *could* have managed. We could have modified the Indonesian dishes to our milder palates. We could have manouevred our way around the lack of privacy. Blue, our driver, was scheduled to take us on a tour of the east of Bali which would have satisfied my own explorer spirit and we could have arranged it for the next upcoming day of scheduled cockfighting. (But to add icing to the cake as it were, Niall was nearly clobbered when a huge coconut fell from the tree and missed his head by a foot. Then, the chair he sat in at the only table in the villa collapsed under him as he pushed back to stand up after dinner.) But truly, our decision to leave was governed by the lack of information with a capital 'I'. With the world in turmoil and with a family to protect, Niall and I needed to know what was happening, not only with the war, but more importantly, we needed to know how SARS was affecting travel to China and Hong Kong. We watched televised images of the Chinese wearing masks in Hong Kong which suggested the virus was spreading, but the words and text were in Indonesian. We sat hunkered on the bed, the four of us trying to decipher the Indonesian news which ran clips from Arabic televisions stations about the war. It was unreal. Blue appeared on Wednesday and drove us back to Ubud but not before the entire staff: the cook, the maid, the manager, the gardener, and the security man stood by the car to see us off. Niall gave each of them a customary tip of 20,000 rupees and they bowed humbly in response. They were sorry to see us go and we asked the manager to please explain that while, yes, it did have something to do with the cockfighting, it had nothing to do with their hospitality. We were sorry we said but really we needed to get back to Ubud. Our scheduled flight to Hong Kong was four days away.

~

While Indonesia is mostly Muslim, Bali is 90 per cent Hindu and when you understand that you understand that it is also the reason why the Balinese are considered a gentle, peace-loving society. (You can even understand the nature of the cockfighting as a kind of wayward, relatively harmless release.) The Hindu religion is central and their ritualised way of life may be the only thing that hasn't changed in Bali since tourism became the number one industry.

'Tourists love Bali and Bali loves tourists,' is how Blue put it.

Balinese Hinduism is different from Indian Hinduism and incorporates more of a Buddhist philosophy. The Balinese focus on pleasing God through aesthetic rituals and ceremonies. They believe in *dharma* and *adharma*, order and disorder, and the need for balance between them. There can be no good without evil. To achieve harmony, the forces of good must be saluted with offerings while the forces of bad must be appeased. Niall and I very much liked this idea of offerings. Plaited baskets of palm-tree leaves filled with flowers and herbs and a bit of rice and incense lie on the sidewalks, on the dashboards of cars, on prows of fishing boats, on bridges, in markets everywhere. These offerings are made to placate evil spirits and honour helpful ones. Some are left to decay naturally. We pictured ourselves making similar containers from rushes, like the Saint Bridget crosses we make on 1 February. Only, we'd need to find a few statues to make the offerings to. The balance between good and evil is the lifetime work of every Balinese. So now it was time for some good for us. The playful but evil demons of the North of Bali had successfully expelled us; now it was time for an offering to the helpful gods.

During our first visit in Ubud, Deirdre and I battled the Ubud market and were hassled and beleaguered by dozens of Balinese merchants. One of our guidebooks, obviously outdated, said not to enquire a price of something unless you intended to buy it. *Insight Guides* neglected to point out that bargaining has become part of the buying. Our experience in Cusco hadn't prepared us for what we experienced in the Ubud market. It was appalling. I hated it. On the ground floor of the market we bought a sarong for 80,000 rupee. I bargained the shopkeeper down 5,000 thinking it was the best I could do. The prices were already inexpensive. This is not my cup of tea. Tell me what the fair price is and I'll pay it. We wandered upstairs past women in stalls begging us to come look. Hundreds of tiny stalls lined in a darkened maze selling the arts and crafts of Bali: basketry of every utility, wood carvings of every description, shoes, batiks, silver, discounted CDs, spices, beaded everything, and kitsch galore.

'It's free to look, Madam.'

'How much you will pay?'

'Nice sarong for you. You buy two.'

One lady asked me, 'How much you pay, Madam?' pointing to my bag.

'75,000 rupee,' I said, opening my bag innocently and showing her the sarong.

'20,000 too much,' she replied shaking her head.

'I give you same for 55,000.' It was no use trying to explain that we had only wandered up trying to keep out of the heavy shower that was falling and that in fact we had no money. She didn't believe me.

'Okay, I give it to you for 50,000,' she said, pulling my arm into her section of the dark market.

'No really I don't have any money left. I will have to go to an ATM,' I said backing away from her. 'You know, an ATM?'

'Please Madam, give me some luck. I give you for 35,000,' she pleaded thinking this was *my* way of bargaining. If she only knew what a pushover I was.

'Look,' I said exasperated, 'I really don't have any money now but I will come back later and buy one. But not for 35,000. For 40,000. Okay?' I could see that she didn't believe me but the fact was that I had spent my money already.

Eventually Deirdre and I made our way back downstairs and into the rain-swamped streets. The pretty beaded sandals I had bought the day before were falling apart in the rain. Deirdre was delighted because, using the same tactic, she managed to get a sarong for 20,000. I was disgusted. How the same thing upstairs can cost less than half of what it costs downstairs annoyed me no end. I vowed to find an ATM and go back to the lady upstairs and buy one of her items. I believed in karma. When we eventually returned after walking a mile around the town looking for a working ATM, the lady must have heard my voice echoing down the long lines of sarongs and cloths and shirts saying, 'No thank you very much. I already have many sarongs. But thank you so much.' She peeked her head around the corner and shouted to me.

'Hello Madam, you come back.'

Deirdre laughed. She couldn't believe that the lady had recognised my voice.

'Yes,' I said. 'I said I would come back. Now I will buy one.'

'Please,' she said, 'you buy two from me now.' Was there no letting up? No, there was no satisfying them. Infuriated and defeated, I bought two from her. She took the money and, saying thank you, waved the rupee notes along the line of her hanging sarongs anointing them with luck. We left her and braved past the many merchants who sensed a catch and tried to haul us in but we maintained our downward gaze and steadily forged ahead, emerging into the hot, busy, wet crowded streets. I was pleased at least that I had fulfilled my promise, even if I had been snookered downstairs. I was not one of the tourists looking for a bargain; I was looking for a cultural exchange and a Balinese product to remind me of our travels when I got back home to Ireland. (It didn't matter to me that these sarongs were a dime a dozen on the streets of New York. It didn't matter that most of the cloths are made in Java and shipped to Bali.) Hindu dogma teaches that the soul can be released from the wheel of life (a cycle of five: birth, happiness, burden, illness and death) only by the observance of *dharma* – doing one's duty according to one's position in life. I felt that it was my duty to buy one sarong from the pleading lady upstairs at the Ubud market.

Would I be rewarded in the next life? Maybe, but I'd settle for a reward in this life; in fact, for this moment.

In between Niall falling on the floor from partial electrocution and falling off the broken chair, we had rung Ardani at John Hardy's factory from our cell phone. He briefly told her that our rented villa was not working out. Did she have any suggestions?

'What is your budget?' she asked.

'At this point, we could pay as much as $250,' Niall said.

'$250 per room?'

'No, I'm afraid not,' replied Niall. '$250 between both rooms.'

Whether it was good karma coming back at me, whether it was the good grace and good connections of Ardani, or whether it was the luck of the Irish, who knows? But when Ardani rang back, she told us that she had managed to book us two suites.

'Excellent,' I heard Niall say, and then after a pause, 'Sorry, Ardani, where?'

Deirdre and I watched his face.

'At the Four Seasons in Sayan in Ubud?' he said, so we could hear him. Open-mouthed, jaws dropped, we squealed like kids at a birthday party. He waved us to be quiet and reacted like a picture of composure himself, like a man born with a silver spoon. 'That's grand,' he added. 'That'll do nicely. Thank you, Ardani.'

The Four Seasons turned out to be a slice of heaven as one might expect. We couldn't believe our luck. It was everything you imagine a resort in Bali to be. Best of all for us under the circumstances was satellite television with CNN, BBC and MSNBC. We were scheduled to fly to Hong Kong four days after we tucked ourselves into the Four Seasons. Ah Chun in Beijing was still encouraging us to come, but we put a call through to Jeffrey in LA. We awaited his response hourly. Meanwhile, we had the number of an Irishman in Hong Kong and we attempted to make contact with him only succeeding in awakening a young woman who said he was out and didn't know when he was due to return. She said it was business as usual as far as she could see in Hong Kong. It was conflicting news from what the news channels were showing. Fifty dead and another 1,500 infected worldwide. WHO officers had not been allowed to go to the Guangdong province, possibly at the heart of the virus, to investigate. What was the real story? The Chinese government was officially saying that the virus was not a great cause for concern.

Often these things are blown out of proportion. And people take unnecessary precautions. We had come this far: China was always going to be the highlight of the trip. One minute we were going, the next we were cancelling. Ambiguity, defeat and disappointment loomed with every headline. Was it alarmist or not? We were counting on Jeffrey to help us make the best decision. After four days in Hong Kong we were due to fly to Beijing on 3 April. It was only a week away. Our itinerary included: Tiananmen Square and the Forbidden City; Mao's mausoleum; the Cultural Revolution Marketplace; the Temple of Heaven; the Beijing Fish Market; the Great Wall; and dinner in a local home and an evening in a local neighbourhood. It also included: a visit to an Art/Dance Studio with An Chun and lunch with the students and teachers, and a music concert; TianJin and shopping for tea sets; The Llama Temple; a trip from Beijing to the cities of Hang Zhou and Suzhou, where our itinerary was being organised by the art community; the train to Shanghai; a river ride with a visit to Pudong. We were then scheduled to take a flight to Guangzhou (Canton, to explore Old Canton and Antique Alley, dinner on the Pearl River and, finally, the train back to Hong Kong.

Although it was not of any real consequence when one considers the life-threatening epidemic that was possibly emerging, it did bear some consideration that we had, in fact, paid *in full* for our private tour of China. We should have known better, but we took Jeffrey Cheen at his word. It had been a kind of gentleman's agreement. We had no cancellation clause on that handshake. A huge slice of the pie had gone into our food requirements, all travel arrangements, and the contracted services of Ah Chun who would be with us for our entire stay in mainland China. We wouldn't mind forfeiting a deposit, but not the whole balance which we had, foolishly, paid before it was due, a tactic of my over-trusting husband. All the previous year we had planned to celebrate our April birthdays in Hong Kong and mainland China in the Year of the Dragon. It was an exciting itinerary and had been worked and reworked half a dozen times since we had met up with Jeffrey in LA. The idea that it might have to be shelved was not only massively disheartening for all of us, but it also left a three-week hole in our schedule, not to mention the budget that had already been spent.

Talk about good and evil, and black and white, and offerings to appease the gods and honour the gods! Between watching the war in Iraq from a largely Muslim country where the leading newspaper called for boycotts of American products and businesses and where 400 volunteers had signed up to join the Iraqi forces, and deciphering the news of what was being called a deadly virus, we were glad to be 'holed' up as it were in a resort in Bali. We felt protected and didn't regret for an instant the price tag of that protection.

Two days before we were due to fly Cathay Pacific from Denpasar to Hong Kong, Jeffrey returned our call and said he thought it was best not to go. The agent in Hong Kong who had booked our hotels advised the same.

'I looked at the schedule and it's just where we were sending you guys. You can't go. Look, I'm a parent too and I wouldn't let Justin go right now. If Joseph suffers from respiratory infections, we just can't take a chance.'

Niall got off the phone and told me the news that I suspected was coming all along. We couldn't risk it. (We agreed that once we got out of Bali and back into Europe we would connect again and see where we stood contractually with the finances.)

Deirdre cried at first. She didn't want to believe it. She had been saving her money for shopping in Beijing and had been looking forward to seeing the Great Wall and even to playing her flute in China. Ah Chun had promised to take Joseph to fly kites in the Beijing park and he was disappointed not to get to meet her. The rest of the trip was just pictures in our head. We were looking forward to an idea we had of China that we had seen on television shows and from *National Geographic Traveller*. What had drawn us to China in the first place was the total foreignness of it. We had planned to visit at least one destination that would challenge us in terms of its vastly different culture, food and customs and we had chosen China. We had specifically asked Jeffrey to organise the tour with a slant on music and art and gardens. As we had already learned from nearly seven months of travelling, it's the people that make a country come alive and it seemed we would probably see more culturally of China than perhaps we had experienced anywhere so far on the trip. Expect the unexpected rang in my mind. But a worldwide health scare *and* a hugely unsupported war in the Middle East was more than anyone might expect.

We called Cathay Pacific and cancelled our flight, neglecting to transfer that leg of the journey to Singapore as we were entitled to do and buying tickets to Singapore instead. As far as we could tell, it was the only viable route out except through Bangkok.

～

The aim of each existence is to perform the *dharma* of that life so correctly that the soul will be rewarded with a higher station in the next life. It was our duty now to protect our children and behave appropriately to the world situation. It is imperative to maintain a proper reverence for all the gods and spirits who dwell on the island for their anger can be very destructive. Had we not been doing so? Balinese Hinduism has absorbed so many local island deities that it has very little in common with Hinduism as observed by other communities in Southeast Asia. We were in a world of its own now. Having decided to cancel, we asked the hotel if we could stay on for a few more days. At one point, it seemed as if we were the only four guests in the Four Seasons hotel, and of course they were happy to assist us. In fact, staying on there was a kind of unreal heaven. We wandered from the sumptuous rooms in grass sandals, clip-clopping along teak walkways and out beneath the palm trees down through rice terraces to the pool. We were treated like a family of some obscure royalty, and not just ones who had lost their way in the turbulence of the world.

The two most famous local deities of Balinese Hinduism are the witch Rangda and her adversary, the lion-like beast called Barong.

The Barong Keris dance is a modern secular version of the very sacred Calonarang exorcistic dance drama that is used by the Balinese to protect their villages from evil. Calonarang is rarely seen by outsiders because it is performed at midnight at village crossroads and in graveyards. Both versions depict a struggle between Rangda, the personification of darkness and evil, and the protective Barong. The struggle always ends in a draw, because in the mortal world neither good nor evil can completely triumph. We had seen this dance in Ubud a few nights before and again at the hotel. Another style of dance known as the Legong is the epitome of femininity and grace and we had the pleasure of seeing this performed on the grounds of the Four Seasons one evening. The young girls who are training to be dancers are exquisite and endearing to behold. The large, round, made-up eyes move like flying darts as they follow the direction of their daintily turned-up hands. The story unfolds in the flicker of the eyes and the fluttering hands and the dancing feet, all dancers mirroring each other. They are costumed in gold, mostly, with crowns of flowers. They throw flower petals before them and move to the ding-dink-dong of the gamelan.

We took full advantage of our time in the Four Seasons and were treated like dignitaries by the staff members who were happy to have someone to take care of. Our immense rooms had two bathrooms apiece and two balconies per room. The whole ground floor of our cottage in Kiltumper would fit easily inside just one suite. In the morning, fresh flowers were brought in by the hotel employees who left their shoes outside as, barefoot, they tidied the rooms. Every night another flower lay on the pillow with a little note wishing us a good sleep. Cool, fresh herbal tea with ginger was always available to us and the music of the gamelan filled the open dining area while we ate by candlelight. Swimming in the pool, which we did every day, we were served poolside with dishes of fresh fruit. By our loungers, laid with two towels, were cold bottles of spring water and face spritzers. Niall kept reminding me that it would never be like this again. So many had cancelled their visits because of the war and because of the virus, we had the place to ourselves and we walked in paradise, through tropical plants and frangipani trees dropping their star-shaped fragrant white blossoms before us. The river valley bordered the hotel and its gently rushing water was a meditation in itself as I studied it from my place in the pool. Had we died and gone to heaven? In emails home we wrote:

Stuck in the Four Seasons in Bali. Can't go to Hong Kong or China. Know anybody in Singapore?

Joseph's twelfth birthday was quickly approaching, but we wouldn't be celebrating in Hong Kong after all. We told the staff about it and they prepared the most wonderfully exotic looking chocolate cake for him. The Hindu New Year coincided with Joseph's birthday and, in celebration, the island of Bali had been preparing for parades for weeks. 2 April would see the whole country close down for the observance of *Nyepi*, the Day of Silence. No flights in or out of the country. No taxis. No shops open. No lights or fire except in hotels, where candles would be used as much as possible. All families consent to stay at home and refrain from any physical activity to prepare together for the New Year in meditation. It is the custom and strictly followed and enforced by the each local community's elders. We felt privileged to be a part of it. The day before Nyepi is probably the busiest day in Bali when the Balinese engage in ritual activities around the temples, in their villages and in their homes. Giving offerings and sacrifices to the evil creatures and asking God to return the evil creatures to where they belong.

After Joseph's birthday dinner, some the staff walked with us to the road where we positioned ourselves to watch the parade of the Ogoh-ogoh, the statues that symbolise evil spirits. We had seen these being made from our first arrival in Bali throughout the villages. Giant statues finished with papier-mâché constructed mostly of bamboo and palm reed. Huge devil creatures with horrible faces. Outside Ubud there was a long pink dragon made from painted sponges. The artistic nature of the statues was remarkable and constructed in the community by the villagers. Artistic ability seems to ooze from every Balinese person. The Ogoh-ogoh are the reflection of the creativity of the Balinese in combination with their religious values. The Ogoh-ogoh are carried through the streets of each village in order to keep down the chaos. The village boys and men carry the devil creatures through the streets, preceded by noise-makers and fire crackers and candles. It was dark by the time they reached us, and we could just barely make out the evil face on the monster, but there was no shortage of loud noise and shouting. Joseph tucked in behind me without meaning to shy away, but it was a bit scary, as it was meant to be.

'Look Joseph,' I said. 'They've all come to wish you Happy Birthday!'

'Yeah, pretty cool, I guess,' Joseph replied, not exactly sure if he was happy to be missing China in order to escape SARS.

'*I'd* still rather be in Hong Kong,' said Deirdre in a tone that revealed that she was beginning to accept the reality of our decision. 'But I'm glad you had a nice day, Joseph. Some April Fool's Day though, huh?'

'Jojo,' said Niall grabbing him around his shoulders and cuddling him, our birthday boy, as best he could, 'tomorrow begins another year for you just like for the Hindus.'

'That's right, Joseph. And we are helping to banish all the evil spirits back to their places in the underworld,' I said walking up alongside him as we crossed the bridge back into the haven of the Four Seasons.

'Think of it this way, Joseph, maybe the good news is that we saved ourselves from a worse disaster and that there really is good at work on our behalf,' Niall said. Always the man with the positive word. In the spirit of the Hindu New Year, we offered our sacrificed trip to the gods and hoped they would be appeased. We would rest like the Balinese for Nyepi and board the plane for Singapore, where who knew what awaited us.

The New Year begins…

Singapore

April, the month of three of four birthdays in The Breen Williams Family Travelling Quartet, was supposed to see us arriving in Hong Kong and touring mainland China from Beijing to Guangdong. At the planning stages a year ago I thought it might be the highlight of our trip. Instead, we were going to Singapore from where we would eventually return to Shannon in less than eight weeks. We were on our way home, but a month too soon.

SARS had reached the status of an epidemic, even while news of its origin and its contagion was still being proclaimed as alarmist by the Chinese government. We had made the right choice, considering the circumstances and the risks involved. Those two extra weeks we had spent in New Zealand turned out to be heaven-sent because if we had stuck to our original itinerary we would have *been* in China only days before the virus reached the world. Where would we have been then? Probably at panic stations, queuing for a flight on British Airways to London with suspicious eyes and ears and wearing masks. So a little bit of flexibility had worked toward our benefit. Would it work for us now? Our plans for the next month were a little sketchy and we had to be flexible. We considered travelling by train through Malaysia to Bangkok until we heard that arriving passengers from Singapore had to wear masks and tags, like branded cattle. No, there were not many places within Asia we could go. Cathay Pacific was cancelling flights left, right and centre. The risk of contracting SARS dictated everything in that part of the world. Until you find yourself in a similar situation you might not understand the confusion and isolation we felt. Halfway around the world, suddenly itinerary-less and wondering when we arrived in Singapore what would we find: masks and quarantine?

We had sent emails from Bali to family and friends asking if anyone knew anyone in Thailand or Singapore, or even Japan, explaining that we had had to cancel our trip to China because of health risks. One reply stuck me as extraordinary, and illustrated how non-global we are at times in the supposedly sophisticated Western World. An American friend assumed it was the war in Iraq that made us change our plans. She wrote, *I can't understand why you are cancelling your trip to Hong Kong. The war in Iraq is a long way from China.*

'Guys,' I said in disbelief, 'wait till you read this. They obviously don't understand what's happening.'

'What news channel are these people listening to?' asked Joseph.

Even our travel agents in Ireland were slow to respond when we asked them for help in rerouting our trip. The emergency situation that we felt we were in was definitely losing something in translation. So we made our own plans in the end with a lovely young travel agent in a hotel in Denpasar. He explained our limited choices.

'I am so sorry you are disappointed,' he said, 'I am very pleased to help to make things little better for you. We see what can we do.'

He was sporting a tie and crisp white shirt and black pants and sat behind the British Airways desk like a kind of saviour. His Balinese face showed white teeth when he smiled. Beside us was a British family cancelling their trip to Hong Kong and booking for London.

Flying from Denpasar was one hurdle to mount: We could only go to Singapore or Bangkok according to our tickets. (Or to Sydney, he explained to us, which was available as a route but would cost a fortune because we had already left that continent – there's no going back unless you pay for it.) Having forfeited nearly $7,000 already (which we perhaps foolishly still hoped to get back from Jeffrey), it was not our first option. Once we had cleared that hurdle, we had to decide where to next. From Singapore, we had only three choices on the Oneworld Alliance Round the World ticket: Frankfurt, London, or Rome. Unable to decide ourselves, we left the choice up to Deirdre and Joseph and rang them from Denpasar.

Nyoman thought this was wonderful.

'You let the children make this decision for you?' We nodded and he laughed and dialled the number for us.

'They won't choose London, Niall, because it's too close to home,' I said as he waited for one of them to answer the phone.

'Hiya, JoJo? Is Deedee there? Tell her to get on the other line.'

'Hi, Dee. Yes, yes, we're here now with the travel agent. He tells us we have three choices and we're leaving it up to you guys.'

'Yeah?' said Deirdre hesitantly.

'Ri-ight,' said Joseph, a bit chuffed.

'So, we're going to Singapore on Wednesday. Right?' said Niall.

'Hmmm,' they replied.

'So, then, the story is… we can go to Rome, London, or Frankfurt after a few days in Singapore. What do you say?'

There wasn't much of a pause on the other end. Their mental calculations simultaneously ruled out London as I suspected, and Rome was out because we had travelled to Italy before. They chose the third option.

'Frankfurt!' Was their resounding answer, followed very quickly when the penny had dropped by Deirdre shouting excitedly.

'Then can we go to Prague?' She had been looking at the map already and was figuring out a possible itinerary.

'Yes, probably so, Dee. We could be there for your birthday, in fact.'

'Cool,' she said.

'Can we go to Salzburg?' asked Joseph.

'Of course we can,' answered Niall. 'I mean I think so,' he continued, laughing as he moved the phone away from his ear so I could hear the shouting in the background. 'We'll decide the rest of it when we get back. Mum and I will book the tickets now and see you in about an hour.'

I was imagining them in their room at the Four Seasons with the map of Europe spread out before them marking a route across as many countries as possible. We were committed to only one destination before taking up residency for a month in the south of France and that was Paris, where we would arrive just in time to meet up with my sister and her family and, separately, Deirdre's classmates. Meanwhile, Joseph and Deirdre would have fun making a route from Frankfurt to Prague to Paris while Niall and I figured out the logistics. Our smiling agent rewrote our tickets and made the bookings. The waves rolled in along the Balinese beach in the distance as Niall and I looked at the map of the world, tracing with our eyes the route back home.

~

Arriving in Singapore was not without trepidation. Travellers from Europe and America were advised by their governments not to travel to Hong Kong, China, Vietnam *and* Singapore. Toronto had been added to the list of infected cities as well. It was like opening the door to a darkened room, not knowing if the floor would give way beneath you as you stepped across the threshold. Disembarking, we looked suspiciously around us for signs of the contagion, but were met by a rather empty arrivals terminal. Some of the customs' officers were wearing masks, some were not. It seemed eerie and vacant. A car was arranged for us by the hotel and the driver greeted us.

The emptiness of the airport was echoed in the empty streets as we drove from the airport through the tree-lined avenues of jacaranda trees. Joseph announced that he loved Singapore even though we had only just arrived. The feeling was one of whiteness. Not a scrap of rubbish in sight. As the city came into view, tall gleaming skyscrapers, the buildings Joseph loves, lined the harbour. Perhaps he said he loved it straight out because Singapore is most like the cities he draws from his imagination. Indeed there is a sense that grows on you while visiting Singapore that it is the city of someone's fantasy, a city drawn on white paper, on the edge of the water. A city that seems to work from A to Z. Arriving at the Ritz Carlton only furthered our sense of the ideal which was welcomed considering what we had prepared ourselves for. The people in the city were not all wearing masks as the Western press would have you believe. The city hospitals had the SARS infection under control and had located every person who had been in close contact with anyone who had become infected. Quarantine was being well enforced. There was nothing for us to fear. If you had to be in Asia during the SARS outbreak, then there was one place to be: Singapore.

We were greeted by a line of navy-blue uniformed hotel personnel as we came through the door. Perhaps it was the well-documented Singaporean welcome, the tradition of hospitality, or else it was because SARS had created a dearth of guests, but we were grandly welcomed. We rode up the elevator looking at each other with the uncertain expression of people who find themselves somewhere they never really planned to be. We had booked the Ritz Carlton Millennia because, with hotels in Singapore operating at less than 20 per cent capacity, there were some very good deals to be had. And I mean very. And if there was ever a time that we needed a little comfort it was now. The Ritz in Singapore, recently voted the sixth top hotel in Asia and the twenty-fifth best hotel in the world by *Conde Nast Traveller,* boasts the best bathroom view in the world. From our tub we could see the whole of the skyline of Singapore. It was one of those hotels with all the glamour you associate with the romantic name: luxurious towels, slippers and bathrobes, mahogany furniture. There was Internet access in each room and plush white carpets and full, gold-tinted drapes. Dinner, a lavish display of an Asian smorgasbord of food, was definitely an experience of indulgence.

Still we couldn't help feeling conspicuous. There was a great sense that SARS was *out there*, that so many businessmen and other travellers had cancelled, and here we were, a Western family of four, right in the thick of it. We had met an extremely tanned English woman by the pool. A blond in her sixties sipping a drink, wearing gold bangles. She told us that she had been staying on the top floor of the hotel for weeks because there was nowhere for her to go. There was an eerie sense of strangers on a ship in a storm. Only here the storm was nearly invisible, but definitely insidious. It may be hidden in an innocent cough. The lady we met was living at the Ritz after she and her husband had been advised to leave Jakarta five months ago because of the increased risk of terrorist attacks on English and American businessmen. Her daughter in England was supposed to come for a visit, but had decided against it because of SARS in Singapore. She confessed she was heartbroken. I told the lady that if she wanted to have her daughter phone me at the hotel I could tell her that the media had blown it a bit out of proportion and that, in Singapore at least, she would have very little to fear. But sometimes people need drama in their lives as a way of functioning and I guessed it suited both the daughter and the mother in this case.

The contrast between the unreal world of luxury that we had been experiencing since we left Sydney, first with the Four Seasons in Bali and next with the Ritz in Singapore, and the world of anti-Americanism abroad in the hot air was something we wouldn't have been as aware of back home in Ireland. I doubt if we would have turned on CNN every morning to see what was happening in the war in Iraq or what new developments were occurring with the SARS virus. It was a lesson not only in world geography for Deirdre and Joseph but probably an eye opener for them in terms of feelings of anti-Americanism. However, unlike the edgy wariness of being in Bali with terrorism in Indonesia, there was never a sense of feeling unprotected in Singapore. Yet, there was a feeling that Big Brother was watching. Nobody put a step out of place. After all this was a Singapore where chewing gum was still illegal.

We took a bus tour of the city one hot afternoon, taking a rather long, circuitous route to arrive at the station because we could tell that crossing the road anywhere other than at a pedestrian crossing was a no-no. A few passengers were wearing masks when we boarded the bus. We kept our faces to the window. A Singaporean voice came across the sound system to tell us which stop was next. The points of interest we were hoping to hear about were not exactly on the itinerary. The faceless voice told us which shopping mall was next, rather than pointing out museums or places of cultural interest such as the parliament house building. It was baffling and prompted Joseph to say, I think, 'Singapore is more western than America. Look, they have shopping malls on every corner.'

He was right. If there is one thing Singapore has, it is shopping malls, ranging from the budget to Tiffany's: a shopper's haven. As one travel guide put it, in Singapore, shopping is a sport. From the time of the British East India Trading Company, Singapore has been a free trading port. And now one might say it has gone over the top. It is not just foreigners, but Singaporeans themselves, spend a lot of their time and money in the shopping malls. The hippest place is Orchard Road and Deirdre and I went along in a downpour to search for some Asian fashions, which were hard to find because of the amount of Western imports and outlets. She did end up with a very cool bag and a wraparound skirt without buttons or zips, similar in style to Alistar Trung's designs in Sydney, only much more affordable.

After Orchard Road, there was Little India, Arab Street and Chinatown to visit. The heat was oppressive as we tried to follow a map around Little India where Niall bought Deirdre a blue and yellow fresh-flowered necklace and we sweated past silk sarongs and cashmere shawls and little hanging elephant strings and spicy aromas until Joseph could take no more and insisted he should be sitting by the hotel pool. Deirdre and I then set out by ourselves to see Chinatown which, according to our taxi driver, was too clean. I liked it being clean but I understood what he meant. It was a bit like a shopping street you might find in *It's a Small World* at a Disney theme park. But most bizarre was the picture of the old town with its Chinese language signs and colourful shop fronts dwarfed beneath the skyline of crisp, tall silver buildings. The mom and pop shops have long since been squeezed out, but for us it was still a thrill. Chinese herbalists selling dried sheep dung and shrivelled-up pigs' ears and every kind of powder and dried leaves and hanging organs you can think of. We stopped by one little shop to buy my friend Marie's three daughters some Chinese dresses and, as I was doing so, I knew that these things could be just as easily bought in New York City or London and probably for the same price, but at least I knew they were as real and as close to China as I was going to get. Next we went in search of a three-legged frog which I understood from my limited knowledge of Feng Shui would bring good luck and which, no surprise, I had failed to find in Ireland. I found one here without much searching. Maybe Chinatown was too sanitised, but it made an impression on us anyway, as we wandered around in the humid heat, and with nearly 80 per cent of Singaporeans being Chinese, it was easy to half-imagine ourselves on Mainland China.

I had a chat with our taxi driver and asked him why the taxi fares were so cheap. He told me that it was partly because there were over 10,000 taxis in Singapore and also because the government prided itself on an efficient yet affordable transport system.

'Why is giving tips discouraged?'

'The government does not want us to earn unaccountable wages that they cannot tax us on,' he said matter-of-factly, but with a certain resignation.

'Oh,' I said slowly. It was starting to make sense.

'The government takes care of us, but does not let us get too far ahead.'

'Why don't you complain?' I said innocently but realising at the same time that I had not seen any signs or posters advocating or protesting against anything and it must be for a reason. Maybe it was illegal to protest.

'What is the use? Where would we go? Singapore is a small country. There is nowhere else to go.'

'I see. Kind of like you're caught between a rock and hard place,' I said.

The taxi driver looked at me in a way that made me think he probably didn't understand what I was talking about. Most

Singaporeans speak a version of English learned from Chinese, Malaysian and Tamil English speakers, called Singlish, and it has a certain style to it. My slang saying was not in his vocabulary.

'But it is not so bad. We are selfish. In Singapore, we are just interested in making money.'

I could have stayed talking with him, but we had reached the hotel. I was interested in where I could learn something more about life from his viewpoint.

'Are there any writers here in Singapore?' I asked, as if I had suddenly had a brilliant idea. I wondered if there was any sort of underground movement of social protest and that maybe the writers of the country had something to say about it. 'I'm just a taxi driver. I don't know,' he said as we pulled up to the great foyer of the hotel.

'Well, good luck, then,' I said handing him the fare and a tip besides. 'I hope you make lots of money.'

'Thank you very much,' he said, smiling. 'I hope I do too.'

Later, I thought about the lack of indigenous culture. It felt to me that imagination was not part of the curriculum. Singapore is about commerce and efficiency.

~

The driver's tone revealed to me that he knew his opinion couldn't change anything. It was a curious thing about Singaporeans. They have this kind of resignation. As if their own opinions don't really matter. And why change the status quo? Their health care was taken care of, likewise their education and housing. Government in Singapore is the mother and the father. And like Big Daddy, takes care of everything, but taxes income at source. Its unique structure of capitalism from the West and Communism from China seemed to me at this point in time working for the good of the people. Their basic needs are met. But in a very pronounced way, it seemed to me that the only goal of every Singaporean was to make money. Singapore ranks third after the US and Finland in terms of global competitiveness in business.

~

It is a thing that happens when you are travelling on a long journey like ours. Sometimes you are filled with excitement and anticipation; you arrive in the places you imagined and they fire you. Other times, you are simply travelling, simply a body in stillness or in motion. Back in Singapore, Niall and I knew that we needed to rally the troops. The year's journey had just begun to feel long and we were still feeling the disappointment of losing China. Singapore, with its super malls with Burberry and Christian Dior and white Mercedes, then Little India, with its colours and smells and flowers, clothes outside windows, Indian music and food, and then Chinatown, was perhaps a good transition. Bittersweet because of the missed opportunity to go to China. A hint of what might have been and what was ahead. Travel always has this element of elsewhere, this sense of the far hills being greener. It is a constant test to be in the now. Deirdre was often best at this, happy to be walking through new places keeping her eyes open to new designs and fashions and what she could bring home, and in Singapore happy to visit the fabulous empty gym in the hotel and later swim in the millennium pool with its great waterfall. She could lie there at ease in the time itself. Still we needed to look ahead and, to do so, booked an Afternoon Tea in the famous Raffles Hotel.

We arrived early, passing rows of glamorous cars and some turbaned doormen to enter the old-world atmosphere that lingers in the foyer of Raffles. Despite the arrival of many chic boutiques tucked into the corners of the Raffles arcade, it is impossible not to still feel a sense of age and history. Here you step away from the white towers and the glamour malls, and with a little imagination you can glimpse the colonial world when the hotel was a stepping-off point for the likes of Somerset Maugham and Joseph Conrad. Passing a couple who sat like a kind of living sculpture, he with a hair-sprayed helmet of yellow-blond hair, dressed in white down to his shoes, she in silver with matching blond hair, we went into the famous Writer's Bar and I ordered a 'Singapore Sling'. As soon as it came, Joseph asked for a sip.

In his white shirt and combed hair he cut quite a picture lifting the narrow stemmed glass and sipping with eyes squinting. He put back the glass and licked his lips.

'Mmm. I like it,' he said. 'It tastes like Christmas.'

'Joseph, you're dead right.' I laughed, after taking a sip myself. 'It tastes exactly like Christmas. And like Christmas it's got everything in it. Look at this recipe.'

We read from the complimentary card on the round glass table: Gin, pineapple juice, lime juice, grenadine, Benedictine, cherry brandy….

My father, who spent part of his life as an international real-estate lawyer, sent us a wonderful email when he heard that we were going to Raffles. He wrote that he had been there in 1981 for a much-needed lift after his embarrassment over dropping a fish-eye back into his shark-fin soup which then splattered all over a senior delegate of the Singapore Investment Authority during lunch at The Peninsula. He wrote:

> *If you can keep your health*
> *When all about you are losing theirs*
> *(and getting an Asian flu),*
> *If you can skirt the globe*
> *When most won't dare*
> *(And have a sling in Raffles when half-through,)*
> *If you can fly and not get tired of searches*
> *And wear the same old things from week to week,*
> *If you just laugh when ports are shut against you*
> *And things begin to look a little bleak,*
> *If you can watch your plans and reservations get screwed up*
> *By vile goons and killjoy's germs*
> *And start again without much hesitation,*
> *Then yours is the world and everything that's in it...*

> *...Love to all, Dad*

Three o'clock came around and we began to observe the arrival of the Afternoon Tea brigade. I had to smile to myself, for they were a troop, coming in out of the tropical heat for that most English of repasts. We followed them and sat in the long dining room where waiters in white jackets attended us, bringing silver teapots and filling our cups time and again. At the head of the room was a lavish buffet with everything from hot meats and salads to the traditional finger sandwiches and scones. It became a kind of comedy for us, watching the middle-aged ladies and gents going discreetly up to fill their plates a third, fourth, even fifth time. Soon it became clear that, for some, Afternoon Tea at Raffles was lunch, dinner and supper too! Before long, we were giggling and I had tears of laughter in my eyes whispering to Deirdre and Joseph not to stare or comment.

'Where is she putting it though?' I couldn't help wondering aloud as one particularly trim-looking lady came back to her table with a fifth helping, this time just a selection of cakes and cream.

Deirdre puffed out her cheeks and we all laughed. And the good humour ran through us like a warm breeze. All right, so, we were not going on to China. But Europe had things to offer, and in the sated feeling of the white dining room of Raffles Hotel with its long windows viewing a courtyard garden, we talked ourselves back into excitement. We spoke of places we didn't know yet except by reputation, of the castle at Heidelberg, of Salzburg, of the Alps, and of taking another long train journey, this time to arrive in Prague for Deirdre's sixteenth birthday. The waiters came and went from us with polite smiles, clearing away plates and bringing fresh forks for more. Being from Ireland, I think we savoured the copious cups of tea more than the food. And so on into the late afternoon we sat there, talking of the next step on the journey, raising a finger occasionally and watching as, out of the silver teapot, came another cup of the good stuff.

Europe

I awoke in the middle of the night flight and looked out the window. Little nests of lights in scattered piles flickered thousands of feet below. From the map on board, I could tell that we were somewhere above Kabul. Deirdre had been worried that we'd fly into Iraqi airspace and I assured her that we wouldn't. Joseph had a surgical mask half on, half off his face, just in case, even though we had already learned that the masks were of little protection. But every time somebody coughed, up went the mask. Deirdre had hers in her hand, at the ready. In fact, about 35 per cent of the passengers were wearing masks, but it was more for peace of mind than anything else. I suppose it was a bit like wearing a T-shirt over a naked body in the freezing cold. We all slept fitfully as you do on long flights. It was not a scene set for slumber. Added to the wariness of SARS, the uncertainty of the war, was our own painful acceptance that we had left the Asian continent for good.

It was five in the morning when we touched down at Frankfurt's International Airport. Expecting to be observed for possible signs of SARS, we instead retrieved our bags and passed through customs and its harsh fluorescent lights as if we had just walked in from next door. We stood in the darkness in the cold morning air of Germany waiting for a taxi in a kind of depression, a kind of anticlimax. Fifteen hours earlier we had been sweltering in the tropical heat of Singapore. I had expected to feel sullen, in fact anticipated it, but as we drove from the airport through the grey light of an early spring morning, I had an odd sensation. Something was vaguely familiar. I found myself thinking of Westchester County, of all places. The suburbs of New York City. How could I be thinking of Westchester? Then it dawned on me, we were back in the Northern Hemisphere. It was the *trees*. The tree landscape was similar in the frosty dawn along the *Autobahn*. The trees were in their first flush of greenery just as they would be in New York, just as they would be in Dublin, just as they would be in Kiltumper. There were daffodils in the undergrowth, and tulips. Germany was so much more recognisable than Bali or Singapore in a way I had not expected. Like *Hello?* What was I thinking? Sometimes I do laugh at myself. But it was suddenly that simple, and I gave into the feeling and let myself be lulled in a familiarity that was comforting.

We had booked a hotel in Frankfurt at rather short notice. Considering we had arrived the day before my birthday, it was a bit of a letdown. I could tell Niall was disappointed because, although the hotel he had picked had 'grand' in its name, it didn't live up to it.

'I'm sorry, Chris,' he said. 'I was hoping for something better for your birthday.'

'It's okay, honey. We're here now. Safe and sound. To ask for anything more would be pure juvenile,' I said, trying to hide my disappointment.

Joseph was not easily comforted either. He was dealing with what he called 'huge surges' of diarrhoea.

'What do you expect, Mum? Coming from a diet of steamed rice and vegetables to this – pork and pastries.'

Deirdre, for some reason known only to herself, had always wanted to come to Germany. I asked her how she was feeling.

'I'm freezing and tired!'

'Right,' I said. 'Of course you are.' And pulled out the jacket we had been saving for the cold springtime of Beijing, that was last worn in Glacier, Montana. Finding yourself and your family at a Frankfurt hotel at six in the morning on a cold, grey day after a twelve-hour flight was not the most inspiring of arrivals. It could only get better, I hoped.

Still, it was an interesting situation to find ourselves back in Europe. Joseph said that he felt too *normal*. It was weird, he said, because since we had left the previous September we had not been normal.

'How do you mean?' I asked.

'Well, in some places we looked different, like in South America.'

'Hmmm.'

'And in New Zealand we were different from them.'

'How's that?' I asked, curious as to how he was going to explain that one.

'We wore shoes!'

'And now we're *normal* again.'

From the mouths of babes. What a delight it had been to have Joseph's running commentary on the trip. What was also fascinating was that Joseph considered himself European. In a way, he was already at home.

~

Because of Frankfurt's development as a money metropolis and centre of international finance, it is not a city for tourists unless you're interested in the Trade Fair Tower – until ten years ago the highest building in Europe – or the European Central Bank, or the Bundesbank. There is little evidence of an old-world charm and much of the old city was destroyed during World War II. After a lavish breakfast that only the Germans can offer, we set off on foot with our jackets and hats and what scarves and gloves we could find amongst our pile of mostly lightweight clothes for the main shopping district of Frankfurt. To our delight, there was an open-air market in the famous pedestrian zone known as *Fressgass*, meaning Glutton's Lane. Scents of enormous hot pretzels and hotdogs and steaming cups of cider and cold beer and mulled wine wafted in the air. Baskets of tulips and daffodils and herbs from organic growers decked little stalls. Painted eggs with pretty blue ribbons hung on small twiggy trees and sold for €2. We bought four of them and a pretzel for Joseph. The wealth of fresh produce and cheeses and salamis and beer and wines from Bavaria in the second week of April was impressive. In the shops, the impact of the war was seen on short-haired mannequins clothed in army fatigue pants and camouflage-style T-shirts. Germany, like France, was against the war in Iraq and, in the morning, we awoke to a small demonstration across the street.

We decided to make the most of our unexpected visit to Germany, so we rented a car and planned a route along the Romantic Road down through Bavaria. We were recovering well from our jet lag and culture shock, although Deirdre couldn't keep warm and Joseph's tummy was aching for plain food. Looking for a day trip from Frankfurt in order to honour my birthday, we chose to head to Heidelberg, one of Germany's most romantic locations. After all, I was embarking upon my fiftieth year and it was only fitting that we should visit the famous city with its red-walled castle, a city that is renowned for its dilapidated beauty and long history of capture and plunder though its 800 years, when I, too, was feeling a little like an old wreck myself, albeit a gracefully ageing one. Manouevring ourselves out of Frankfurt without a word of German among us was its own little adventure and we drove down the wrong road in the wrong direction more than once.

'So much for Europeanising the road signs,' said Niall in exasperation as we drove the long black Mercedes station wagon that Avis had given us.

Only 80 km from Frankfurt, we arrived in Heidelberg by lunchtime and followed signs for parking, eventually finding our way to the old part of town to the Hauptstrasse – the long, cobbled shopping street closed to traffic in an area famous for its Christmas market. Although clearly European, Germany was at first indecipherable to us. We found that the road signs and directions and tourist information were not exactly visitor friendly. Without the benefit of having done a little research, as I had with the rest of the trip, we were winging it and just followed the pedestrian traffic down what seemed to be the longest shopping street ever, to the base of the 315 steps that led to the castle, and began the climb. I read somewhere later that it is a breathtaking view because by the time you get to the top, 640 feet up the hill, you are *literally* breathless. Mark Twain wrote about his visit to Heidelberg in *A Tramp Abroad*, saying that 'a ruin must be rightly situated to be effective' and this one certainly was. High on the hill with a commanding view of the River Neckar and the Neckar Valley and the city of church spires and old painted buildings sits the Heidelberg Castle. It is said to be one of the sights of Europe to see the castle illuminated, as happens on special occasions, with fireworks and lights displaying a blinding spectacle of crimson and gold. We were too jaded to investigate the library, which has a document signed by Charlemagne, or the famous laboratory. But we did take a look down into the cellar to see the legendary Grosses Fass, the biggest wooden barrel in the world ever to have been filled with wine, capable of holding approximately 221,000 litres. Made in 1751, it was built from 130 oak tree trunks. Like some wines that only get better with age, the Heidelberg Castle has a beauty that comes from decay and ruin, with nature softening its collapsing corners and adorning it with crowns of greenery and birdsong. We found an attractive spot to sit outside with a stein of beer and a frankfurter, where we sang 'Happy Birthday' quietly.

~

The Romantic Road, so named because of the old castles, historic towns and pastoral landscape beloved by German poets of the 'Romantic' period, was probably coined by a tourism director from Augsburg in the 1950s. It follows a medieval trade route and part of the old Roman Road from Augsburg to Rome. The twenty-six towns along its route are among Germany's best-preserved medieval walled towns, one thousand to two thousand years old. The trail begins in Wurzburg and ends 290 km later at the foothill of the Alps in Fussen. The travel books caution you against travelling during the high season because of traffic congestion along the two-laned highway, but in mid-April we had the road to ourselves. There was no rain on the horizon and, in our black Mercedes, we cruised through the Bavarian countryside in sunshine. I have to say Germany was a surprise to all of us. We loved the landscape of rolling hills and green fields dotted with slender clock towers, their painted obelisk tops rising from the centre of every small village. It was a fairy-tale setting. Gothic architecture from the medieval period garnished every town. Our first stop was the walled city, Rothenburg ob der Tauber, which, unknown to us at the time, is Germany's best-preserved town. A treasure we stumbled upon in our ignorance. Known as a free imperial city since 1274, Rothenburg is a delightful city to wander around, with its houses half timbered and wooden-shuttered and its steeples and highly pitched roofs and cobbled streets. We were dismayed to find a McDonald's in the middle of the central marketplace, and I guess the Germans are as much entitled to a Big Mac as anyone else, but in such a historical setting it looked a bit comical to say the least.

We spent the night in Augsburg, which in 15 BC was a Roman military camp and was, by the 1500s, one of the largest cities in the German-speaking world. We stayed in an immaculately clean small hotel near the cathedral, the Dom, where the earliest settlements in Augsburg are to be found. Augsburg was the birthplace and home of Mozart's father, and the hotel we stayed in had been remodelled from a wealthy merchant's house where Mozart spent the night during some of his many visits to the city from nearby Salzburg. In the morning we headed straight for Austria with great enthusiasm because it was like an adventure inside our adventure, setting out for Salzburg skirting along the German Alps, taking full advantage of our year of holidays and leaving behind our disappointment of China. Our drive took us past Chiemsee, Bavaria's largest lake, and then just before the Austrian border to Bad Reichenhall where a stretch of road takes you along the German Alpine Road to Berchtesgaden, said to be one of the most panoramic routes in the entire Alps and home to Hitler's famous Eagle's Nest. We lunched in bright sunshine in a café in a square overlooking the painted façade of the Zum Hirschen, formerly a hotel, painted from base to roof with scenes from Bavaria. Beautifully painted buildings appeared around every corner and from everywhere the snow-topped mountains came into view. Stunning scenery abounds in the Berchtesgadener Land, the largest and oldest nature reserve in the

German Alps, and we all wanted to come back in winter to see the fairy-tale land come alive in the snow. In less than an hour, we reached the city of Salzburg, home of Wolfgang Amadeus Mozart and *The Sound of Music* and one of UNESCO's World Cultural Heritage Sites. Another unplanned destination and another enchantment. As we approached the city we were amazed how easy the drive had been from Frankfurt and how easily we found ourselves flowing in the traffic across the river looking for our hotel.

Our time was short in Salzburg, but among our wishes was to visit the Mozart Museum, do a little shopping for Deirdre's sixteenth birthday which was two days away, hear some music, return the car and figure out how to get to Prague. I had planned our trip pretty efficiently up to this European leg and suddenly found myself without information on where to eat, where to shop, where to stay, and most important what to see. For an efficient planner like myself, I felt like an unprepared girl scout. Still, we allowed ourselves to be taken along with the flow, as if we were in a kind of lazy river where we moved along without much effort in the same direction as everyone around us. This is how we found ourselves at No. 9 Getreidegasse, the Mozart Museum – without a map – and up the stairs and into the house where he lived for many years in Salzburg. We saw his first violin, Deirdre and I standing in front of the glass box in which it was suspended as if the air around it held it magically in place. It was probably the reverberations in the room from people's footsteps, but as we looked, Mozart's violin seemed to pulse and we imagined that our own meagre harmonics were somehow in tune with the great composer's. The Mozart family lived at the Hagenauer House for twenty-six years. Manuscripts, opera sets and original portraits of the family are displayed along with his first viola and his first clavichord piano. The museum has been lovingly and systematically renovated to reflect with accuracy what it would have looked like in Mozart's time. Mozart felt at home in Salzburg – that alone bestows upon the city an air of beauty and harmony that is unrivalled in the world. The old town with its magnificent architecture and the new town with its chic shops straddle both sides of the River Salzach. A city of white gold. As salt is vital to life, I thought, Salzburg is vital to European culture.

We booked tickets though our hotel for the Mozart Kammer-orchester and Festival Ensemble which performs regularly in the Prince's Chamber at the Festung Hohensalzburg, the famous fortress that sits high on the hill overlooking the city. Built in 1077 by an Archbishop, it is possibly the largest, fully preserved fortress in Central Europe. During its long history, the fortress has remained unconquered. And no surprise; it is not easy to access. Instead of conquering the steps, we arrived by funicular, the easy ascent to the white fortress, just in time to see the sun setting behind the Alps. Inside, the chamber orchestra was tuning up beneath a blue and gold ceiling, comprising 3,000 gilded bosses. We sat in the Prince's Chamber and listened as the Salzburg Festival Ensemble opened the evening's programme with a serenade by Mozart, his famous *Eine Kleine Nachtmusik*. I was enraptured and thought again, as so often on this trip, of the wonderful experiences Niall and I were making possible for our children. I didn't care if the five-member ensemble played the Mozart with a little too much polish. Or if the cellist was overly dramatic as Deirdre felt. It was still Mozart being played in his city. I knew it was a bit too nicely packaged, too staged even. One might be tempted to say, 'give me a break, isn't this a little OTT?' Another time I might agree, but not this night, this exquisitely clear night with an almost full moon rising above the beautiful white city in the Alps. *Eine Kleine Nachtmusik* lingered in the air as we left the fortress. The white moon rose above the citadel of the Salzburg Cathedral, its glimmer lighting up the wrought-iron, gilded signs along the Getreidegasse, down the narrow street of shops and houses, past courtyards and passageways all tightly nestled together like quavers and crochets on a clef.

~

When we awoke on 16 April, it was Deirdre's sixteenth birthday. We were in Salzburg. By late afternoon we would be arriving in Prague, the Czech Republic. But first we had to return the car, find the train station, load all our bags on board the train and take an eight-hour journey, changing train four times. We hadn't antici-pated that it would be such a tiresome trek, but flying from Salzburg was exorbitant and Avis wouldn't let us drop the car off in Prague. So training it was the only way. Deirdre was determined that we should go to Prague. It had the sound of mystery to her. And it was her birthday after all. It was as good a substitute as she was going to get for the dinner with a record producer in Shanghai that had been bumped from the schedule on account of SARS. Niall and I were impressed that she didn't mind spending most of the day on board trains. We took a photograph of Deirdre reading an Austrian paper with the date clearly visible so we could take another photo of her reading a Czech paper (or pretending to read it) in the evening, reminding her in years to come of the riches of that special day.

We marked the long journey by transfers and the time seemed to pass quickly enough. Our second transfer had to be managed in six and half minutes at the Czech border. We devised a system where I would throw the bags down to Niall who would carry as many as he possibly could, locate the train and come back for the stragglers. Deirdre and Joseph were weighed down with knapsacks and their own pulley bags. I was wearing a bag across my front and back and pulling two bags. It really showed that we had too much stuff. It was a scene from a comedy, the four of us dragging our world-weary luggage down the steps to cross under the tracks and back up again, huffing and puffing, pulling and sweating and swearing in six minutes flat. Not a porter in sight. My shoulders and elbows were nearly pulled from their sockets. Joseph was cursing. Niall was red as a beetroot. Deirdre accomplished her feat with style. Hair untangled, smile on her freckled face, poised as befits a good princess who is asked to perform a peasant's tasks. What a trouper. After the Olympian achievement, we rested and ate what we had gathered from breakfast, some bread and apples, passing Czech villages and train stations with unpronounceable names, hoping for a tea trolley that never came.

We arrived in Prague by early evening. Into a cold, low-ceilinged, red-and-black checked (or at least that is what I remember) train terminal. Our pile of luggage in disarray at our feet, beginning to show signs of weariness. Zips coming apart on dusty and blackly marked canvas duffels, and crooked wheels. People in dark leather coats smoking cigarettes and ladies with black eyeliner and dyed hair eyed us blankly as they passed. Half a dozen taxi drivers descended upon us. The only thing I had managed to read from the guidebook said not to trust the taxi-cab drivers in Prague. They will take you the long way around and charge you double. Rather, we waited for a man with a sign to appear to bring us to our hotel on the river, aptly named the Riverside Hotel. We had been waiting at the wrong end of the station, it seemed. Finally we heaped ourselves into an enormous black limousine, a limousine fit for a queen's entourage, and were driven through the late afternoon traffic of the city through somewhat drab streets with faceless concrete buildings flanked by parked cars. It wasn't until we neared the river that we began to see the splendour that people speak of when they speak of the magic of Prague. For it *is* a magical city, a fantastical city, a city of sandcastle spires and Gothic steeples and turrets. Pastel-coloured buildings reflect their aged beauty in the fast-moving waters of the Vltava. The same fast-moving waters of the Vltava, meaning wild waters, that had carried with them baby grand pianos during the floods of the summer of 2001.

We were grandly welcomed at the Riverside Hotel by Petr, the manager, a very tall, erect Czech with a head of black hair immaculately in place. He glided rather than walked. We were brought up in a smoky, golden elevator to an elegant landing with big white doors and golden knockers. He showed us to a beautiful suite in the corner of the hotel with one window overlooking the river and the other facing Charles Bridge. The children's room was adjoining ours. We were perched on the banks of the river's edge. I had booked the rooms on the Internet, explained who we were, that it was the tail end of our trip and that it was also Deirdre's birthday. We felt that we were being treated like royalty. The staff presented Deirdre with a birthday cake and the four us with decorated Easter eggs. We felt anything but bohemian in Bohemia.

～

The way to get to know any great city is either to fall in love or to get lost. And the latter is just what Deirdre and I did when we couldn't find anyone who spoke English to direct us back to the river after a visit to the New Town, founded in 1348 by Charles IV after the Old Town had become too crowded. So we just kept going until we could walk no further, feeling cold with the cutting wind blowing in our ears. We walked along narrow sidewalks with little closed-looking cafés and veered further and further away from Wenceslas Square. We finally found a taxi which took us just around the corner – we had been very near – and we were charged an appropriate and reasonable fare. So much for the guidebook's warning.

We had seen some of the city's famous sites the day before when we engaged a guide, at the recommendation and insistence of the helpful, but slightly obsequious, Petr. Her name was Irina. She was tall and thin with lank blond hair and a yellowy pale complexion. A lady in her fifties, she appeared to wear no make-up but lipstick. She had studied Spanish and drama at university and was hired as a translator and employed as an independent guide. To say she was not cheery would not be exaggerating. She had, after all, survived Communism, but it had knocked something out of her, unless that's how the Czech people are by nature. She was intent on showing us St Vitus Cathedral, the jewel of Prague, and pointing out where you could see the Gothic architecture, then the Baroque, the Romanesque, the Renaissance, emphasising the remarkable co-existence of the many preserved buildings and monuments dating back a thousand years. She showed us the squares used in the filming of *Amadeus* and the house where Mozart stayed. We watched the changing of the guards at the government buildings with their smart blue uniforms and horns blaring. Down Golden Lane, where the alchemists used to live and where Kafka lived at No. 22 for a year. She was less keen on showing us the crowded shopping markets where an abundance of shops were selling garnets. She warned us away from the shops displaying Russian dolls.

'You can't trust those. It's hard to buy genuine Czech products now with too many Russians here,' she said with some disgust.

She explained to us that in the Communist hangover, 70 per cent of the Czech people were atheist. I could see Joseph totting this up in his mind and wondering then what all the churches were about.

'And why don't they believe in anything?' he asked later. 'I want to know.'

'Joseph, for many years Prague and the land known as Bohemia was like a chessboard for rulers. Religions came and went for hundreds of years. Then they had Hitler, followed quickly by Communist rule. Until recently the Czech people have felt powerless to effect any change and now that it has finally come to them they are too wary to align themselves with any religion and are only interested in self-government.'

'Ah huh,' said Joseph nodding his head.

'The history of Bohemia in less than a nutshell, I'm afraid, Joseph, but that's about the gist of it.'

In the boutique streets of Prague, the scent of money changing hands was undeniable, and there was, I thought, a palpable sense of a people making up for lost time. A kind of aloofness in the population was also tangible. What people call the magic of Prague may be in danger of getting tarnished as commercialism and tourism take over, but there is something about the city that I think will never change: the fairy-tale setting of music pervades everything. As you walk you see posters announcing concerts on every wall. There are trios and quartets and quintets playing every night. There are operas and ballets and orchestral performances. From high windows you catch notes escaping from rehearsal. This is something that links the city to its past in a living sense.

'Here,' Niall said, stopping the children, 'here is the theatre where one of my favourite pieces of music, and which you've both heard playing in Kiltumper, Mozart's *Don Giovanni*, was performed for the very first time.' We stood before the old building, in a hush, imagination filling the air, thinking for a moment of that man whose home and first violin we had seen a day before, and who is to say that some ghost of the music did not float on the air?

~

The great astronomer Johannes Kepler lived in Prague for twelve years, from 1600 to 1612, during which time he formulated and published the first of his three laws of planetary motion. He was the Imperial Mathematician to the half-mad, half-wonderful Emperor Rudolph II during the time when Prague was the centre of Europe.

Kepler's work was inspired by the beauty of structure in the universe and he created his theories because he believed in a divine order of the heavens. In the development of astronomy there would have been no Kepler without Copernicus, but no Newton without Kepler. During his years in Prague, although plagued by personal misfortune, he also conceived a fantasy, possibly the first work of science fiction, called *Somnium*, or the 'Dream' in which he imagines a trip to the moon and writes about what the first visitors there will encounter. In my imagination I see him strolling along the Charles Bridge with its thirty statues and gargoyles of gothic proportions through a frozen fog above the icy waters of the Vltava ruminating on the orbits of Saturn and Jupiter and Mars and watching the phases of the moon with his renowned double vision.

In my own efforts to find symmetry and connectedness in the universe, I was delighted to rediscover Kepler in Prague. For in this magical city, the golden city of one hundred spires, Deirdre was turning sixteen. It was a stage set for a princess. Petr had booked us a table at one of the nicest restaurants in Prague, the fashionable French La Perle de Prague, which sits on the top floor of the architecturally whimsical glass building known locally as the Dancing Building or as 'Fred and Ginger' because it resembles a couple dancing. Designed by Frank Gehry and Vlado Milunic, it was directly opposite the hotel on the other side of the river. We arrived by walking across the bridge in our finest clothes as the sun went down, the April evening cooled by the chilly waters of the river. Once inside the Dancing Building, we understood where its name came from. It not only commands a fantastic view of the city but as Deirdre said, 'It feels like I'm inside a pearl.'

The interior was white with white linen tables, each laid with four glasses per setting so everything seemed to sparkle with a luminescence that bounced from glass to silver to window, down to the river water and the lights of the bridges, and back again. Deirdre, sweet sixteen, beamed like a pearl's essence. She was illuminated from within and, I hoped, feeling special. She had crossed a threshold into young womanhood and looked every inch a princess and we her adoring subjects.

During dinner I kept leaving the table to visit the rooftop from

283

where I hoped to see the full moon rising for the eighth time since the start of our journey.

'Yes, my wife too, she is much affected by the moon,' said the maître d', as I came down the stairs from the roof with its spectacular view of Prague Castle shaking my head and feeling a wee bit dizzy from champagne.

'I will keep a look for you and tell you when she is rising,' he said, accompanying me back to our table.

And so we dined, as Niall pointed out, in expectation of the moon as our guest. And in that mood of expectation and birthday excitement and the gladness of travellers newly arrived in a wonderful city, we ate in a kind of warm glow, the little band of our family treasuring the moment of Deirdre.

'Not bad, eh Dee? The moon over Salzburg and the moon over Prague in the last twenty-four hours,' I said, as we left Fred and Ginger behind in The Pearl of Prague.

'A birthday moon just for you,' said Niall giving her a kiss and pointing to the orange orb that had finally floated into the midnight blue sky above the hundred gold-tipped steeples.

The cold air was sobering, but the night was alive with excitement and wonder, and belief in ourselves and our journey. It wasn't Beijing or Shanghai, but it was more significant in a way because it was a reconnection with our roots as children of a great European culture, a culture of music and literature and art. As the great Newton said of Kepler, it was because he was standing on the shoulders of giants that he was able to advance in his studies, and in some small way we were recipients of that legacy.

'You can't tell me there's no harmony in the universe!' I said, giving Deirdre a big hug as we walked back across the bridge arm in arm, cuddling each other against the cold night, our April birthdays over for another year and wondering where we would be this time next year because surely the world was our oyster.

~

The month of April had seen us in Bali, Singapore, Frankfurt, Salzburg, Prague and finally Paris and there were still two weeks left before the start of May. Our final destination in Plascassier in the south of France awaited us. We flew on Easter Sunday to the city of lights, shamefully unobservant of the day that was in it. Although, in our defence, we had prayed the afternoon before to the Infant Child of Prague in the first Baroque church in Prague, The Church of Our Lady Victorious, in the Little Quarter, feeling ourselves somewhat resurrected in front of the tiny statue with its cloth cloak and gold jewelled crown, and its child's hand raised in sanctification on Holy Saturday. We were blessed.

My mother had a special reverence for the infant child, not surprisingly as she birthed six of us infants in seven years, and kept a statue by her bedside. When she died, I took the statue of the Holy Infant of Prague and brought it with me back to Ireland where it stands now above my bed. I made mental note to pay more attention to it when I returned, for its legend of miracles was long and worthy, especially now that I had seen the real thing. I think my mother must have been smiling down from above that Easter evening as she watched from her heavenly realm the international, circuitous routes that brought her two daughters and their families together in Paris. My mother had never been to Paris or seen the other great cites of Europe, but I like to imagine that she was cheering us on and revelling in our adventures.

We met with my sister Deirdre and her family in the evening in an apartment they had rented for the week, off Saint Germain. As soon as we knew they had settled, we taxied over from our own rented apartment in the 15th arrondissement. It was our second visit to the apartment, having been there two years earlier. The rent was very reasonable, which helped because we certainly needed to relax our expenditure before the final splurge down south on the Mediterranean, and we were happy to be staying there again. Bernadette had left a bottle of wine for us on the dining-room table with a note welcoming us back to Paris. She was from County Monaghan and had married a Frenchman, but they lived in London. They kept his apartment from his bachelor days and visited regularly. It was perfect for us with two small bedrooms, a large living/dining room area, kitchenette and a full bathroom. It didn't have great views but it was only a five-minute walk to the Eiffel Tower and less to the metro station. We felt like old hands finding our way around. Niall speaks French quite perfectly so we felt doubly at ease, and looked forward to two weeks in one of the greatest cities in the world, unencumbered in a way because we had no agenda. Our only commitment, besides spending time with my sister, was to bring Deirdre to meet her classmates who had travelled from Ireland to be in Paris for five days as part of their 'transition year' programme, a reunion for Deirdre that we hoped would go well for all concerned.

For their part, Deirdre and Larry had been sceptical about coming to Paris. The war in Iraq was a month old and not going according to Bush's plan for the soldiers to be in and out and back home already. Some of Larry's acquaintances had queried his judgment in deciding to travel to Europe. With a name like Bernstein and an American passport, travelling to the country in Europe most against the war whose capital was home to five million Arabs – was it wise? Anti-Semitism had provoked several riots on the streets of Paris already. This was a time in America when Chirac was being called everything from a coward to a heretic. Americans were denouncing everything French. Champagne and Bordeaux were being removed from the shelves. Naturally, the Bernsteins had some reservations, but in the end they threw caution to the wind and came to Paris, warning Niall that he might find himself the French-talking Pied Piper with seven of us marching behind him, keeping our American mouths shut. As it happened, when they arrived there was little anti-Americanism in the air that was truly offensive, except for some petitioners outside the metro stations asking that Bush and not bombs be dropped from the planes. Some of the Arab taxi drivers were vocal about the war and, along the Champs Elysées, there was a definite dearth of American films in the cinema. But The Gap was still crowded with customers and Disneyland, Paris, was as busy as ever.

Full of excitement and stories to tell, we knocked on the door of their apartment and, when it opened, we shrieked with delight. It was one of those moments loaded with so much to say that you say nothing. Daniel looked at Joseph and Julia looked at Deirdre. I hugged my sister and she me. We shuffled our feet and inched our way into the rather elegant apartment, finally sitting down. It was the first of what was to become many such meetings when we reunited with our life in Ireland where there was just too much to tell and where it was impossible to make known how we really were after all that we had experienced. It was a time if ever there was one to employ the mind-meld custom (the wordless joining of minds) of the great Vulcan nation, used so often by Leonard Nimoy as Spock in *Star Trek*. But, having only my feeble words, I had to make do with, 'Sure, we're fine. We've had a great time.'

Without delay we handed out some gifts that we had brought with us. A wooden flying lady for my sister from the Ubud market in Bali, meaning beautiful woman. A skirt and T-shirt for Julia from Singapore. A bottle of wine for Larry. And souvenir patches and money for Daniel from nearly every country we had been to.

There was nothing I really wanted to do in Paris except to visit the Rodin Museum and revisit the Musée d'Orsay. There was an exhibition of Michelangelo's drawings at the Louvre that I thought Deirdre should see as she would be starting to get her portfolio ready for art school. And I had half an idea of finding our way to Giverny to see Monet's garden. Would the irises be in bloom? As a family we were happy to follow Larry's lead because we were plum worn out from *seeing and doing* according to the guidebook. Also we had the benefit of having been to Paris before and had the good fortune to live in Europe with Paris only a two-hour flight away. It was my sister and her children's first time to Paris. Julia was learning French at school, so she was encouraged to speak with Niall and to order for herself at the restaurants. Not a shy child, she rose to the task and giggled when she got it right. Daniel, the youngest of us, was simply in awe of being transatlantic. He had been given a camera by his grandfather and took as many pictures as he could. He had been promised to get to see the Eiffel Tower and the Arc de Triomphe and Napoleon's Tomb and war museum. Someone else had told him to be sure to see the Mona Lisa at the Louvre. As with so many of us, our first visit to Paris revolves around the age-old list of must-sees. And everyone has a slightly different list. My first trip to Paris was when I was a student travelling in Europe. I was twenty-one. I didn't see the Eiffel Tower then. I didn't take a cruise down the Seine. I was there long enough to take a zillion photographs of gargoyles at the top of Notre Dame and head straight for the train station for a journey to Nice where a friend of mine was studying art and learning French. The more I visit Paris, the more I am struck by its beauty. The more I visit other cities, the more I appreciate Paris.

As Niall said to us while we were eating in a street-side café on Saint Germain, 'There is a reason why Paris is Paris and one of the top-ten places in the world to visit. It has grandeur and hauteur. It has a sense in which it knows it is beautiful. French arrogance is understood in these terms. The French have got one of the best cities in the world and they take care of it. It's one of the few cities where the practical was given as much importance as the beautiful, with its straight avenues and tree-lined boulevards and expansive vistas before its monuments and great buildings. In Paris, everything is a picture.'

Considering the short amount of time the Bernsteins had to spend in Paris it was remarkable what we accomplished with eight of us. An evening cruise down the Seine. A trip up the Eiffel Tower. Two visits to the Musée d'Orsay to see the Degas, the Monets, the Manets, the Van Goghs and the Bonnards. A trip to see the Mona Lisa including a side search for Dutch seventeenth-century paintings that Larry was intent upon finding. The Arc, Concorde and the Tuileries. Notre Dame and Sainte Chapelle. The sound of coins dropping as offerings for candles in the Sacré Coeur with its brilliant gold mosaics. Searching Montmarte for a place to eat. Shopping down Saint Germain for Julia and Deirdre and visits to the pet shops along the Seine for Daniel and Joseph. An afternoon in the garden at the Rodin Museum proved to be a favourite among all of us, Daniel and Joseph and I playing hide and seek in the great green garden and shade of the plane trees under the steady gaze of *The Thinker.*

Even though at the time it couldn't be understood how important it was to me that my sister and her family came to join us for part of our journey, albeit the second to last stop, it was like a great blanket that we wrapped around us all. We were able to share in their excitement at their first European trip together as a family and it didn't diminish in measure to our trip. For their part, they were able to imagine what it had been like for us. The excitement they had felt for Paris we had been feeling for the previous eight months. It was nearly too much for my sister. I could sense her shaking her head and musing to herself *how did they do it?* Because organising the week's trip to Paris had been enough for her.

As Joseph remembered, the day my sister and her family left Paris to return to New York, it was as if the sky was crying. We were crying and it was raining heavily. We were soaked waving them goodbye as Niall hailed a taxi, and we felt a bit like orphans in a foreign city. But the feeling didn't last. After all, the south of France awaited us. Still ahead was Deirdre's reunion with her classmates and a trip to Giverny which I was suddenly intent on doing. The gardener in me was in need of a fix.

~

Giverny is only forty-five minutes away from Gare de Lyon. A short taxi ride leaves you at the café and shops just in front of the gardens. It was the third week of April and the irises were still a closed fist, blue-tipped and green. Not a one had opened. The famous rose pergolas were naked awaiting summer. A spring sea of tulips, pink, red, white and purple black in long borders stoutly saluted our visit. White hyacinths and wallflowers and forget-me-nots were like coloured down feathers beneath them. Clematis and wisteria bloomed along pergolas. Hundreds of pansies, like a poor man's heart, posed for my camera. It was drizzling as we walked along the great gravel paths. But it was still a paradise. The flowerless lily pond was not blue but grey and green and brown reflecting the grey day around us in the shelter of green wood and flowering azaleas. Yet the Japanese bridge with a great weeping willow cascading beside it looked just as it does in Monet's numerous paintings or was I imagining it? I was painting with my mind's eye. It was as exciting as standing in front of Mozart's violin. The ivy-covered pink farmhouse with the green shutters sits facing south towards the unseen Seine.

'I could live here,' I said to Niall, tugging on his arm under the umbrella.

He laughed. 'But you, my dear, have Kiltumper,' he said to me without pause.

'Yes, yes, I do,' I said, smiling back. 'And if you say it with a French accent it'll sound even better.'

'Killtoumpear, hey? *Ah oui, oui, Madame tu es folle…*'

~

Plascassier was the last stop of our journey around the world. Another Internet find, we had booked it back in New Zealand with an English woman named Juliet who had married a Dutchman and lived in Monaco. This was their summer house! On the Internet it looked fantastic. Large swimming pool and pool house. Large lawn area dotted with towering cypress trees. Renovated kitchen, and six bedrooms. Maybe it was the address which was not quite Valbonne, not quite Mougins. Maybe because it was the month of May but the rental cost was reasonable and we jumped at the chance. Initially we had thought we'd be arriving from Hong Kong after a month in China and we had thought we would need some time to wind down before landing home in Ireland. We likened it to a decompression chamber. We could not imagine leaving Shanghai for Shannon and chose instead the south of France as a kind of gathering place. Niall to finish his novel. Me to continue writing about our trip. Deirdre and Joseph to reacquaint themselves with French for their studies, as both would be taking honours French when we returned. Finally it was a place to which we had invited half a dozen friends and family, although most of them were going to miss out it seemed.

We rented a van from Nice Airport and arrived in the late afternoon. Not a cloud in the sky. Unlike Paris where it had been raining intermittently for the last two weeks of April, Plascassier was warm and brilliantly blue. Juliet met us at the door and welcomed us in. She was a petite woman with golden red hair. Very beautiful and young. *Now if I could look like that after a month in the south of France*, I thought to myself. Wouldn't that be icing on the cake? She confessed herself to be a bit of a scatterbrain and wasn't sure what we had agreed contractually. It was one of the things I had discovered during our many Internet dealings. The less money you paid up front, the better it was. Twice when we had paid fully up front it turned out disastrously. You'd think it would be the other

290

way around. It gives me no pleasure to note that our Internet disasters were with Americans.

We couldn't get over the size of the villa and once Juliet had left, Deirdre and Joseph ran from room to room laying claim to their bedrooms. First we had to decide where to put two of Deirdre's friends who had accompanied her from Paris and, once that was organised, we set aside the yellow room with en-suite bathroom for Lucy and Larry, our oldest friends from Kilmihil, who were due to arrive within hours. With the sun streaming through the porch doors it looked like the inside of buttercup. I hoped they would like it. Joseph could move into the girls' room upstairs when they departed a few days later. Meanwhile, he found a place for himself downstairs.

Deck chairs and sun loungers were spaced around the pool and laid out carefully every other morning by an old Frenchman who arrived before we got up and left before we had time to chat with him. Juliet said he kept an eye on the pool and swept the porches and she kept him on out of friendship. He arrived by motorbike and disappeared quietly. The pool was freezing but the kids' Irish bodies were used to cold Atlantic water even in summer and couldn't resist. Deirdre's friends, Vanessa and Sheila, were beside themselves in quiet awe of the villa and their south of France experience. We were happy to be able to provide it for them. Niall and I decided to let them have the run of the place to sunbathe and chat and catch up on all that Deirdre had missed from a year away from school. It worked like a charm. For her part, Deirdre felt like one of the group again and, after meeting her classmates in Paris, was not in the least hesitant about rejoining them for fifth year. It had always been our biggest concern how our children would resume their lives in Ireland and, from the looks of it, Deirdre at least wouldn't have much difficulty.

For the first week we entertained and were entertained by Lucy and Larry, who are also Deirdre's Irish godparents and acted on her behalf when we had a ceremonial welcoming and christening party for Deirdre all those years ago. Larry used to be principal of the school where Niall teaches. During the years we have been much connected with them and they have always been available to us when in need. Lucy was one of the stars of the Kilmihil Drama Group and her penchant for liveliness makes any occasion with her spirited. She was like a mother hen to the girls, warning Sheila to put on more sunscreen, and going to the shops to keep our refrigerator stocked with French delicacies. It was wonderful how well we all got along for the week, but that speaks too of the villa itself, large enough to accommodate our different temperaments, and the weather which held warm and sunny day after day. Lunches saw us eating alfresco beneath the purple wisteria, eight of us around the wooden table, passing the baguettes and cheese and tuna fish and fresh tomatoes and haricots verts and fresh fruit. Evenings saw the four adults sitting in the dining room by candlelight with yet another bottle of wine that Larry had brought back from the village. We didn't talk that much about our trip, but shared more in the moments that were before us. The weather was incredible. The food fantastic. We didn't think of the numerous summer barbecues down at Blakes' that Larry had cooked outside but that had to be eaten indoors on account of the Irish weather. We didn't think of the times we yearned for the freshness of vegetables we found at the markets in Valbonne. We didn't think of returning to Kilmihil. We savored every moment in a way that was like opening a good bottle of Cabernet, knowing you still had a case of it to enjoy. Before the end of the first week, we lost no time in phoning Juliet to book a month the following summer.

When our visitors left, we determined not to go anywhere. We had already been to Grasse to the Fragonard perfume museum; to Cannes on the eve of the film festival where we all lounged beside bare-breasted thin Frenchwomen and hairy-chested Frenchmen on the beach; to Mougins for ice-cream; and to St Paul de Vence. It was our third visit to this part of the world and this time we had not come to spend hours driving the windy roads through the beautiful hill villages following the tourist trails. This time we had come to live a little, in the style of the French, so we spent the next two weeks sitting by the pool day after day. Niall continued to write in our bedroom, which overlooked a handkerchief of a garden with irises in bloom across the lawn to the pool. Deirdre sat reading and sunbathed, or listened to music in her blue room with its four-poster iron bed. She had a small balcony in her room and I imagine she continued to feel like royalty. Sometimes the sound of her flute flew like a pursed-lip breeze out across the garden. Joseph drew in his room or read or swam in the pool and munched on *pain au chocolat* and baguettes. There was a dilapidated tennis court next door that we had the use of and, some afternoons, with the sun filtering through the cypress trees, we pretended to play. We revelled in our good fortune and were grateful.

Occasionally we took trips to the wonderful old town of Valbonne, just a few minutes away, to walk up and down the quiet streets and to buy food. We found an English bookstore where we could rent English-language videos and buy English-language books because Joseph had quickly run out of reading material. We found him *Kim* by Rudyard Kipling and *Huckleberry Finn* and the *Life of Mao*. And when he had finished those he read *The Poisonwood Bible* by Barbara Kingsolver, which Deirdre was reading for next year's honours English class with Niall. When the owner discovered that it was Niall, she was disappointed that she had none of his books, but said she had had them and would make it her mission to have plenty when he visited again the following June. Would he mind signing some then? The English are much in evidence in the south of France and while it does give you pause to wonder how anglicised France is becoming, it also makes for a pleasant holiday. We had spent all our money, so window-shopped instead, envisioning what we would buy the following year to bring home. Friday is market day and the most wonderful French market is set up in the main streets off the square, selling everything from teak hairclips from Bali to fresh olive oil from the region. French linen tablecloths and bedding hang along the stalls and you can imagine you are in some Arab bazaar with carpets of colour lining the streets and scents of spices and sausages and cheeses and herbs from Provence feasting on each other.

We looked in estate agents' windows for the current prices of villas and imagined ourselves, like everyone else who stopped, owning one. The prices were on par with what we would want to buy in Dublin if we were to buy a second house. Most people buy down for a second home; we'd be buying up. I can't imagine that one would ever tire of living in Valbonne or Plascassier or Grasse and so I put the thought out there in the universe. If I wanted it bad enough the universe would have to conspire to help me. But, as Paulo Coelho says, only if it is my destiny. And my destiny at the moment was the very thing I was intent on discovering. It had taken me around the world and taught me that you can live a little bit beyond yourself, if you dare, and in so doing reap a multitude of rewards. I wasn't entirely sure if all this time I had been running away from something or towards something. Time would tell. The end of the beautiful month of May was approaching and the first of June was nearly upon us.

Ready or not – it was time to go home.

Kiltumper

We had five hours to pass in the coffee dock at Heathrow before we took our final steps around the world. Joseph says we didn't really go around the world, but of course we did. We started nine months previously from Ireland and we went west, zigzagging north to south sometimes, but all the time going west, and we were still travelling westward. Travelling to the western edge of Europe. Back to Ireland. Back home.

'I'm glad that I'm not getting on a plane again too soon,' he said, exasperated as we navigated the hot tunnel-like corridors of the Irish section of Heathrow. 'I couldn't take it!'

He bobbed along heavy-footed with his knapsack full of books on his back.

'I'm glad we're going home, too,' Deirdre said a few minutes later. 'I couldn't *wait* to get out of that house. I was really scared. Every time I went into the bathroom I had to check the shower first in case anyone was hiding.'

She was referring to the house in Cap d'Antibes where we had been robbed a week earlier. We had been able to rent the villa in Plascassier for only three weeks and, partly because I wasn't ready to go home, we decided to rent another villa for a week. Finding one hadn't been all that easy, but when we did we thought we had lucked out as the saying goes. Our new villa overlooked the Mediterranean at Cap d'Antibes. However, it turned out to be pushing our luck. It was I who seemed to fall into the proverbial pitfalls of travelling and, if something untoward was going to happen, the gods had already bargained with me that I would be the target in exchange for the wellbeing of my family. So it was that one day when the four of us were sitting by the pool, someone, nimble and thrifty, climbed over the walls, scaled the high house and invaded our bedroom where two laptops were sitting and our wallets lay in our bags. They left the laptops, didn't find the cameras, took our cash and robbed me of all my jewellery which was in a little leather pouch in the bathroom. When we discovered it shortly thereafter we were horrified and frightened. We got not an ounce of satisfaction from the agent or owners, even though we had abided by all their cautions and locked all the ground-floor doors and windows while sitting at the pool as they had warned. Nothing to be done. (Needless to say we won't be referring any clients to them.) It was as if the gods still needed to be paid. We had less than a week of time left on our forty-week journey and we had been blessed with mostly good luck. It was time to pay the piper before our trip was through, and I was just the one to do it. Unfortunately, I lost all the jewellery that Niall had given to me on the trip and nearly all of my little treasures that I have been collecting through the years. There was a special silver hanging orb that opened that Niall had bought in Bali for my birthday. Nothing too expensive, which was the irony of the thing. I'm sure the robbers were anticipating some emerald rings and diamond earrings considering the location. Mostly they got fine silver jewellery with a bit of funk added as is my style. I kept imagining the thieves would take pity on me and throw the red pouch back over the high gates. But no such luck. We nearly left that day for home, but decided it was not the right way to finish such a feat as ours. We took it on the chin, or I did, and instead tried to be thankful for all the times things could have gone wrong and didn't. Joseph couldn't believe that we should be robbed in the wealthiest place we had stayed in our entire trip. He recounted the less affluent places we had been and all the times we could have been robbed. He was outraged. Deirdre was very frightened and when Niall left midweek for Ireland she hesitated and nearly went with him until he convinced her that he wanted to prepare our homecoming and to let him do this last thing.

The heated, infinity-style pool in which we swam every day, with its cypress-framed view of the Mediterranean, did little to lift our spirits. In fact, nothing about the Cap could impress Deirdre or Joseph then except the high walls of the houses, the cameras hidden in the trees, the sensitive lights, the gates and the dogs behind them. I told Deirdre that I had seen Pete Townsend in the supermarket. Who's he? Big deal. She couldn't wait to get home, this child of mine who had loved every minute of our journey. I busied myself reading Margaret Atwood when I should have been preparing my return, but with the wind knocked out of me all I could do was to take the final days as they came and try to let go of my attachment to my things. I don't think if we hadn't experienced life in Bali we would have been able to understand the robbery in larger terms. Although it was a bitter pill to swallow, I understood there must be balance in everything, otherwise things fall apart.

Despite my own mixed emotions, I was relieved that both Deirdre and Joseph were ready to go home, even if I was not. I cannot exactly say why I was not ready. There were too many thoughts running around in my head, like so many participants in a marathon. It triggered an uncomfortable response in my own being. An uneasiness in my chest and pit of my stomach. I have been learning to shift from my over-active thinking mind into a more *feeling* state of being. A friend of mine calls it sensing. It's not an emotional kind of feeling but a physical body feeling. It was painful. But I understood there was a back catalogue of similar feelings attaching themselves to this one and that all that was required was for me to be still and feel them.

We had left Nice Airport that morning, the kids and myself. Niall was already in Kiltumper preparing the way, softening the blow. We returned the rental van we had been driving for a month in a hectic atmosphere as hundreds were arriving and renting cars on their way to the Grand Prix at Monaco. Half a day later we arrived at Heathrow only to wait another half day for our plane to Shannon. It was unpleasant because the truth was *the trip was over*; yet there we were, stranded between the journey and its ending. Playing a waiting game. Entering Limbo. Finding ourselves at the eleventh hour. Like *Jumanji*, the game had gone on and my turn was up. I was reminded of something I had thought about already – that our trip comprised a thousand little journeys. This wait at Heathrow was a journey too of sorts. I didn't want to think about it. I didn't want to be there. I wanted to be somewhere else. I was not ready to return, plain and simple. Not ready either to embark on this final journey: the journey home. The only comfort was in understanding that my place at this point in time was alongside Niall in Kiltumper continuing our lives with Deirdre and Joseph – *not* somewhere else, but home.

Meanwhile Niall had given me his finished novel, *Only Say the Word*, which he had completed a few days earlier before he left France. I admired him enormously and was pleased that he had managed to write continuously during the nine demanding, exciting, emotional, exotic months we had spent together as a family that year. It occurred to me only then that he had been on his own journey as well. I thought about how difficult it must have been for him at times, and that I had perhaps demanded too much. At least he'd have three months of the Irish summer to complete the final draft and his need for continuity and sense of place would be satisfied. More importantly, however, his well of inspiration and creativity would be brimming. I was confident that the time away would show itself in a hundred positive ways. I was grateful to be so engrossed in it, but I found the endeavour a greater responsibility than I was prepared for. He hoped I'd have finished reading it before I got home but it was unlikely. My focus was too scattered. I was still reeling from the robbery in some respects.

When it was time to board and we reached the door of the plane my throat constricted. I felt like I was entering a dark tunnel that would take me to a place I wasn't entirely happy to be going to, a bit like an animal being shepherded into a pen. I tried not to be too obvious about it, but Deirdre was not long figuring out that something was wrong. 'What's the matter with you?' She asked when we had sat down.

'I guess I'm just feeling anxious about going home. That's all. It'll be all right.'

She looked at me with those large grey-blue eyes, stunning with a deep tan. My daughter had grown up before my eyes into a poised and beautiful young woman. I guessed she was deciding whether to be sympathetic or tell me to get over myself. She had the good manners and inner wisdom to choose the former.

'Me too, Mum. But you'll be fine. We can't leave Dad over there on his own now, can we?' she said.

'No, I guess not. You're right, of course. I'll be fine once I'm there. Not to worry, Dee. And thanks for asking.'

I was thinking of all those times down through the years that I have been *returning* to Ireland. Of the many times I had left my mother's home or my sister's home and cried once we touched down on the Tarmacadam of Shannon Airport. Of the many times I longed to be elsewhere. I buried myself in a house-and-garden magazine. There are times when you can give in to your feelings and times when you have to get on with it. Self-indulgence was not an option. For Deirdre and Joseph, I put on a smile and said, 'Everybody okay?'

They nodded equally. The plane took off. It was time to prepare myself. We would arrive in Shannon in an hour.

In mid-air you have thoughts that are partly dreams. On that flight, mine were mostly in the form of questions. I wondered if my sister's string on the map in her kitchen marked the journey in different colours for the different continents we visited. How many postcards had she received? Would I get to see the world map that Sarah Nestor, the art teacher in Kilmihil, had made for Deirdre's class with its collection of postcards sent from *every* destination? How many photographs had we taken with our five cameras? Was it ten or twelve boxes we had Fed-Exed to Kiltumper? How was Huckleberry? Were the cats, Neidín and Freckles, still alive? Had Diarmuid managed to keep the cottage from falling down? Was the new glasshouse up? And of course: How was my garden?

~

No fanfare, no trumpets, no drums, no banners flying. We arrived home pretty much as we had left, quietly and among many. For me it was overwhelming, but the kids took it in their stride which I was at once both grateful for and a bit saddened by. Grateful that they were not weighed down as I was with the idea that something monumental in our lives had just ended. Like a falling star, it was extinguished as soon as we stepped from the plane. But saddened that the final steps were being taken without some ceremonial closure. Outside passport control, on our way to get our bags, a small table greeted us, attended by one lone person sitting behind a sign that read: 'SARS Information'. It made the three of us laugh and momentarily lifted me. It was as if it had a subtext just for us that said: *We* know you've been away in foreign parts and welcome home. I took it as a sign, a gesture of Irish hospitality that was warmly welcoming. It struck us as both endearing and humorous. For from Paris to Prague to London there was nothing about SARS. We had arrived in Frankfurt from Singapore in the middle of the epidemic and not so much as a leaflet was passed to us warning passengers of possible symptoms, and here we were in Ireland, half way around the world from the hotbed of SARS, being reminded to take care. It was downright sweet. And if the universe sends signs to cheer us up, then this one I couldn't ignore. And that more than anything seemed to hail our arrival home. It is impossible to explain how powerfully I felt cushioned by the impact of our homecoming just then.

Our bags arrived for the final time all accounted for. We loaded up and went out to find Niall who was waiting with Larry, our old friend. Standing beside each other they seemed like two pillars through which we could navigate the last docking. Although at times to see the two of them standing side by side is comical – Niall is over six foot and Larry is half a foot shorter; Niall is balding and Larry has a healthy head of silver hair. Larry, to some degree, understood something of what we must be feeling, having seen us at the start of our trip in Amagansett with our dear friend, his wife Lucy, and at the end of our trip in Valbonne. It was another sign I thought to myself. A true connection with our growing roots in west Clare.

Niall hugged both his children at once and said, 'Welcome home.'

Larry hugged us as well, greeting us with a bit of a laugh as he always does. His immensely cheerful nature left little room for negativity.

'How are ya now, lads? Welcome home!'

I knew that I needed to be alert to the positive signs that were all about me. Otherwise, I would never survive. The sweetly sick perfume of spread slurry greeted us when the automated doors slid open. It was cold. Misted grey skies and a thin veil of rain mildly assaulted us. Summer in Ireland. We were undeniably home.

~

We had taken the last plane from Heathrow to Shannon and arrived in Kiltumper Cottage at twilight. Huck was there to greet us. He swathed Deirdre and Joseph with his great white furry body. He circled the cars. Ran into the garden and back to us. *Life is now as it should be* I imagine he was thinking as he led the way to the front door. Deirdre and Joseph were giddy. There wasn't an ounce of evidence that they had anything but joy in their hearts. The garden was spectacularly in bloom with poppies and tall pink foxgloves. The Japanese cherry, Mt Fuji, was completely covered in white blossoms, the wispy branches nearly touching the ground. The landscaping firm had done a wonderful job maintaining it. I was thrilled to see it looking so well. Things were falling into place. I couldn't deny it. I had to read the signs and line them up. Together they spelled: *welcome home*.

Niall had performed his usual mastery of setting the house as if it were a theatre set. Candles were ready to be lit on the table that was spread with a feast. He had bought a good bottle of champagne when leaving Nice Airport. Our four-page itinerary of the trip was laid carefully on the table, scribbled now with a new heading. *Been There. Done That!*

'Welcome home, honey,' he said, and hugged me as I came in the glass door from the garden into our front kitchen. 'Everything will be fine. You'll see.'

He knew without me telling him how I was feeling. He knew me so well. His warm embrace radiated with an understanding and an empathy that acknowledged that while the adjustment would be hard for me it was also going to be okay.

'Wait till you see the glasshouse,' he whispered and held me as the kids ran past us straight up to their rooms, Joseph shouting, 'I'm home! I'm home. Deirdre, we're home!'

Lucy arrived up from working late at Fitzpatrick's grocers in the village and the small homecoming party began. We toasted with champagne and ate Irish smoked salmon on brown bread in the conservatory, the garden laid out in splendour all around us.

'The garden is looking lovely, Chris. Isn't it?' said Lucy.

'She'll be out first thing in the morning, Lu,' said Niall.

Larry laughed and Lucy said, 'Yes, she'll have to get weeding if she wants to keep it looking like this,' she looked my way and continued pointedly, 'No time to feel lonesome now, do you hear me?'

As we had just seen Lucy and Larry a few weeks ago in Valbonne, they were the perfect couple with whom to celebrate our return. I was glad that Niall had asked them to come up and felt myself sharing deeply my growing joy to be, if not be back in Ireland, at least to be 'home'.

'It's not such a bad little house, is it, Lu?'

'No, no, Chris, it's lovely. That young man Diarmuid kept it very well.'

'But I mean, it's so... Well, it's funkier than I remembered. And so colourful.'

I amazed myself in my fondness for my own house. It was like celebrating a part of me that I had taken for granted. I toured the back kitchen and the front kitchen and the sitting room where Niall had set a blazing turf fire in the open hearth. Its fiery light in the yellow room made it glow like gold, and was like a heartbeat. Every room spoke of creativity and imagination and homespun cosiness Kiltumper style. It was another sign. I have to say, admitting to a certain amount of sentimentality, that I did feel a bit like dear old Dorothy when she awakens from her dream and is glad to be home and tells Auntie Em, 'There's no place like home.' Having no Auntie Em, I told Niall instead.

'You know, Kiltumper is really quite a nice place. I'm not going so far as to say that I'm glad to be home *in Ireland*. But I am more than happy to be here in *our* home. We've built a world for ourselves right here and it's beautiful.'

Niall looked at me with the knowledge that yes, he had known that all along and, a bit like the Scarecrow, he nodded his head in agreement.

'Hmmm... We'll see how I get on with the rest of it. Okay? Too early to say.'

'You'll be fine. I'll help you.'

~

'Welcome back.'

'Are you delighted to be home again?'

'What was the best part of the trip?'

'What did you like the most?'

'You missed the summer – we had it back in March. March was lovely.'

How *did* it feel to be home again? I watched Deirdre slip easily and comfortably back into her life, a fluid transition I think because of the reunion in Paris with her classmates. Joseph didn't return to school, which ran for only one more month, so he busied himself watching his favourite television shows and drawing on the big table in the front room. He was just happy to be home and didn't expect anything more from it than the comfort he felt. And Niall too seemed settled back in Kiltumper. Maybe he was just pleased to have anchored himself so he could re-draft his novel which he hoped to send to his, agent, Marianne, in August. Glad too not to be moving. Glad not to be carrying the bum bag. Glad not to have to find a taxi, and glad to give our bank account a rest. A decent cup of tea was all he asked for and some of our friend Auntie Mary's brown bread. It occurred to me that it was easier for my family, Niall, Deirdre and Joseph, to come home, because Ireland had always been their home. It was a bit different for me. Ireland was my adopted home. Although I had adopted it for some very good reasons, in a way, the last part of my journey was to re-discover that place that was nowhere else but where I was, and, more powerfully, to accept it.

~

It took me nearly a month to begin to feel integrated and to let go of a resistance I knew was impeding my settlement. A friend said to me that this part of the trip – the returning – might be the hardest journey of all. I wrote to my sister in an email:

Having some re-entry problems. Feel like a space capsule that has just re-entered earth's orbit and has fallen into the sea with a crash and loud thunder. I'm bobbing along in a tiny space floating on the water. Between two places. Waiting for the outside to open the hatch.

I don't want to say that there wasn't a great welcome for us when we came home, because in people's hearts and minds I'm sure they were all glad to see us. Niall was certainly missed at the secondary school. My friend Marie who had stayed in touch throughout our trip had warned me not to expect that people would make more than a passing remark and bid a warm welcome. When she returned from nearly two years away that is what she found. It was as if we were slipping back into *their* lives, like cogs on the wheel. We had been missing, but it hadn't affected the daily movement of the life that moves unstoppably forward, although sometimes it appears to move round in circles for most of us.

'Nothing has changed,' Niall said to Martin who had picked him up from the airport.

'Yes, isn't it great? That's the beauty of living here,' he replied smartly.

~

The often-asked question: 'What did you miss the most?' started me thinking. What *did* I miss the most? Maybe it would be through the things that I missed about living in Ireland that I could find my way back into life here. The month of June had passed. The glasshouse was christened and a long yellow banner with the words 'Welcome Home' had been cut and the door opened to the tomato plants that the gardener's wife had left for me. We added cucumber plants that we bought from an organic grower in the Saturday market in Ennis, and pumpkin and courgette plants. Another friend, Liz, had grown some aubergine and cherry-tomato plants for us and came by just after we had arrived to say hello, well done, and glad you are back. I was happy to be working in the garden again and knew without asking myself that that was what I had missed maybe most of all. June was split between sunshine and rain and I spent hours in the glasshouse staking and tying and training the tomatoes and cucumbers, delighted to have somewhere to go in between the showers. Delphiniums had been lost during the winter along with other perennials and I wasted no time in replacing them. The freshly mulched beds were a joy to weed. Neidín and Freckles followed me to the garden and chased each other across the lawn.

Nothing more caught my attention in terms of what else I missed about living in Ireland. There wasn't a great sense of community that missed my company or Niall's or the children's for that matter. There were no invitations to dinner, no opportunities for slide shows. A few people dropped by, and that was it. It was clear that in order to participate in my local community I would have to make an effort. The choice was up to me. In a way this realisation brought with it a certain amount of freedom. When and if I was ready.

At first I was reluctant to go down to the village. I was a little nervous. Even with the re-introductions over it was still discomforting how easily things returned to normal. It was like we had never left. When we went to Ennis it felt like some of the shopkeepers had missed us only when they suddenly realised that they hadn't seen us. Like, 'Hey, I haven't seen you for a while. Where you been?' It was amusing to explain to just about everybody we met that we had indeed been gone. Had travelled around the world in fact. I felt at times I was asserting myself in a new way. But also I felt I was having to impress people with the idea that we had achieved something of stupendous proportions. If truth be told, the excitement of others was not matched by our own. Our photo albums remain largely unopened by visitors. We told a few stories, like the one about the Bolivian boatman, or the time we saw the great grizzly, or how we had to cancel our trip to China. But it was mostly to ourselves that we would say, 'Hey, remember when…' Deirdre received some wonderful recognition because four articles she wrote for *Face Up* had been well circulated. She was even mentioned on national radio when a lady phoned in to say that she wished there were more stories in the teenage magazines like the ones Deirdre Williams was writing. Deirdre was so pleased with herself and more people seemed to know about our trip through her than through our own acquaintances. It was a positive affirmation for her.

Meanwhile, I felt as if I was weaving a cocoon around myself, my family, our home and the garden. Perhaps making more conscious choices about how we lived. There was too much to think about. And the trip itself was still so fresh in my mind and already I was reliving it through memory. As I continued to write about our experiences I understood its meaning to me was threefold. To keep a record of this extraordinary year in our lives, to celebrate it by writing about it – a kind of ceremonial closure, and perhaps most importantly, to find my own voice in the process.

~

We had come home in time for summer. We had taken a whole year off from wintertime and it felt good. I was hopeful the summer wouldn't turn out as badly as the previous two but after June, July was not looking promising. Not as far as I was concerned anyway. The tractors in the fields were buzzing with their first cuts of silage. Our neighbour PJ Coughlan had begun his machines for cutting turf and its constant hum wafted like a melody on the warm though drizzled air.

In the first week of July, we decided that Deirdre and Joseph would take classes at the Willie Clancy Week in Miltown Malbay, just up the road. Neither of them particularly wanted to go. Joseph eventually said he'd go if Seán McNamara was his teacher. Seán spent his life playing fiddle with the Liverpool Céilí Band and had taught Joseph at the summer school the previous year, but we had heard that this year he would be assisting and not teaching. He was in his early eighties and, like several of the teachers there, he had given his life to Irish music. Deirdre said she didn't want to go and that was that.

'Well, guys, listen to me. You are both going and *that's* that.' I said.

'Why?' asked Joseph. 'When we don't want to?'

'Okay, here it is. You are going for several reasons. One, because you live in West Clare and if there is anything we learned from our trip around the world it is how important local culture is. Remember the Peruvian band in Aguas Calientes? Or the Chileans at Ian and Maggy's at Christmas?'

'Ah huh,' they nodded.

'Yeah, well, while it was fun to hear him play Elvis, we enjoyed the Chilean music much more. Traditional Irish music is part of your heritage.' I was on my soapbox now and they would have to grin and bear it.

'And what else?' asked Deirdre.

'Secondly, because it's a bit of a challenge for both of you. Sorry, but you need experience in doing things you don't necessarily want to do. You'll need that skill in your lives.'

'Go on, what else?' asked the disgruntled teenager and her younger brother.

'Well, finally and not least importantly, because I said so and sometimes, just sometimes, Dad and I know what is best for you.'

'Yeah, right,' said Joseph.

'And just maybe,' said Niall, 'who knows, you might even like it.'

So off we went our first morning to Willie Clancy. I went to register Deirdre at the primary school in Miltown where the concertinas, flutes and whistles were set up and Niall took Joseph to Spanish Point to register for fiddle classes. There are always more fiddlers than any other musicians. The classes occupy the whole of the Spanish Point secondary school, known locally as 'the convent' because it was run by nuns. As well as music classes, there are set-dancing classes, traditional singing classes and Irish-language classes. The whole of the small village of Miltown and Spanish Point, perched on the Atlantic, becomes a mecca of Irish traditional culture for one week in early July. Musicians and students appear from around the world, in rain or shine, in anoraks and Irish knit sweaters, carrying pipes, fiddle cases, concertina boxes and flute cases. Whistles stick out from back pockets. Some are wearing dreadlocks, others are bald. Some are nicely turned out, others have just woken up and emerged from tents. They all come together regardless of age or nationality or expertise. Needless to say, the traffic is cumbersome, but we were lucky to sneak in to the car park of the primary school after dropping off the boys at the convent. Registration for the flutes was efficient and I left Deirdre in an intermediate class and said I'd see her again at one o'clock.

'Have fun, sweetie,' I said, smiling.

'Yeah, thanks Mum,' she said. 'Can't wait.'

It wasn't like I had to drag her there. I think secretly she wanted to see how she'd get on compared with traditional players. Having studied classical music for the past eight years, she felt inferior when it came to Irish trad, as it is called. But I knew she was underestimating herself.

'It will be a good challenge for her if nothing else,' I said to Niall when I found him at the convent.

Seán McNamara was there and Niall had spoken with him but he said he wasn't teaching this year. He was sure that Joseph would find a class for himself.

'Let's stay until the break and see how he gets on,' said Niall.

'Just in case,' I said.

'Hmm. Do you want to walk along the beach road?'

'Yeah, okay,' I said. The breeze buffeting us, off we went.

We had a tea at a small grocery shop overlooking the beach and watched the brave swimmers in their bathing suits on the grey day. I couldn't help but feel the buzz. Miltown was alive with energy. I told Niall that while I had been waiting for him I had watched a mother with five children. Three small ones in shorts and T-shirts and two older girls, one as tall as her mother, carrying fiddle cases. The older girl had a small golden-coloured knapsack on her back and her hair in a pony tail. She must have been about thirteen. The three little ones ran behind their mother like ducklings while she wordlessly ushered her way past the queue to drop off her two daughters. She had had the good sense to pre-register them. She was coatless and purseless in a red T-shirt. Her untanned skin looked pale against the red of her shirt. Her bobbed black hair looked as if she had combed it in a hurry and I imagined that she had probably left the breakfast things on the table and whooshed her kids from the kitchen to the car. I was thinking that she was one of the many quiet-spoken mothers who bring their children to cross-country clubs and Irish music classes, down to the library in the village, and to the community hall for games. Living her life from deep roots, bearing fruits and growing more roots. A sense of being defined from a secure sense of place, a lucky woman. Did she know it? I wondered.

Niall and I returned to the grey convent on the hill to see how Joseph was getting on. Something like twenty-three rooms trickled and oozed with fiddle notes escaping from the gaps in the building. As I walked down the corridor looking for my son, I could see, through the small square windows in the wooden doors, bow arms going this way and that. Some heads bobbing back and forth to the music. Some musicians standing, some sitting. And there, in a small room amongst a dozen fiddlers, mostly young adults, was Joseph. He smiled broadly as the boy to his left spoke to him. He was connected to a greater experience and, whether he knew it or not, he was enriched. I watched for a few seconds and nodded to Niall. All was well. We felt confident that, with his fiddle under his chin and his bow in mid-air, in a few hours he would have begun the process of re-discovering a part of himself. We were confident too that Deirdre would rise to the challenge and enjoy herself. We went away feeling a quiet pride that we had been the instrumentalists in this concert of reconnecting our children with a sense of themselves: an awareness that they are Irish and musical and playful and joyful. For all the rest of that week the mornings would see our musicians heading for classes, and the evenings would see them fiddling and fluting new tunes until fingertips were red and the house abuzz with notes flying.

308

A July that was too wet and cold to match the enthusiasm I had for the garden turned the corner when August arrived. The sun fully appeared in an Irish blue sky. We were into our eleventh month of summer. We watched the moon rise at the southwest corner of the garden, illuminating a large-petalled, salmon-pink oriental poppy. Niall sent the final draft of his novel to his agent and went about pottering in the garden as never before. He built a path through the boggy end of the vegetable garden and cleared a hedge of brambles and nettles so we could see clear across the top into the grove where three apples trees struggled beneath the sycamore and ash. He played football with Joseph and brought me cups of tea while I was writing. At times it felt like our first days together in Kiltumper when our only commitments were to each other and to making a garden and a home. Like we were the point of stillness in the turning world. The days were easy and filled with a kind of wholesome nothingness. Resettlement for Deirdre had been easy and Joseph was content in his home, as if the whole of Kiltumper Cottage and its garden had become his nest and he needed nothing else in those moments of continued summer. I watched with some jealousy how well Niall and Deirdre and Joseph adapted to being home again. Jealous because I was not quite settling. Transplantation for the three of them was successful, whereas for me there was some rejection. It was as if the life I had been living in Ireland before the trip had been ruptured. I was becoming deeply aware of an inner disturbance that wanted my attention. In some ways I felt that I was being given a choice to continue as before, or not.

My friend Marie was anxious for me to resume my practice as a homeopath and offered me the use of her office again. She was eager to refer some of her clients to me. 'C'mon Christine,' she said. '*When* are you going to start back?'

'You know, Marie,' I said, 'it would be the easiest thing in the world right now for me to go into homeopathy. Apart from the actual work of it, I could very easily pick up where I left off.'

My petite friend, ten years younger than me, with her short brown wispy hair and grey eyes, listened to me. I found it difficult to explain. Homeopathy had become practically a way of life. But I knew that it was a distraction, a way of channelling energy *away* from myself. The fact that it was a wholesome endeavour was the seductive part. As if I could fool myself into believing that the work was important and ultimately for my highest and greatest good. The work was important, there is no doubt in my mind about that. But I wasn't sure if it was the best choice for *me* at this point in my life.

'I think it would be better for me to take this time that has been given to me, to address this inner place. If I go back to homeopathy it will be from the perspective of my whole person if that makes any sense to you.'

I paused and watched Marie. 'In half a year I'll be fifty and I want to be able to say to myself that I am confident that what I am doing with my life is authentic and genuine and that I am expressing myself with as much wholeness as I can muster. I have had too many obligations and those obligations have eclipsed *me*. As if I am constantly in a shadow.'

She nodded and I knew she understood what I was saying.

'Take your time,' she said, smiling.

~

Joseph went away to summer camp in America, to Vermont for three and half weeks, and Deirdre returned to her eighth year of Summer Music on the Shannon, held at the University of Limerick for three weeks. It was residential and she stayed in the student lodgings overlooking the Shannon. She was excited to be back playing flute with her friends and having some much-needed time away from her parents and brother. Joseph had been seduced by an idea of what he thought an American summer camp would be like and had been pleading to give it a try with his cousin Daniel in New York. We agreed that it would be a good experience and thought it might make the transition between a year away and the start of secondary school in September easier for him. Niall accompanied Joseph to America and didn't return for a full week. I was home alone for the first time ever. I was free to potter around the house and garden on my own. I made a few phone calls to friends, but as luck would have it they were all out and about on holidays or busy at work. So for a week I ate the dinner I had harvested from the vegetable garden alone. The courgettes were ready for picking and, together with basil and cherry tomatoes, I ate as if I was back on the Mediterranean. For lunch there were cucumbers and lettuce and rocket salads. I started to look upon this time alone as a kind of cleansing, a reacquainting myself with the things all about me. I had no responsibilities and it was both freeing and terrifying.

I had said to Niall before he left that I was determined to get my house in working order. There was so much clutter and too much unused, but crammed-full, storage space. I started opening cupboards and presses and throwing away unused clothes and shoes and old copies of magazines. I tidied the kitchen cupboards from top to bottom. I used to joke with Niall that what we really needed around the house was a wife. Now in part I was *becoming* that wife. And it was okay. I didn't have anything else to do. It was enough. I didn't have to juggle a career, a job, motherhood, and wifehood. For that short time I was a housewife. It didn't escape me that getting my house in order involved some inner work as well. I accepted that there was probably an equal share of cupboard-cleaning and crammed-full storage space *inside* my head that needed attention. And even though at times I felt like a racehorse at the starting gate, I resisted the urge to gallop away.

~

Nearly every day of August brought sunshine. We couldn't keep the tomatoes in the glasshouse watered and everyone looked like they had returned from a holiday in the sun. A few evenings I went to the National Concert Hall at the University of Limerick to hear Deirdre and the woodwind orchestra in concert. She was greatly enjoying the company of the boys from Artane as I came to call them. The Artane Boys' Band from Dublin was part of the Summer Music on the Shannon programme. For three weeks her days were filled with playing music and her evenings filled with concerts. In between, she was experiencing herself as a teenager and was clearly having enormous fun. She never called home and when I phoned her she'd say, 'What is it, Mum? Yes, I'm fine. Don't worry. Bye.' I was so proud of her and trusted her completely. Niall returned from New York and we heard that Joseph was having some difficulty adjusting to camp life, American boy style. But we believed that all such experiences are positive in some form or another and we knew he was learning how to handle himself away from home. I missed him incredibly. It broke my heart at times to think of him struggling, but I knew him to be in good hands and believed the counsellors would help him. We believed that for both our children a little time away from us would be beneficial. After all, we had lived in each other's pockets for quite a long time.

Then my brother Stephen, who had been telling me for years that he would come to visit us in Ireland some day, finally arrived in the middle of August. He was the only one of my five siblings who had yet to visit and I was eager to see what he would make of our life and home. Oddly enough, although Stephen hadn't been during the eighteen years that we had been living in Ireland, he had in fact been a visitor to Kiltumper Cottage many years before when we were both in our twenties and living independently in Europe. I was a student at UCD at the time and Stephen was modelling in Europe. We met up and travelled for a week around the southwest coast including a visit to Mary Breen, the then owner of the Kiltumper Cottage.

'He won't believe the changes,' I said to Niall before he came. 'Back then, there was no running water. No central heating. No telephone. Mary was milking a cow by hand in the cabin when we arrived that time.'

'Twenty-five years sees a lot of changes in rural place like this,' he replied.

'Yeah, and your old house in Kilmacud in Dublin probably hasn't changed a bit in that same time.'

Stephen arrived with his two teenage sons, Kellen and Ryan, who were delighted to be in Ireland after touring in the sweltering heat of Europe. Kiltumper was a world away from anything they had seen before and I took great pride in being able to show them where their great-grandfather had grown up. Teenage Californian boys are not easy to impress, but I think the open hearth with turf fire, the quiet green of the landscape, and the *céilí* evening in the square in Kilrush did the trick. When eventually Stephen's sons returned to San Francisco, we had a few gentle days together.

Stephen had relocated to San Francisco from Seattle a few weeks earlier and was in between jobs as a financial consultant. He had never taken so much time off for himself and there were times during his visit with us that I could feel his restlessness. I think he was largely unaware of it. People in the business world get so used to multi-tasking, to cell phones, laptops and airports, that pure quiet can sometimes be unsettling. And that is what we have here in Kiltumper. For myself, I was absolutely delighted. For in a way, I got to show him around my world. He was in awe of the garden and how much the house had changed since his visit back in 1980, but yet how its core was the same.

'Chrissie,' he said to me, 'your home is beautiful.'

'You think so?'

'Yes, I do. Seriously, you and Niall and have done an outstanding job.'

It's all I needed to hear in a way and very affirming. Stephen was well travelled himself and knew a good thing when he saw it. In a way, he is like my twin brother, although eighteen months divide us. We feel the same way about a lot of things and share some private wounds that separate us from our four other siblings. He is Deirdre's godfather and Niall and I are godparents to his twin daughters. We have a link that binds us across miles and years. To finally have him in Ireland to see what I had made of my life these past eighteen years married to the same man in the same house in a country not my own was a necessary part of my journey back to resettling. It was as if I could see Ireland afresh through his eyes. And in the August summer I have to admit it looked tremendous. Stephen was aware of the Celtic tiger and of the high reputation of its education system. He was impressed with the housing and the character of the towns that we drove though, many of them retaining their charm by not replacing their shop fronts with plastic neon frontages. He thought it was remarkably clean, which surprised me.

At the end of the week, we decided to take a few days down in Kerry. Half our lifetimes ago, we had been two American students abroad, he and I travelling with backpacks and hitchhiking around Slea Head. We had tucked ourselves into a rocky cove overlooking the Great Blasket Islands before finding ourselves a B&B for the night. It too had been August. Now here we were again, brother and sister, this time in a hired silver car driving the same route. Gone were the backpacks. We sported expensive sunglasses and shirts of finer cloth, but the jeans were still the same. Although our lives had changed immensely since then, we shared a felt sense of connectedness. It was as if we could look at each other's lives and see the *road not taken*. In a way it was comforting because I think I understood then that I had taken the right road for me. And, as the poet says, 'that has made all the difference.'

~

Two weeks after my brother left, the first of September rolled around. We acknowledged to ourselves that a year had passed since we had departed. It was just us, as it had been for most of the trip. It quietly came and I wondered if in another year we would turn to each other and say, 'Remember? Two years ago we left for our trip around the world...' Probably so. And the year after that. Meanwhile, Ireland was turning out to have the best summer in years. Certainly the best summer I could remember. The days held warm and blue. I was in paradise in the garden. But soon it was time to get ready for returning to school: Niall as a teacher in the afternoons, Deirdre as a fifth-year student in the first year of her final two-year course, and Joseph as a first year.

My baby was going to high school. It didn't seem possible. In some ways I wished Joseph wasn't as advanced as he was because then we could have had him return to primary school and complete the last year that he had missed during our travels. But it would have been counterproductive. He was reading the same books as Deirdre and had devoured her geography textbook already. There was nothing for it but to send him to school and hope that he would get on all right.

I remembered back to when Joseph started primary school. We had taken a photograph of him standing next to a sunflower that towered beside him. He was in a yellow tie-dyed T-shirt and shorts and wearing a beige baseball cap. He had his small schoolbag on his back. He was full of excitement.

Today, eight years later, both of my children head off to school together, with their father, on another September morning – this time after fifteen months of holidays. A sunflower that Joseph planted in June stands outside in the open porch, just waiting for a photo opportunity, as if to say, 'Wouldn't it be nice if we only had to measure our years against the indubitable growth of a sunflower.'

As I snap the photo I have tears in my eyes. It was a long time ago that Deirdre left in her blue and white polka-dot dress for her first day of school, and as they stand there beside the sunflower with the morning sunlight in their excited eyes, Niall waits on the edge of the garden and nods back to me. 'Don't worry,' his look says, 'I'll look after them. This is just the next journey, the next adventure.'

And I blink back the tears and smile and hug my children one more time. 'Okay,' I say silently, 'here you go, travel on, experience, and feel my love.'

Another year is beginning.

Epilogue

The night of the total lunar eclipse, 9 November 2003, sees the end of this story. Niall's publisher in England made an offer on his novel. The Italians bought it a week earlier. He is returning to playwriting now that he has finished his fourth novel His fourth play, commissioned by the Abbey, will be a play with music. Winter arrived in the beginning of November and it was time for me to finish my own book about our year of holidays in the summertime around the globe. In the theatre of the heavens, a grand sextile appeared above the earth with the alignment of the sun and the moon, Jupiter and Saturn, Mars and finally Chiron, which the spiritual astrologers claim provides a crystal rainbow bridge between physicality and the spirit, the inner and outer planets. A performance of the universe where the unique and very rare alignment of the planets presents a matrix of timeless symmetry, where we, the audience on earth, are invited to co-create and to open ourselves to a mutual and harmonious flow of energy which hasn't been seen for 6,000 years. As Plato says: 'Perhaps there is a pattern set up in the heavens for one who desires to see it, and having seen it, to see one in himself.'

Among the things that I recognised for myself during the previous year was that I needed to take some time off, away from homeopathy. I wanted to be home for my children. I wanted to be there when Joseph came home from school with his ups and downs. And at the beginning there would be more downs than ups. I wanted to be available to Deirdre and help her prepare a portfolio for art school. In two short years she would be gone from our home and, like the previous year, I didn't want to miss a day of it.

Somewhere along the way I had another little epiphany and I understood that it was no coincidence that we had taken nine months to travel. Not a year. Not half a year. But nine months. And although it has taken more than nine months to write the account of our journey, it was the journey of nine months that gave birth to a more complete awareness of myself.

A journey without to travel within.

Things are becoming clearer to me and I have reconnected with a buried part of myself. The self that is re-emerging is finding contentment in the being-ness of what is around me. As a wife. As a mother. As a gardener. And as a writer. But apart from my own journey, the nine months that we spent with our children – day in and day out, twenty-four hours a day, seven days a week – have been a tremendous gift to Niall and me. When I think of it now, writing these last words at the table here in Kiltumper, I think that in a way we were able to reclaim those nine months when our children were not with us. Those nine months when they were journeying in the wombs of their birth mothers. That was their first journey, and one that would eventually lead them to us. Yes, that is how I shall always think of it, that year and this one, a journey that became the gift of a lifetime.